Reaganism

&

the **Death** of
Representative
Democracy

WALTER WILLIAMS

GEORGETOWN UNIVERSITY PRESS
WASHINGTON, D.C.

For my granddaughter
Boo Williams
with love

Georgetown University Press, Washington, D.C.
© 2003 by Georgetown University Press.
All rights reserved.
Printed in the United States of America.

10 9 8 7 6 5 4 3 2 1   2003

This book is printed on acid-free recycled paper meeting the requirements of the American National Standard for Permanence in Paper for Printed Library Materials.

Library of Congress Cataloging-in-Publication Data
Williams, Walter
Reaganism and the death of representative democracy / Walter Williams.
        p.   cm.
Includes bibliographical references and index.
ISBN 0-87840-147-4 (cloth : alk. paper)
1. United States—Politics and government—1945–1989.
2. United States—Politics and government—1989–   I. Title.
JK271.W554 2003
320.973`09`048–dc21   2003006471

Contents

Acknowledgments

I am most indebted to Bryan Jones, who not only read more than one draft of the manuscript but also became my main sounding board for discussing ideas and working through problems. Seldom is one fortunate enough to have a colleague both willing to give his time and able to provide insightful comments. I benefited from both the critique by William Andersen, a constitutional law scholar, of my chapter on representative democracy, and the comments by the media expert Margaret Gordon on the chapter analyzing the media and political information. Rebecca Crichton and Victoria Kaplan offered comments on the manuscript from the generalist's perspective. I am much indebted to my editor at Georgetown University Press, Gail Grella, who provided an extraordinary amount of assistance in helping me clarify points and make the manuscript more readable. Finally, as with earlier publications, my wife Jacqueline (Jackie) Williams pointed out unclear ideas and garbled sentences and paragraphs that found their way into the manuscript.

The dedication is to Jackie's and my first granddaughter, who started life with the names her family gave her and an expected nickname. Born on Halloween day in 1998, she soon became Boo, and the other names faded from view. She and her brothers Charlie and Peter, born December 14, 1996, have brought me great personal joy as this study made me increasingly concerned that the nation was on a frightening path away from democracy as conceived by the Founders.

one

A Radical Transformation

During the second half of the 1990s, the American economy performed at a pace comparable to the first twenty-five years of the postwar era, with high growth, low unemployment and inflation, and a remarkable 3 percent productivity growth rate. A veritable cornucopia of goods and services poured forth, as the United States rushed past its main rivals to again become the world's economic colossus. People spoke of a "new economy," driven by lean, mean corporations utilizing the fruits of the technology revolution. In sharpest contrast, the federal institutions of governance had been deteriorating since the start of Ronald Reagan's administration. This decline was consistent with the prevailing political philosophy that an active national government would do harm by undermining the economy through its misguided policies.

Reaganism had proclaimed: Get the federal government off the backs of the people—cut taxes deeply, particularly at the top, where high rates discourage entrepreneurs; deregulate business; devolve power to the states—and the nation will flourish again. President Reagan's political philosophy, which replaced the New Deal thinking of Franklin Roosevelt, held that unfettered free-market capitalism could serve the dual role of providing the economic bounty and of sustaining democracy far better than the politicians and bureaucrats in the nation's capital.

This book offers a different view. First, the economy surged so mightily in the second half of the 1990s despite, not because of, Reaganism's antigovernmentism and market fundamentalism. Second, the new political thesis that dominated the last two decades of the twentieth century became a central factor in the severe deterioration of the federal institutions of governance after 1981 and stands as a major barrier to the reform of the American political system. Third, money politics prevailed as members of Congress paid more attention to corporate America, their campaign finance paymaster, than they did to their constituents, and the nation slipped into early-stage plutocracy. Although the United States had not become a full-fledged plutocracy with total control by the wealthy, America's weak brand of democracy is far different from the representative democracy supported by the strong federal institutions conceived by the Founders. Government for the wealthiest citizens and major corporations had replaced government for ordinary Americans.

Finally, the declining capability of the institutional means of governing materially increased the likelihood of developing unsound policies, mismanaging new and existing programs, and failing to achieve the nation's most important domestic policy goals. I will argue that the harm inflicted by Reaganism on the critical institutions of governance created by the framers of the Constitution has undermined the U.S. political system and turned the federal government away from the major domestic policy problems facing the nation.

Putting the structure and processes of the national government at the center of the analysis reveals a critical sea change in the American political system: *In the years since the coming of the Reagan administration, the United States has undergone a transformation in its political institutions and its philosophy of governance of a magnitude not seen since the 1930s.* An important and related point is how little attention has been paid to the changes in the central institutions of the American political system that have made the current system fundamentally different from that of 1980.

In the upcoming chapters, the in-depth analysis of these institutions will make clear the profound changes in less than a quarter century under Reaganism that have done untold damage to the structure of governance created by the Founders. It also provides evidence to make the case that restoring the institutional efficiency of the federal government must be the pivotal first step toward greater effectiveness in achieving America's domestic policy objectives of personal safety, economic security, individual freedom, and full political citizenship.

The last paragraph raises the need to distinguish between the nation's ends or goals or objectives (the three will be interchangeable for our purposes) and its institutional means. The former set out what people want; the latter are the organizational structure and staff, the policies, and the procedures to be employed by the federal institutions in seeking to achieve the desired goals. The Founders clearly and eloquently captured the relationship between means and ends in the single sentence that constitutes the Preamble to the Constitution: "WE THE PEOPLE OF THE UNITED

STATES, in order to form a more perfect Union, establish justice, insure domestic tranquility, provide for the common defense, promote the general welfare, and secure the blessings of liberty to ourselves and our posterity, do ordain and establish this Constitution for the United States of America."

The Founders could not have been more straightforward. Here in the Preamble are the several objectives the nation sought and the means or designated instruments for achieving them—the structure and procedures for the new government and its central institutions as originally set out in the Constitution. September 11, 2001, exposed the weaknesses in the federal government and underscored that the machinery of government must be in good working order if the nation is to accomplish its objectives. Repairing the inadequate means is the first necessary requirement. Only after that can the larger issue of effectiveness in fulfilling the nation's major unmet needs be achieved.

Two Earthquakes

As I was well along the way toward finishing this book, two political earthquakes shook the country—the September 11 terrorist attacks, and the Enron scandals that began with the bankruptcy of that company and involved malfeasance by a number of major corporations. Until September 11, the end of Bill Clinton's presidency seemed the right cutoff point for the study, because ample available evidence showed how poorly the deteriorated federal institutions of government had served the American people. Then came the earthquakes, which yielded pure nuggets remarkable for the breadth of the pristine examples of the deep decline of the national political institutions. Moreover, the terrorists crashing airliners into the World Trade Center towers and the Pentagon figuratively jumped off the political Richter scale and instantly brought the national institutions of governance and the question of their competence and capacity to center stage.

Like children lifting a rock to discover the slimy, slithering bugs hidden under it, September 11 and its aftermath exposed for all to see a frightening level of inefficiency in the federal government. Since the 1980s, critics had observed the deterioration of the federal government institutions in the domestic policy arena; yet these problems of inadequate capacity seemingly did not register with most of the electorate or else struck them as unimportant for their well-being. In sharp contrast, the rock lifted up by the terrorist attacks delivered a message to the American people that could hardly be missed: Their safety, both at home and abroad, depends on the competence and commitment of their elected representatives in Washington and the federal civil servants working there and throughout the United States, as well as the men and women in the uniformed services.

Enron symbolizes a level of corporate malfeasance like that of the Gilded Age and the 1920s, two other periods during which plutocracy reigned as unfettered capitalism controlled the political system. Some of Enron's top executives seemingly combined excessive greed with a total lack of scruples. They "cooked the books" to falsely show rapidly growing profits in order to produce a striking run-up of Enron in the stock market that, in turn, enhanced the value of their stock options. Yet they could not have succeeded without collusion by accountants, stock analysts, and other private-sector gatekeepers charged with keeping the system honest. These gatekeepers had been freed from supervision by federal oversight agencies such as the Securities and Exchange Commission starting with the Reagan administration's massive deregulation effort. No president since the 1920s had been nearly as strong in his support of business as had Ronald Reagan until his disciple, George W. Bush, picked up the banner of Reaganism.

Democratic capitalism requires a balancing act. On the one hand, democracy must not place too many constraints on the incentives needed to stimulate the private-sector firms lest strong economic growth be held back. On the other hand, capitalism must not stifle the democratic institutions so that they lack the commitment and capacity to maintain political equality and sufficient economic opportunities for all to prosper with hard work. In the most entrepreneurial of nations, balancing has been complicated by the bias toward unfettered free-market capitalism. Democracy needs all the help it can get to avoid being dominated by corporate capitalism.

John Judis has argued that a factor in the "triumph of business and Republican conservatives" had been a lack of constructive leadership during Reaganism:

In the past, elites and elite organizations have remained steadfast in their support for policies that sought to reconcile democratic ideals of equality with the facts of corporate capitalism. Even in the hostile environment of the 1920s, the elite organizations had persevered. But that did not happen in the late seventies and the eighties. Far from providing a counterweight to corporate individualism and to the attack against pluralism and government, they came to reinforce it.[1]

Yet viable federal institutions of governance are a necessary element in the balancing act that keeps capitalism from crushing democracy and must be strengthened if the nation is to move back from plutocracy to representative democracy.

Failed Means and the Policy Window

By the end of the twentieth century, two viruses—*polarized politics* and *institutional deterioration*—had sickened the U.S. political system. The main institutions of national governance had been caught in a vicious cycle of deterioration that carried them to the lowest point in the postwar era. The White House had become a spin machine, spewing out misinformation and less-than-truthful commentary to protect or project the president's image and to sell his policies.

As bipartisanship withered away, Congress increasingly failed to function as a deliberative body seeking reasoned policy compromises for legislation that meets the nation's pressing domestic needs. Most federal agencies suffered from some combination of an insufficient number of competent staff members, pay schedules too low to attract outstanding specialists, and ancient computers and financial systems that were seldom able to produce enough sound, up-to-date information to support efficient management. The American political system became entrapped in the most polarized decision-making process of the postwar era. Risk-averse politicians concentrated mainly on reelection and voters lacked the political interest and knowledge needed for responsible citizenship. Reaganism—with its antigovernment, antiregulation, antitax, and probusiness philosophy—achieved its objective of hamstringing the federal institutions concerned with domestic policy. The pre–September 11 period offers a vivid portrait of damage wrought by this brand of political think-ing. The national institutional structure of governance had gone into a free fall, with nothing on the horizon to stop the decline.

The attacks by Osama bin Laden's al Qaeda terrorists—the rare cata-clysmic event capable of propelling institutions and individuals toward fundamental change—opened a policy window offering the opportunity to restore the capacity of the weakened public institutions to operate ef-ficiently. Suddenly, Americans saw that inadequate equipment, poorly paid and trained personnel, and private contractors that cut necessary outlays in pursuit of higher stock prices provided grossly inadequate airport se-curity to protect against terrorists and hijackers. Nor did the federal se-curity system have the vital information needed to track down possible terrorist attacks on bridges, ports, and nuclear facilities or the release of anthrax or other diseases into our air, food, and water. The Enron bank-ruptcy provided a reinforcing major aftershock that opened the policy window for institutional change even wider. The collapse showed that in-adequate federal regulatory efforts could both undermine the basic data needed for financial securities markets to have credibility with the pub-lic and fail to protect stock investors, including Enron employees, some of whom saw their entire retirement savings wiped out.

The terrorist attacks brought immediate changes in attitude by Wash-ington officials and the public. Greater cooperation came both in the po-litical and operational arenas. The president and the majority and minor-ity leaders in the House and Senate quickly displayed a patriotic spirit of problem solving to counter the terrorists. No change came as a greater surprise than the striking positive shift in how the people viewed their government and its main institutions and top political leaders. Citizens' trust in the federal government to do what is right, just about always or most of the time, had been in a long decline from its high of 76 percent in 1964. Vietnam and Watergate appeared to have brought a large per-manent drop in the public's confidence in the federal government. The trust measure fell to 19 percent in January 1999, the lowest point ever recorded.

Two weeks after the terrorist attacks, a poll indicated that more than 60 percent of the respondents trusted the government to do the right thing, by far the highest level of trust since 1966. Although September 11 challenged the strongly held views about the irrelevance of the federal government, deep institutional rot had already occurred. Seemingly without concern, citizens and their political leaders before the attacks had mouthed the shibboleth that the federal government is a necessary evil and should do as little as possible. At the start of the new millennium, the damaged institutions could not be fixed without costly new investment and a dramatic reorientation of the nation's attitude toward them. These changes required committed political leadership marked by boldness and honesty.

A symbiotic relationship exists in which strong leaders are critical for the operation of sound institutions and such institutions are needed as the support base for strong leadership. Institutions may be likened to vehicles that must have capable, responsible drivers who determine their direction, take care of their maintenance, and operate them to stay on course and reach the desired destination. The other side of the coin is that leaders need well-functioning vehicles that have the capacity to carry them where they want to go. A sound institution can provide the organizational structure and processes and the personnel and nonhuman resources, such as computers, that facilitate and sustain the exercise of leadership over time.

The policy window opened by the attacks on the World Trade Center and the Pentagon brought forth a bold, committed leader against terrorism as President George W. Bush, less than a year into his first term, rallied America and a number of other countries to fight the threat. As a true believer in Reaganism, however, President Bush was the wrong leader at the right time to push for broad reform to strengthen the entire institutional structure. In addition, the war on terrorism pursued both at home and abroad called attention away from the strong legislation to curb corporate corruption that had been passed at the height of public indignation about business malfeasance. Terrorism stayed in the news. Corruption faded from view. The anger subsided. Business leaders persuaded politicians that a forceful implementation effort was not the way to treat their big campaign contributors.

The bill passed to prevent future Enrons had been particularly important. It offered the best opportunity since corporate America had gained excessive power in Washington to move back toward representative democracy supported by efficient federal institutions of governance. But big business's fierce objections to its stringency brought a pullback from strong implementation efforts. The policy window—which looked so promising after September 11 for initiating broad institutional reform to revivify the American political system—slammed shut as the president and Congress restricted significant institutional changes to the homeland security area, defined broadly to include efforts to deter terrorists and supporting regimes wherever they might be.

Challenges to the Institutional Reform Thesis

Does the health of the nation require an efficient federal government with the capacity to carry out its legislative mandates and to develop and implement new policies that address America's major needs? That is the question. This book's basic premise of the pivotal need to strengthen the federal governance structure is not without challenges. The fundamental one comes from antigovernmentism, which holds the Washington government to be a "necessary evil" only to be trusted in the areas of national defense at home and abroad and of monetary and fiscal policy. Those who make the second challenge argue that the highly polarized ideological conflict over the philosophy of governance is the dominant factor; the collapse of the federal government institutions is simply one of the effects. Neither challenge holds up, but considering them illuminates the basic structural issues that the United States needs to confront.

Government as a Necessary Evil

At the heart of the first challenge is the fundamental clash of two political philosophies of national governance: the New Deal and Reaganism. The former cast the federal structure as the main problem solver in the public sector. In direct contrast, Reaganism, the modern articulation of antigovernmentism, had as its dominant tenet that the federal government loomed as the main barrier holding back free-market capitalism from overcoming the nation's major socioeconomic problems and must be both reduced in size and severely constrained in its efforts.

The early 1980s provided adherents of Reaganism with the perfect opportunity to use this political philosophy to sweep aside the New Deal philosophy. Not only was the United States experiencing a recession and unprecedented double-digit inflation and interest rates, it kept falling further and further behind its two biggest economic rivals, Germany and Japan. Washington could easily be blamed for crushing American capitalism. Thus the facts accorded with the emerging antigovernmentism philosophy.

In the 1990s, the superb aggregate performance of the new economy challenged the argument that the federal government had to be cut back severely before American capitalism could rise again. Traditional federal government macroeconomic management made an important contribution to strengthening the economy in the 1990s. In particular, the Federal Reserve Board, led by Alan Greenspan, gained such great acclaim in keeping inflation contained and fostering rapid economic gains that Greenspan became known as "the second most powerful man in Washington." In the early 1990s, Presidents George H. W. Bush and Clinton joined with Congress to enact major federal tax increases and budget caps on spending that helped stem the unending stream of huge deficits unleashed in the early Reagan administration. In contrast, the states and localities and the private sector did not step forward to fill the gap, especially in the declining domestic policy arena. Antigovernmentism could be put in the docket as one of the culprits holding back the needed federal investment to support long-term social and economic progress.

On one level, that of actually reducing the size of the federal government, antigovernmentism did little. The theorists pushing antigovernmentism did not take into account the underlying institutional and political difficulties and costs of reducing the size of the national government. No remotely acceptable political means existed at the start of the Reagan administration for moving from a large to a small federal government.

Twenty years later, much the same could be said, despite President Bill Clinton's sizable reductions in the federal workforce. His boast that the era of big government had ended in his administration was mainly sound without any real substance. Whatever antigovernment rhetoric came forth from ordinary citizens, they wanted their favorite programs protected or expanded. Washington understood fully the dangers of doing specifically what the electorate called for generally. Even though antigovernmentism did not visibly shrink the size of the federal budget, adherence to the philosophy of limited government produced great damage to the body politic. The simplistic Washington-is-the-problem argument tended to dull the public's awareness of or interest in the serious domestic policy issues that needed to be addressed and blocked any institutional efforts to realistically debate them.

Although there has been wide disagreement between those who have praised Ronald Reagan and those who spelled out the harm he did, both sides should agree without qualification on one critical assessment: Reagan had a big presidency, a dominant presidency. Both his programs and his political philosophy have been major factors in shaping the U.S. economic and political systems in the decades since he came to the presidency. The power of Reagan's political leadership is clear; the extent to which it benefited or damaged the nation is the issue. My claim that Reaganism blighted America rests on the tremendous impact of Reagan's own actions during his two terms and on the continuing wide influence of his political philosophy. Antigovernmentism has had a lasting effect by greatly diminishing the capacity of the federal executive agencies to operate efficiently. Reagan's political thought brought forth policies that short-changed low- and middle-income families and favored business and the wealthy. In sum, a powerful president adhered to a wrongheaded political theory of governance and, on the basis of it, pushed through policies that did harm to the nation and the Constitution.

President Reagan inherited a government that had a number of institutional deficiencies, but it still functioned moderately well. Then, during the next two decades, his brand of virulent antigovernmentism weakened the institutional capacity of the federal government to develop and implement sound policies to a point where it had ceased to serve the domestic policy needs of the public. Sean Wilentz, a professor of history and director of the program in American studies at Princeton University, made this key point in discussing the Enron bankruptcy: "It signals a crisis in modern conservative thinking and politics—a crisis that has less to do with bad character than it does with scandalously bad federal policy. . . . [Enron] stands as a monument to the era of deregulation and laissez-faire business politics that has endured for more than 20 years."[2]

The weakened federal government in the last two decades of the twentieth century pursued the highly flawed policy of deregulation without strong monitoring that became one of the main culprits in both the savings and loan scandal and the Enron bankruptcy and generally facilitated deleterious business practices to increase reported profits. Whatever the appeal of Reaganism's modern antigovernmentism as a political philosophy for its time, it in no way refutes the thesis of the pivotal need to restore federal institutional efficiency and has made any effort to do so far harder in both political and structural terms.

Polarized Politics as the Dominant Factor

The problem with the assertion that the polarized politics caused the decline of the federal institutional structure is that the dynamic interaction of the two simply cannot be unraveled. The ideological conflict over governance and the ailing federal system are *joint* products of the traumatic years from the mid-1960s to the close of the 1970s. In striking contrast, the 1950s and the early 1960s, before the assassination of President John Kennedy, had been an exceptional time of domestic tranquillity and political peace exemplified by the remarkable bipartisan cooperation under the leadership of Republican President Dwight Eisenhower and two towering Texas Democrats—Senate Majority Leader Lyndon Johnson and House Speaker Sam Rayburn. The institutions of national governance appeared to be operating just as the Founders had envisioned. In 1964, as was noted, Americans recorded their highest level of trust in the federal government. Government worked, and the now pejorative term "liberalism" reached its high point in the postwar era.

Then came a veritable eruption, unleashing forces that battered the economy, the social structure, the political institutions, and civil society for nearly two decades. The late 1960s were beset by conflicts that many saw as threatening the American way of life (at least in the prevailing 1950s version). The urban riots and unrest in numerous large cities brought open animosity between blacks and whites and devastated the social fabric of the central cores of numerous cities. The rights revolution, which empowered racial and ethnic minorities and women, also created deep concern and hostility. Many reacted negatively to what they saw as unfair gains from affirmative action and to the perceived breakdown in the social order from rising sexual promiscuity and sharply increased drug use.

The Vietnam conflict—the longest war and only one lost in U.S. history—took the lives of more than 50,000 Americans and stirred up angry political protests, particularly on college campuses. In the 1970s, Vietnam continued to tear at the American psyche, and the Watergate scandal made

Richard Nixon the first president ever driven from office when he resigned to avoid impeachment. The 1973 price hike by the Organization of the Petroleum Exporting Countries marked the end of the postwar boom, with the remainder of the 1970s bringing appreciably lower rates of economic growth and productivity, double-digit inflation and interest rates, higher unemployment, and falling real wages.

The tumultuous events came one upon another like the afflictions of Job and blighted the years between the mid-1960s and the close of the 1970s. In the 1980s and beyond, the earlier traumatic times influenced how Americans thought about the federal government and filled the political environment with deep political animosities. As a result, the United States still suffers from two political afflictions: extreme polarization and deteriorating national institutions of government. Opposite sides of the same coin forged in the fire of intense socioeconomic and political turmoil, the two interact over and over to wreak havoc on the U.S. political system.

In rejecting these two challenges to the main premise that the collapsed national political institutions are the pivotal starting point for intervention, I need to be clear exactly what is being argued. The claim is not that the damage to these institutions constitutes the nation's biggest problem but rather that they do offer the best starting place to confront the failure to treat the most critical domestic policy needs of the American people. The national political institutions are part of both the problem and the solution. Significant positive change remains unlikely as long as they are inefficient. These venerable institutions, placed by the framers at the heart of the Constitution, continue to be the primary base for deliberating on the major public problems facing the nation and for exercising the high level of presidential and congressional leadership demanded for sound governance.

Democracy in Peril

When Benjamin Franklin came out of the final session of the Constitutional Convention in Philadelphia, of which he was the most famous resident, an onlooker, Mrs. Samuel Powel, asked, "Well, Doctor, what have we got, a Republic or a Monarchy?" The venerable statesman and scientist, then more than eighty years old, replied, "A Republic, if you can keep it."[3] In 1789, the American Republic emerged as the world's first representative democracy. The several elements of that concept, however, were not laid out in the Constitution itself, so I have drawn mainly on the writings of James Madison to indicate the *rights* of citizens, the *obligations* of the electorate and its chosen representatives, and the *relationships* between the electorate and the members of Congress and among the latter that can be summed up as "Madisonian representative democracy":

- All eligible voters will have an equal chance to participate fully in the national electoral process.
- Citizens must expend the effort to gain sufficient political information and knowledge for reasoned voting behavior.
- Members of Congress must serve their constituents as their agents, with the primary obligation of faithfully representing their constituents' specific policy concerns and their broader political interests during deliberations in Congress.

It needs to be noted that Madisonian representative democracy requires full political citizenship to be earned by the electorate through the acquisition of enough political information and knowledge to understand the relevant policy issues in the election. Although voter competence is a necessary requirement for full political citizenship, it is not sufficient. The electorate also must have an equal opportunity to participate in the process of selecting candidates and officeholders, and this requirement demands more than an equal chance to vote. A blocked process can keep even the most conscientious citizen from obtaining full political citizenship—a situation that became increasingly likely during the last two decades of the twentieth century in the wake of big-money politics.

Costly election campaigns give major contributors greater and greater power in the selection process as their contributions determine which candidates will have the resources to compete in the election. Given the political power of big money, it is no surprise that members of Congress listen more to their major contributors than their constituents, so that political equality for ordinary citizens has declined severely. The link between politicians and the people necessary for Madisonian representative democracy to work has been severed. At the same time, the American public does not perceive democracy to be in trouble. A December 14–15,

2000, *Washington Post*–ABC News poll, conducted just after the Supreme Court decision on the Florida vote recount that gave George W. Bush the presidency, found that nine out of ten Americans remained confident that the United States still has "the best system of government in the world."[4]

Citizens now subscribe to a newer, far less demanding concept of democracy that will be termed the "Democratic Ideal." The current notion has two main components. First, the public views the Constitution as the nation's secular bible, which created America's unexcelled brand of democracy. This superiority of American democracy stands as an article of faith and is not susceptible to challenge.

Second, the newer concept places personal liberty above political liberty, with the former reflected by the degree of individual freedom of choice. Political scientist Andrew Hacker has argued that "America's obsession with shopping" is ingrained deep in the culture, "the freedom to shop ... is the choice Americans cherish most," and "possessions, carefully selected, become dimensions of our identities."[5] The earlier obligation of the electorate to acquire sufficient political knowledge to make reasoned voting choices has ceased to hold. Attaining full political citizenship under the Democratic Ideal has become a "right" much like becoming legally able to buy alcohol upon reaching a specified age. There is a big difference, however. At the required age, people can actually purchase alcoholic beverages. At the specified age to vote, the mantle of full political citizenship will not necessarily buy real political equality. The product received could easily turn out to be the equivalent of nonalcoholic beer.

The American people have much to answer for in the loss of representative democracy. Although they are victims of both the information overload and distortion generated by the electronic revolution and the misinformation and misleading commentary of polarized politicians, citizens generally have failed to seek needed political information to comprehend the meaning and implications of proposed policies. Moreover, the striking lack of political information and knowledge has not stopped the American public from believing themselves to be well prepared to cope with policy complexity, and such overconfidence has eased the way for governmental and nongovernmental entities to misinform them.

Despite concerted efforts by their elected politicians to mislead the American people about policy proposals that are not in citizens' best interests, they never doubt that democracy works and their system remains the best in the world. Pundits and politicians continue to praise the wisdom of the people, but what stands out in recent years is their political ignorance coupled with their susceptibility to dishonest information and slanted commentary that plays to their cherished myths. Democracy still survives in the United States, but it is a pale version of the brand needed to sustain Franklin's Republic.

Looking Ahead

The book's next three chapters will discuss the main concepts to be used in the analysis, delve more deeply into the Reagan presidency and Reaganism, and consider the nature of federal governance, concentrating mainly on the Constitution. After that, the focus for several chapters will be on the details of the decline in the key institutions of the American political system—the presidency, Congress, the agencies, the parties, and the media—and the increasing difficulties faced by the electorate in fulfilling its responsibilities as citizens. Before doing so, the stage needs to be set by laying out the major charges in the bill of indictment of Ronald Reagan and Reaganism. As to the economy during and after the Reagan administration, it will be argued that President Reagan's policies did more harm than good and were particularly damaging in materially increasing the maldistribution of income and wealth. Nor did Reaganomics stimulate the 1995–2000 boom and could have deterred the strong economic growth if presidents George H. W. Bush and Bill Clinton and Congress had not enacted major tax increases and stringent budget caps to contain the yearly deficits.

I will level five main charges against President Reagan and his philosophy of governance as principal culprits in damaging the federal institutions. First, Reaganism's antigovernmentism and market fundamentalism (i.e., unfettered capitalism is superior to government in solving domestic public policy problems) convinced the American people that Washington was the problem, never the solution. The Reagan administration reduced the capacity of the federal agencies to manage existing programs efficiently and to provide the sound information and analyses needed for reasoned policymaking. These destructive efforts greatly decreased the ability of these agencies to carry out their legislative mandates and left the domestic policy legacy of a hollow, incompetent federal government.

Second, excessive business deregulation led to major reductions in the size and capability of regulatory staffs and restricted their use in monitoring private-sector companies. The inept federal regulatory efforts made it easy for large corporations to alter their books so as to improve their stated earnings. They were aided and abetted by public accounting firms in covering up these practices and by financial analysts who used the overstated earnings to ballyhoo the stocks. This collusion among corporations, their accountants, and stock market analysts contributed both to the excessive stock market speculation that brought the major bear market that began early in the twenty-first century and also to the overhang of excessive investment by corporations that impeded economic growth.

Third, the hard-right ideology driving Reaganism led to the debilitating levels of political animosity between the president and members of the opposition party in Congress and among the Democratic and Republican members in both the House and the Senate. At times, the bodies barely functioned because of the diminished bipartisanship. Moreover, the ideological battles spawned a plethora of political misinformation and biased commentary that made it increasingly difficult for citizens to interpret political information and to understand the implications of proposed policies.

Fourth, the Reagan administration's deep federal income tax cuts and probusiness changes disproportionately benefited the wealthiest families and greatly increased the financial capacity of large firms to fund the campaign needs of candidates for national office. Senators and representatives became so beholden to the big campaign contributors led by corporate America that they put business interests ahead of those of their constituents and turned the United States into an early-stage plutocracy. This growing maldistribution of income and wealth afforded moneyed interests undue political control and robbed ordinary citizens of their political equality and full political citizenship.

Fifth, Reaganism struck down Madisonian representative democracy by damaging the federal institutions that have historically been inseparably intertwined with it. Madisonian representative democracy depended on the efficiency of these institutions, which had the responsibility to sustain the activities and procedures required for the continuance of this concept of governance. When President Reagan's unrelenting attack on government decreased the capacity of Congress to engage in reasoned deliberations and work out sensible compromises on policies, it undercut a critical decision-making process needed for the viability of representative government. By striking at the institutions that underpinned Madisonian representative democracy, Reagan attacked the basic concept of American democracy, even though that may not have been his intention. Ignorance in this case is no excuse. *No charge looms larger against Reaganism than that its tenets induced federal policies and organizational and individual behavior that led the nation into plutocracy and a much diminished brand of democracy.*

In subsequent chapters, we will find several external culprits—Reaganism, big-money politics, the information explosion, the media, and the electorate—and some internal ones where the institutions suffered harm from within, all of which interacted in battering the federal institutions of government and in crushing Madisonian representative democracy. I will argue that Reaganism should be put at the top of the list of external culprits; however, some clarification is needed. Big-money politics and We the People are not far behind Reaganism. A fair analogy is to a gang of bank robbers made up of specialists—the person who can open any safe, the one who decommissions security systems, and the expert driver. Each makes a key contribution in a bank heist.

Reaganism gets first place because of its influence on other culprits. Its antitax, antiregulation, probusiness tenets helped big business and wealthy families gain the resources to fill politicians' campaign chests and propelled corporate America toward excessive influence in Washington. Reaganism's antigovernmentism, unshakable belief in America's brand of democratic capitalism, and simplistic optimism lulled the public into greater and greater complacency about the direction in which the United States was going. Rating the culprits, however, is not as important as recognizing that the new political philosophy had a major role in the assault on representative democracy and the federal institutions needed to sustain it.

When working on this book before September 11, I sought to make a strong argument that broad institutional reform represented the pivotal first step toward a more democratic federal government that would better serve the most pressing domestic policy needs of the American people. Without strong institutions of government, policies will be badly executed, serious domestic challenges facing the nation will either be ignored or poorly considered, and plutocratic governance will continue. Moreover, the institutional damage is severe, wondrous fixes are lacking, the cost of repairs will likely be high, and the execution of them will be long and frustrating. Whatever the merits of the argument, broad institutional reform had little or no chance of being undertaken in the hostile political environment of the early twenty-first century. Then the al Qaeda terrorists brought a huge opening. But the policy window quickly closed and made the initiation of significant institutional changes extremely difficult outside the homeland security area, broadly defined.

An important difference after September 11 is that the dramatic costs of ineptitude in federal agencies often became major media stories that sent the strong message "inefficiency can cost lives." Although the need to strengthen the operation of the federal institutions became more evident, the most critical problem of the rise of plutocracy mainly stayed below the noise level. Even when the issue of corporate corruption did gain wide media coverage, the story line did not treat the more basic problem that the political environment for such corruption had come about because the U.S. political system is no longer the representative democracy conceived by the Founders and instead is dominated by major corporations and the wealthy. Selling the argument that the United States has become a plutocracy will be an uphill battle; optimism is hard to come by. That does not diminish the need to spell out as best I can that institutional overhaul is pivotal for restoring representative democracy and is a task demanding an immediate all-out effort.

Finally, I need to comment briefly on two important topics that will receive scant attention: the rightward shift of the federal judiciary and the marked decline in voting at the national level in both presidential and off-year elections. As to the latter, there will be extended discussion of whether eligible voters have adequate political information and knowledge to make reasoned choices among presidential and congressional candidates, but only a limited consideration of voting behavior.

A clear marker in the years since the inauguration of Ronald Reagan has been a dramatic movement on the political spectrum toward the right. This shift, which occurred in both national parties to a degree few would have expected a quarter of a century ago, has been a key factor in reshaping the key institutions of governance. Liberal Democrats, with some exceptions, not only have moved away from the left as defined in years past but have dwindled in numbers among national politicians. Liberal Republicans now appear to be extinct; even those of the moderate persuasion in the Grand Old Party are few in number. Ideologically, the Republicans of today are much closer to the thinking of the 1920s than that of the 1960s.

This shift has been at least as strong in the federal judiciary as in other institutions in the American political system. It has come about because a disciplined Republican Party relentlessly pursued a clear agenda while the Democratic politicians have been "astonishingly passive," to quote University of Chicago law professor Cass Sunstein. He observed further that the Republican leadership want a federal judiciary: "to reduce the powers of the federal government . . . to strike down affirmative-action programs and campaign-finance laws; to diminish privacy rights . . . and to protect commercial interests . . . from government regulation."[6] The Republicans' success in getting their nominees appointed to the federal judiciary and blocking those seen as threats to their agenda has been striking.

Sunstein has underscored the same kind of radical shift to the right in the courts as in the rest of the federal government as well as the failure to perceive it: "To a degree that has been insufficiently appreciated, and in some ways is barely believable, the contemporary federal courts are fundamentally different from the federal courts of just two decades ago." [7] Not only is Sunstein's assessment of change correct; so also are his observations about the rapidity of the institutional change and the lack of appreciation of its magnitude. What has happened, however, is a piece of a seismic shift in the central institutions of the American political system.

It is worth noting one facet distinctly different for the courts: A number of the right-wing judges who were relatively young when appointed will be on the bench for many years to come. Although this dimension of a court in which members are appointed for life has major implications for institutional change, we only need to note it without treating the federal courts further because they have been on the same path as the other institutional elements of the overall U.S. political system.

Harvard University professor Thomas E. Patterson writes that "the period from 1960 to 2000 marks the lowest ebb in [voter] turnout in the nation's history."[8] In the earlier year, 63 percent of the citizenry participated; by 2000, the vote declined to 49 percent of the electorate, falling below 50 percent for the first time since the 1920s. Even the close

Bush–Gore election in 2000 only brought out 51 percent of the eligible voters.

Disaggregating the data showed an even grimmer picture. Despite being the best educated groups in history—at least as measured years in school—Patterson observed: "Today's young adults are less politically interested and informed than any cohort of young people on record." [9] The voting rate for adults under the age of thirty years plummeted from 50 to 30 percent between 1972 and 2000. In the world's first great democracy, voters are vanishing at an alarming rate, led in the flight from the polls by the youngest members of the electorate.

Patterson's analysis shows a massive structural failure of the current presidential election system. Little works right anymore, as he noted:

> In 1878, the British statesman William Gladstone declared the U.S. Constitution to be "the most wonderful work ever struck off at a given time for the brain and purpose of man." Would anyone of his stature say the same about the design of today's presidential election system? What words would describe a jerry-built system that includes an outdated Electoral College, a chaotic nominating process, tepid party conventions, and an Election Day administered by states and localities that differ in their registration procedures, polling hours, balloting measures, and commitment to full participation? What could be said of an election process that is easily the world's most time consuming, cumbersome, and expensive? [10]

In short, the many institutional structures and processes in the presidential election system are highly inefficient and often counterproductive, like much of the rest of the American political system.

two

Analyzing Federal Governance

Several important concepts need to be set out to guide this analysis of the national institutions of governance that will move across a number of diverse areas. We start with brief sections on the functions to be carried out by the federal government and the nature of means. Next will be three sections spelling out the organizational concepts—competence, capacity to compromise, and credibility—that help guide this analysis of the federal institutions. Then comes a discussion of the central place of political information and commentary for the federal institutions, the media, and the public in assessing how well the institutions are performing. Finally, the chapter turns to the complex interrelation between the political system and the economy. Both the performance of the economy, particularly in distributing income and wealth, and the dominance of market fundamentalism were critical in the deterioration of the federal institutions during the last two decades of the twentieth century.

Federal Government Functions

Notwithstanding all the ideological battles that have filled the air since the early 1980s, all the jokes about Washington's ineptness, and all the claims that the national government is irrelevant made through September 10, 2001, the great bulk of the specific federal functions now carried out are generally accepted by the American people. To start with, despite the vast number of federal programs, roughly four-fifths of the federal budget goes for retirement income, mainly Social Security; health protection, primarily Medicare and Medicaid; national defense; and servicing the national debt. Except for the final category, which involves mandatory interest payments, the other programs are generally under pressure to be expanded, not reduced. Nor are draconian reductions likely in the wide array of programs that account for the other fifth of the budget.

Disagreements often turn out to be over programs that are misperceived as being expensive, such as nonmilitary foreign aid, or policy issues that have little or no dollar outlays, such as mandating prayer in public schools.

When people call for big cutbacks in Washington, they are seldom specific and generally have a very limited understanding of the many important functions the federal government carries out. As the former Washington correspondent and current analyst of the political system Elizabeth Drew has written:

> To dismiss Washington as "irrelevant"—and therefore unworthy of one's attention or efforts—is to overlook the fact that that's where law and policy are made on taxes, medical care, the quality of our air and water, Social Security, the national defense, foreign involvements, the safety of airplanes, abortion, securities regulation, the release of new drugs, gun control, the soundness of our banks, disaster relief, continuing education and training, to name just some. And it's where the state of our schools, housing, transportation, and the overall economy are heavily affected.[1]

Drew's list could be greatly expanded with more critical federal efforts, such as monetary and fiscal policy, homeland security, justice and public safety, environmental protection and preservation, and public land use, again to name only some of them. When Americans think about what the federal government should be doing to make their lives better, the list, even before September 11, 2001, had been long and costly, with the problem more likely being that too little is being done, not too much. The Florida voting debacle, the terrorist attacks, and the Enron corporate corruption scandal underscored that the federal government should be doing more rather than less to ensure voting rights, provide for public health and safety within our borders, and monitor a variety of commercial practices, including ones that make employees vulnerable to losing all or most of their retirement savings.

The critical issues about functions tend to arise from the unwillingness of the U.S. citizenry to pay for the functions and the incapacity of the federal government to carry them out efficiently and effectively, not from concern about their reasonableness per se. As to the former, citizens' fear of income taxes and belief that people are overburdened by them have led to a tax schedule that is less and less progressive and increasingly inadequate to meet the pressing domestic policy problems faced by the bulk of the American population. As to the latter, virulent antigovernmentism and the ensuing political polarization have made the federal institutions of governance increasingly inefficient. These two issues, particularly government competence, dominate the remainder of this book, rather than the relatively uncontroversial one of the American people's views on the appropriate functions of the national government.

Means Matter

The relationship between means and ends is an often ignored but critical element in the analysis of the federal government institutions. The term *ends,* which will be generally interchangeable with objectives and goals, indicates what an organization desires to accomplish in a particular effort. Keeping the inflation rate below 3 percent, putting a person on the moon, or eradicating the threat of polio have been final objectives. The same ends often guide policy year after year. In the first case, even if the United States has accomplished the goal each year for more than three decades, the federal institutions, particularly the Federal Reserve Board, must be ready for threats, such as rapidly rising oil prices, to a continuing low inflation rate. *Effectiveness* is the measure of how well an organization does in reaching a desired end.

Means are the "implements" employed in seeking to reach specific objectives and can range from a hammer to a governing body with all of its structural elements and detailed procedures. Different as the two may be in a number of dimensions, the hammer and the governing body are both devices or ways that can be used to carry out tasks needed to achieve desired objectives. In this regard, each can be used efficiently, as when the hammer is in the hand of a master carpenter, or inefficiently, as when that same tool is employed by a ten-thumbed weekend builder. *Efficiency* is the criterion used for measuring how well an institution does in executing its organizational tasks. The measure is sometimes described as an "intermediate or instrumental objective" because it is a necessary, but not sufficient, condition for attaining the final objective.

It needs to be noted that the main roadblock to achieving objectives likely will not be the dearth of policy proposals that look reasonable on paper but rather the lack of sufficient federal institutional capacity to enact, implement, and manage the needed policies. A carefully designed policy that looks highly promising on the drawing board may not pan out when properly tested in the field. The hard organizational reality is that inefficient means (e.g., poorly devised laws, understaffed projects) will block policy effectiveness; yet sound means do not guarantee successful outcomes. In light of the deterioration of the federal institutions, however, the first step should be to improve their operation, because organizational inefficiencies block sensible legislation and thwart the execution of laws already in place.

Means Can Be Harmful

Two important characteristics of means are that they generally carry with them known or unknown deleterious consequences and also may be employed for good or evil. As to the latter, the fastest, safest, most reliable automobile may swiftly transport a pregnant woman to the hospital in weather most foul or whisk bank robbers to safety. Another automobile example—the sport-utility vehicles (SUVs) that became so popular among families with children because of their expected safety—illustrates the question of expected and unexpected deleterious consequences. It was clear from the beginning that SUVs would have the undesirable feature of poor gas mileage as a result of their heavy body weight, which came about in part because of safety concerns. But the vehicles also had the unexpected consequences both of crushing the hood of a smaller car in a head-on collision because of the height of the SUV bumper and of rolling over far more often than other vehicles.

Unanticipated deleterious outcomes are the bane of policymaking. The most valuable aspect of analyses of the efficacy of proposed policy alternatives may be uncovering potentially harmful consequences of the proposed course of action that its designers have not discovered or, more sinisterly, have not revealed. Suppose an archetypical policy analyst of yesteryear had heard Shakespeare's King Richard III crying, "A horse! A horse! My kingdom for a horse!" The analyst well might have thought, even if lacking the courage to say it:"Prithee, take a hard look at any proffered steed before turning over the keys to his kingdom and leaping into the saddle." Such skepticism surely makes for poor drama, but it is good advice in considering whether to buy a horse or a proposed institutional structure.

The fact that implements can be used to help or to harm and may have negative side effects embedded in them holds true for governing institutions just as for any other means. The South of my youth is a pristine case of the intentional use of government institutions for evil both through such laws as the poll tax, which in effect barred black residents from voting, and through such administrative actions as different police and judicial enforcement policies for black persons. Growing up during the 1940s in an East Texas city of 35,000 people with a black population of about 25 percent showed me at close hand how highly efficient governing institutions could be. That part of the state was much more like the Deep South than the rest of Texas—East Texas was to Texas as Mississippi was to the South.

In my East Texas hometown, elected officials were expected to maintain the white majority's goals of full racial segregation and to keep the black residents docile and disenfranchised. For example, the city's black and white schools were geographically distant and had no common activities, including sports. The typical white young person would not know any black youths and probably only had much direct contact with black adults working as maids or in menial jobs generally demanding physical strength. As had been the case going back into the nineteenth century, democratically elected public officials used then-legal means to establish clear expectations about the behavior of the city's minority residents. The certainty that the establishment would act swiftly and harshly if there were any violation of the established norms created a level of fear so high that life-threatening physical intimidation of blacks was unlikely to be needed to exert full control.

The more efficient a government's institutional structure, the higher the chances that the elected leaders of that government can achieve their own or their constituents' sought-after objectives, be they noble or ignoble. In the long-established, rigid institutional caste system of my youth, the high level of government efficiency produced an environment without overt violence, so that black people, when observed by white persons, appeared content with their lot. My point obviously is not to condone that vile system of subjugation of the black minority but to underscore the striking operational success of the institutional structure. It is also important to recognize that the South in general and the East Texas city where I lived were not acting on their own. Presidents, Congress, and the federal judiciary all aided and abetted the states and localities in pursuit of these goals. Looking back over fifty years or more, the efficiency of the means employed in this repressive effort still astounds me. Only strong federal institutions and the deep commitment of President Lyndon Johnson to enact and enforce the Civil Rights Act of 1964 and the Voting Rights Act of 1965 made serious progress toward undoing these state and local governing practices.

The Institutions of Government and Representative Democracy

Representative democracy became the Founders' central concept, specifying the desired institutional relationships between the governors and the governed and among the representatives when in session. It can be cast as an end, in that full political citizenship under Madisonian representative democracy is aimed at providing voters with the freedom of choice to determine which particular individuals will be their representatives in the national government. A government of the people, by the people, and for the people is a desirable outcome in and of itself. When full political citizenship under Madisonian representative democracy is considered an end, the federal institutions are the chosen governmental means for sustaining this brand of democracy.

The presidency, Congress, the judiciary, and the executive agencies are all responsible for maintaining the viability of Madisonian representative democracy. These entities' institutional inefficiency in executing this mission can undermine representative government. For example, this will be the case when congressional polarization reduces the bipartisanship needed for representatives to carry out their responsibility under representative democracy to engage in serious deliberations to create a base for developing reasonable legislation and for informing citizens of major national issues. Representative democracy is also harmed if members of Congress pursue the interests of their major campaign contributors at the expense of their constituents. Madisonian representative democracy and the institutions of governance are inseparably intertwined.

Representative democracy can also be conceptualized as a means, in being based on the theory that a governance structure whereby the people choose the executive and the members of the legislature who will represent them in governing will be the superior implement—as compared with a monarchy, whereby a king and an aristocracy rule—in reaching national objectives such as those set out in the Preamble to the Constitution. When representative democracy is conceived as a means for attaining national goals, it and the federal institutions are still crosscutting, and the levels of efficiency of these institutions will continue to be important for the health of representative democracy. Moreover, representative democracy and the federal institutions crafted to maintain it remain so intertwined that efforts to batter these federal institutions becomes an attack on representative democracy and the American Republic as conceived in the Constitution crafted in Philadelphia in 1787. This will be true whatever the motive for trying to weaken the federal institutions.

Three Faces of Competence

Complex institutions generally combine a great variety of skills—from those that have precise dimensions, such as simple clerical and highly technical jobs, to those that involve softer skills, of which leadership is the most prominent one. A static listing of the various levels of competence available to an institution is only one aspect of how efficient or effective the institution will be. At issue is how well the individual members work together. To emphasize the importance of the dynamics of performance is not meant to downplay the role of a highly capable staff but to recognize that individual and institutional competence are not the same thing and may even move in opposite directions. In the 1980s, individual competence in Congress rose dramatically, while institutional competence declined even more rapidly. As individual members of Congress became increasingly competent, they became more independent and often did not want to be restricted by institutional demands from pursuing their agendas, even though their actions might threaten to undermine the standing of the House or the Senate in the eyes of the public. This counterintuitive result of individual and institutional competence not going in the same direction became critical in the decline of the national political institutions, and it is important for gaining a better understanding the dynamics of the institutional deterioration.

In considering the competence factor, three definitions will be used: *absolute,* which is cast in terms of state-of-the-art skills; *comparative,* which sets out the level of competence demanded by the economic, social, and political challenges that threaten the nation; and *perceived,* which is based on whatever criteria, information, and political beliefs that people choose to use in assessing competence. Both absolute and comparative competence rely on a measuring rod, albeit one much less precise than a ruler, to assess individual and institutional competence. Perceived competence, in contrast, may be little more than a "gut" judgment based on misinformation and the politics of unreality. In considering the three definitions, it is best to start with the most straightfoward one of absolute competence, which is based on the actual capability of individuals, organizations, and institutions as compared with existing state-of-the-art capability levels.

The notion of absolute competence is not restricted to specialized technical capability but includes the whole range of policy, managerial, and political skills and knowledge. Competence demands for agency heads and their technical staff members illustrate some of the differences in the breadth and depth of skills and knowledge needed in complex organizations. The archetypal competent agency head would have a profound understanding of how large-scale organizations work, extensive political and managerial experience and know-how, broad program and policy knowledge, the capacity to interpret policy and program information and analysis, and a proven record of success in leading large-scale organizations. In contrast, the needed skills and knowledge of the ideal information specialist are more narrow than those of the agency leader, but far more demanding in the area of technical expertise. Policy analysts, for example, should have mastery of the relevant data, research, and analyses in their particular areas of expertise and the capacity to manipulate information to develop well-reasoned analyses as a basis for higher-level decision making. For large-scale federal organizations, the most important skills will generally be those involving managerial and leadership capabilities. For example, two policy offices with similar missions may have comparable staffs as based on technical expertise, but one may be much more efficient because of the greater capability of the head of the unit to manage the staff and interact with top management.

Comparative competence takes into account the difficulty of overcoming the policy and political barriers to successful governance. The key question is not how able are political leaders and their governments as assessed by state-of-the-art standards but how capable are the individuals and the institutions when their resources are pitted against the demands of the policy and political challenges to be confronted. Raise the policy and political difficulties; increase the level of competence demanded for efficient performance. The end of Dwight Eisenhower's administration in 1961 marked a dividing line between a period of relatively limited domestic challenges and the ensuing one of highly explosive shared governance among federal, state, and local officials brought on by the new social and environmental legislation of the mid-1960s and early 1970s. Nor had the rights revolution yet emerged during the complacent years of the 1950s. The point is not that the problems were absent but that they were unnoticed or ignored. Then policy and politics erupted and produced dramatically increased demands, which overwhelmed the state-of-the-art tools and techniques then available. Thus, a government with the top marks for absolute competence could still be sadly deficient in its comparative competence and hence deemed to have failed to meet the particular policy and political challenges of its time.

Perceived competence is a much slipperier notion than the other two definitions because there need be no tie to reality for people to render a judgment. When the public lacks information or is misinformed about what the federal government spends or does, citizens' perception of the individual politicians and their institutions' competence to govern may be severely distorted. A 1994 poll taken on election night found that 46 percent of people thought either nonmilitary foreign aid or welfare produced the biggest outlays in the federal budget. In actuality, nonmilitary foreign aid equaled roughly 1 percent of the budget, as did what most people thought of as welfare—the (then) Aid to Families with Dependent Children program. Social Security, by far the largest federal program, took 22 percent of the federal budget. Yet many people, whether they knew Social Security claimed more than one-fifth of the entire budget or not, wanted benefits to be increased. The 46 percent of those polled who erroneously believed that the biggest federal expenditures were either nonmilitary foreign aid or welfare in all probability saw such vast outlays as gross misspending that could have been dramatically reduced and used for much more pressing needs such as retirement security. That citizens are badly misinformed about what the federal government spends and how it operates surely helps shape their perceptions of their political leaders' competence to govern and, at times, may be an overriding factor.

Central to the perception issue is whether or not citizens can make reasonable judgments about politicians and policies without having both sound, relevant information on the federal government and the capacity to understand what those data mean. The public's information difficulties have been made worse by politicians' increasing attempts to hide information or overtly distort it as they relentlessly pursue a favorable public perception. This use or misuse of information is part of a larger effort by the nation's political leaders, particularly presidents, to control the public's perception of their performance. Starting with President Ronald Reagan, large staffs began to manage the president's image and reputation. Over time, these image managers have come to package the president's best features in seeking to create an aura of competence and confidence and to distort potentially harmful news to negate its impact. Yet their success is not assured. But in President Reagan's case, these efforts made him look every inch the forceful leader in full command of any situation and often completely covered over his managerial weaknesses. Reagan's handlers adroitly manipulated the public so that they accepted fiction as fact and perceived the president as having great competence in making decisions.

Misperceptions about the competence of political leaders carry two dangers. Gross overestimates of competence can gain strong public support for leaders to pursue wrongheaded policies. Alternatively, citizens' misperceptions about a relatively competent president may cast him as so inept that any leadership effort will be stymied. Such misperceptions can be increasingly dangerous because the actions of government are likely to be more rather than less important. The United States will be confronted in the twenty-first century by major domestic policy problems it has ignored or confronted ineptly in the past, such as an aging population not adequately prepared for retirement, a failing health system that is the costliest in the world, and an increasingly unfair federal income tax structure that unduly benefits the rich and worsens the most unequal distributions of income and wealth among the major industrial democracies. As Peter Drucker has written: "The function of government and its functioning must be central to political thought and political action. . . .

[Efficient and] effective government has never been needed more than in this highly competitive and fast-changing world of ours."[2] In the case of the federal government, it may lose power to the states and have fewer functions, but those it retains will be more critical than ever and require at least as high a level of institutional competence as today, and likely an even higher one.

Compromise

The capacity for reasoned compromise is a tool of the trade that requires a high level of competence for satisfactory performance. It will be treated separately, however, because America's unique system of governance, with its separate powers for each branch, demands compromises for legislation to pass—unlike a parliamentary system, which combines the executive and legislative functions and thus does not need such compromises. The harsh polarization of the American political system that began in the 1980s made reasoned compromises increasingly hard to hammer out as political opponents tended to take positions that were far apart and prided themselves on holding to them. When Speaker of the House Newt Gingrich, the main architect of the Contract with America, considered compromising on its policy pronouncements, the true-believer Republican House members, mainly the first-term representatives elected when their party recaptured Congress in 1994, turned on their former hero. They drove him from the House, despite the fact that he had been the key actor both in shaping their conservative manifesto and in establishing the foundation for the unexpected election victory of many, if not most, of them.

Speaker Gingrich certainly did commit the crime with which he was charged by his radical followers. That he did so is hardly surprising, in that negotiating a compromise that reconciles competing demands had been embedded in the constitutional structure by the framers of that venerable document. Despite this, it became common in the 1990s to label any compromise as a sellout of principles. Doing so showed a fundamental misunderstanding of the Constitution itself, or an exceptionally cynical political posturing, or the debilitating impact of the growing polarization and its accompanying true-believer mentality—or a combination of all these. Whatever the cause, the result was a dangerous Congress that usually fled from needed legislation or enacted ill-thought-through policies.

A careful look at the key elements in the negotiation process and the act of compromise itself begins with setting out the concept's main components: one or more conflicting or opposing claims, principles, or objectives among the parties (using only two parties hereafter, for purposes of clarity); a process whereby the two parties can negotiate mutual concessions, which include both benefits and losses for each; and an acceptance by the parties of a final binding agreement. Although the three required elements in the definition do not address the issue of the quality or the viability of the compromise over time, they provide a useful base for setting out the requirements for an ideal negotiating process for reaching reasonable compromises on major issues. First, the opponents would consider how to reconcile their differences in extended deliberations marked by mutual respect, civility, and the use of sound information and analyses. Second, the compromise would take into account the relevant systemic needs and balance the necessary gains and losses in such a way that the agreement would be acceptable to both protagonists, would hold until environmental changes demanded reconsideration, and would facilitate future compromises. A good compromise requires that the proponents carefully weigh their gains and losses and decide that what is being won is sufficient to offset what is being given up.

The U.S. government has turned out to be more difficult to administer than any other form of democracy, so it is no surprise that other nations have rejected America's complex system of built-in checks on institutional power. Other democracies have instead chosen the parliamentary structure, which lets the government of the day unilaterally pass legislation and thus impose its will on what is often the toothless opposition. Although the latter does not enjoy its powerlessness, such suffering at the hands of the parliamentary majority is accepted because the opposition still wants the system to continue. After all, by winning an election, the opposition reverses the power situation. The oppressed becomes the majority party, which can now run roughshod over the new opposition and pass its legislative agenda without having to compromise. For almost all democracies, possessing either no loaf or a whole loaf seemingly outweighs each party gaining part of a loaf after negotiations or no bread at all unless a compromise is reached.

A successful compromise on controversial policy issues in the U.S. governance system involves a complex operational process that almost always requires extended negotiations in a give-and-take process in which each of the protagonists must make painful concessions. To further complicate matters, reasoned compromises demand two not necessarily compatible agreements during the negotiating process. First, both political parties must find the compromise acceptable so that it is likely to hold over time. Second, such a compromise must ultimately be prudent in facing up to its socioeconomic and political challenges.

Under ordinary circumstances, an incremental adjustment may do the job of allowing negotiators to reach these two agreements. But prudent is not a synonym for cautious. There are times when a major change is the wise course of government action. For example, with the U.S. banking system near collapse in early 1933, Franklin Roosevelt moved boldly in the first week of his presidency to save it. He was able to do so quickly because Democrats and Republicans both recognized the threat and the need for speed. It was the rare case where the panic-stricken Congress perceived the national emergency to be so grave that the usual process of extended negotiations and reluctant compromises would be dangerous. In the much more typical setting, acceptability and prudence will be more difficult to combine.

A prudent compromise can range from an incremental adjustment that barely separates the old and the new points of agreement to a major systemic shift. An unwise compromise arises when the negotiated policy either goes far beyond what is actually needed to cope with the problem at hand or falls well short of the level of effort required to treat that problem. Doing too much can be as deleterious as doing too little. The key variable in assessing the reasonableness of a specific compromise on a public policy problem is the degree of correspondence between the most appropriate feasible policy change for coping with the problem and the government's actual response. The term "feasible policy change" has been employed because what the government can do in seeking a needed major change may be severely restricted by technological and organizational limitations.

When the changes needed go beyond the capacity of available policy techniques, the negotiating process will have worked efficiently if it takes the policy compromise up to or near to the point of technical unfeasibility. In

general, the reasonableness of a policy compromise and hence the efficiency of the institutional process are measured by the degree to which
the actual and the needed policy changes are commensurate. The smaller
that distance between the two, the more reasonable the compromise and
the more efficient the institutional means supporting policymaking.

The passage of the British government's Great Reform Act of 1832 offers a pristine example of reasoned compromise that has gained from historical perspective. It not only brilliantly illustrates the essence of crafting
a prudent bill despite fierce disagreements that often threatened a complete breakdown in the legislative process but is also relevant because the
compromise took place before the adoption of the classic parliamentary
model whereby such agreements became of little consequence. Two powerful opponents with strikingly different views negotiated for fifteen
months to pass the bill.

During that momentous time, the nation's fate hung in the balance.
Britain faced the specter of civil war as British politics revolved around
memories of the 1789 French Revolution that overthrew a king and the
mild 1830 uprising in France that brought needed governmental reforms.
The 1789 revolution raised fears of the mob, whereas the 1830 uprising
underscored the value of reasonable change during a political crisis that
could have exploded. Attention in the early 1830s centered on the ancient system of rotten boroughs. These were usually relatively small geo-
graphic areas that were sparsely populated, perhaps by no more than a
handful of people. The rotten borough might be under the control of a
powerful aristocrat, such as a duke, who had his people elect his choice to
Parliament. In sharp contrast, no one residing in the rapidly growing cities
in the North of England such as Liverpool and Birmingham had a vote.

During the period of fifteen months of rising concern, the government's leader, Charles, Lord Grey, relentlessly sought compromise. But
he never retreated far from the original bold March 1831 bill because he
believed the political environment demanded a truly significant change
to keep Britain from nation-threatening strife. His opponents wanted to
hold fast against enfranchising the new industrial cities, whose urban
workers seemingly conjured up the French mobs of the 1789 Revolution. Lord Grey and his followers, in contrast, believed that the mild 1830
uprising in France, which had brought important and much needed governmental reforms, clearly showed the value of not standing pat or mak-

ing only incremental changes when the political environment demanded that major steps be taken. During the extended negotiations, Lord Grey realized he had to compromise, determined the points in the original legislation on which he could make concessions and not undercut the main objectives, and stood firm where he believed he could not.

The great British historian G. M. Trevelyan wrote of the 1832 bill's abolition of the rotten boroughs that it stood as "one of the most prudent acts of daring in history," and added that "a more perfect Bill [judged by twentieth-century standards] . . . would have failed to pass in 1832, and its rejection would sooner or later have been followed by civil war."[3] Trevelyan and other historians favorably quoted John Bright's statement from an 1864 speech:"'It was not a good Bill, but it was a great Bill when it passed.'"[4] From the perspective of 1864 or 1920, the Great Reform Act of 1832 hardly seemed a monumental step, because it did not broaden the vote to women or other excluded categories. However, such extensions of the vote were not the major political problem in the early 1830s. Putting them on the political agenda would have been foolhardy in asking for what were clearly unacceptable changes that likely would have undermined Lord Grey's main effort. Moreover, Trevelyan's "prudent act of daring"—the reasoned compromise of the 1832 act—set the stage for all subsequent legislation that widened the vote. Here is a classic case of a bold, but wise, compromise in response to a political environment that demanded significant reform to keep Britain from being torn apart.

In a more recent American example, Bernard Asbell saw the enactment of a new Clean Air Act led by Senator Edmund Muskie during a two-year period as a mid-twentieth-century American version of daring prudence. He wrote:"Muskie himself is satisfied that the law has located itself at that magical point of political balance: the boldest feasible act in the public interest that takes into account the relative political strengths and conflicting demands for justice of all contenders."[5]

These British and American examples stand out as prudent compromises that balanced the various competing factors in the equation "by both preserving the most essential elements of the political and social institutions at risk and meeting the demands of the changing environment."[6] A "just right" point of political balance that results in a reasoned compromise will not be known at the outset but will emerge over time in the political process of negotiation, in which the two advocates must make the necessary accommodations to move forward toward the eventual agreement. Successful compromises flow from a dynamic process of negotiation over time, with the final agreement developing during the give-and-take between protagonists who must make tactical judgments about what can be traded, what cannot, and the specific terms that will make a concession acceptable. The dimensions of the negotiated agreement are difficult to predict; however, the sounder the government institutions, the greater the probability that the result will be a prudent one—whether it is only a modest step or Trevelyan's "act of daring."

Credibility

When U.S. treasury secretary Robert Rubin resigned late in President Bill Clinton's second term, Texas Republican senator Phil Gramm, who often had fought with Rubin over policy issues, observed: "Of all the officials in the Clinton administration, he has had more credibility with me, and I think with Congress, than any other official. He will certainly be missed."[7]

If a person who saw only Senator Gramm's laudatory statement knew nothing about the Treasury Department's leader, that reader would not have known which of the two standard definitions of Rubin's credibility—"believable" or "worthy of belief or confidence"—the senator had intended. These alternative definitions may seem similar but can be worlds apart. The first requires belief and belief alone, whatever the source or however unrealistic in terms of available information. Rubin's credibility exemplifies the second definition, with his sterling reputation resting on his earlier experience as a highly successful Wall Street investment banker and his much praised performance as the central actor determining and guiding the Clinton administration's economic policy. Rubin's straightforward, self-effacing approach grounded in sound policy data and analyses earned him his unsullied reputation for honesty with Democrats and Republicans alike in an administration notorious for its partisan spin. "Credibility," according to this more demanding definition, which is used in this book, must be earned by making arguments that rest on sound evidence and/or logic.

To say that a person has credibility or that a particular argument is credible does not imply that either is unchallengeable. Even when the data meet the validity standards used by professional information specialists, the available research methods seldom (if ever) yield definitive data that cannot be legitimately questioned on theoretical or technical grounds.[8] The best that can be done is to produce sound or honest—the two are interchangeable—numbers, defined as those obtained when accepted technical procedures are applied both appropriately and in a nonpartisan manner (i.e., without a political bias).

Such information can still be questioned on the ground of its appropriateness or the quality of the specific methods and processes used to produce it. Honest numbers and analyses also can elicit strong disagreements among competent professional information specialists with no partisan axe to grind on how the data have been interpreted generally or have been employed specifically in an analysis. At the same time, there are widely accepted technical standards for data development and use and strongly held professional norms against knowingly biasing results to fit the predilections of political leaders.

It needs to be recognized that challenging data derived by employing state-of-the-art techniques without political spin does not mean that the disputing policy analysts are questioning each other's technical competence and personal or institutional integrity, which are basic elements in the second definition of credibility. Honest numbers can beget honest dispute (reasoned debate) among honest analysts. This last statement is not a Pollyanna-like claim of the purity of "real" professional analysts, but it does indicate two key aspects of analytic credibility. First, policy analysts individually and their organizations can attain high credibility with analysts of different social and political orientations. Second, credible opponents will be able to engage in reasoned arguments that may lessen the range of disagreement on information and analyses and support realistic compromise. In particular, the inaccurate claims that becloud so much debate can be reduced significantly—a signal achievement.

When it comes to the credibility of the federal government, citizens on the outside and those within may be looking at the same politicians, political executives, career staffs, and institutions, but the external and internal assessors usually differ strikingly. These sharp differences include their levels of interest and effort in making judgments and their resources for acquiring sound information and evaluating it. The starting place is external credibility, which in essence recasts the much-discussed concept of trust in government in a credibility framework. Michael Schudson, a communications professor at the University of California at San Diego, has argued that "trust, so far as the polls are able to measure it, is [not] an intelligible indicator of anything."[9] A low level of trust could indicate either the healthy skepticism that Madison saw as making government better or a dysfunctional cynicism that sees the federal government as irrelevant or corrupt most if not all of the time.

Conceptually, the public's trust in the federal government is like the notion of believability (the first definition of credibility) in not necessarily resting on a solid foundation. In their assessment of the external credibility of the federal government, citizens are likely to face a shortage of reliable information and are prone to rely on such factors as prejudice and ideology in their judgments. Although the public's assessment of Washington's credibility is a technically weak measure, the measure of trust in government seems to be a good proxy for external credibility, whereby the judgment about it rests mainly on limited, not necessarily accurate evidence, and is made without much effort. That is to be expected, in that there may be little reason for serious consideration of this abstract concept. Even when the people have chosen to focus seriously on the question of government credibility, the dearth of readily available good evidence and the amount of time and knowledge needed to dig it out may severely restrict their judgments.

Internal credibility has a different framework and dynamics from those of its external counterpart, in that the internal assessment generally is made by individuals who personally know the people being evaluated and deal directly with the institutions. For example, a member of Congress considering the credibility of individual Republican and Democratic House members, the two parties' leaders, and the president likely will have an evidence base ranging from extended relationships over years to brief meetings, perhaps never one-on-one, as might be the case with the president.

But even where direct exposure is limited, it can be supplemented by information and judgments obtained from respected individuals who have had extensive involvement with the president or others that the assessor does not know well. Moreover, the assessments of the significant individuals and organizations with which evaluators have important transactions, especially if the relationships are extended, are in a special class that justifies the investment of time and money to increase the quality of the information about colleagues' competence and integrity, be it in a public or a private organization.

A relatively high degree of internal credibility would appear to be a necessary condition for Congress to engage in fruitful debate leading to the crafting of a sensible agreement on legislation. Internal credibility is so essential because the final compromise that produces an important bill passed by Congress and signed by the president will almost certainly involve extended negotiations within the parties, among the parties, between the House of Representatives and the Senate, and ultimately between the leaders of those two institutions and the president and/or his delegates. In the political process, it will surely be beneficial if the members and staff people involved, on the basis of their individual scrutiny of reliable information on relevant past performances, consider each other as being capable and trustworthy participants in extended negotiations on legislation and administrative issues. These favorable circumstances should foster reasonable deliberations rather than partisan posturing and lead toward compromises that confront the serious issues involved.

Washington's pervasive polarization in the 1990s, which undermined internal credibility, raised high barriers for developing and passing major legislation to attack domestic policy problems. As the 1998 televised impeachment hearings showed so vividly to tens of millions of viewers, members of both political parties neither believed nor respected each other across parties and quite often within them and considered the president morally bankrupt as an individual. This intense polarization left the political system looking like a World War I battlefield, with both sides dug in and fighting for a few feet of ground.

President Clinton had come to the Oval Office facing a Congress that in retrospect looks almost friendly when compared with the incredible hostility at the end of his presidency. Yet he had no honeymoon period, passed his 1993 tax hike with the narrowest of margins despite Democratic majorities in the House and Senate, and suffered a humiliating defeat on health care when his party still controlled Congress. In looking to the future, September 11 still leaves in question the willingness of members of Congress to work together over time in developing and passing feasible policies that would realistically address the pressing unmet needs of the American people. The internal credibility problem is unlikely to go away without extraordinary leadership and followership within both parties to overcome the lack of trust in the competence and integrity of members of the other party built up in the polarized 1990s.

Data and Democracy

Sound political information and knowledge have a critical place in this study of the national institutions of governance. Political scientists Michael Delli Carpini and Scott Keeter have observed that "political information is to democratic politics what money is to economics: it is the currency of citizenship."[10] The comparison to money recalls an analogy to Gresham's Law, whereby bad money drives out a superior currency. Soft information that involves no verification may force out hard information that is more costly and time consuming to develop.

Political information today can be a base metal or solid gold. Currently, the combination of the increased employment of misinformation in the polarized political environment and the great technical capacity of the various electronic means for information dissemination has made the quality of information more difficult to determine than at any other time. With the media and partisan participants in the political process pouring forth questionable numbers and commentary so rapidly that the means of verification are overwhelmed, this debased currency of citizenship has become one of the main threats to America's brand of representative democracy. James Madison could hardly have envisioned the complexity of the computer age, but he fully understood the democracy-threatening danger of inferior information. Writing in 1822, the foremost architect of the Constitution warned: "The people who mean to be their own Governors, must arm themselves with the power knowledge gives."[11]

The current section looks broadly at the political information that is the primary link between the electorate and its national government by considering the appropriate definition for such information, the professional responsibilities of journalists as the primary suppliers of political facts and analysis to the public, and the relationship between political knowledge and democracy. Delli Carpini and Keeter wrote: "We define political knowledge as the range of factual information about politics that is stored in long-term memory. . . . The emphasis on factual information distinguishes political knowledge from cognitions that are incorrect or that are not subject to reasonable tests of correctness."[12] They elaborate on their definition in pointing out that "long-term memory" implies cognitions not quickly discarded and that "range" is used to set out a broad notion of political knowledge to distinguish the concept from the specific facts it embraces.

Lawrence Grossman, former president of the Public Broadcasting Service and NBC News, defined political information as "solid, responsible, and meaningful information about significant issues in contrast to gossip, sensationalism, personal scandal, and the like."[13] The two definitions differ as to rigor and purpose. In the case of the two political scientists, their definition is more sharply drawn than Grossman's, in part because it has such a central role in the their statistical analysis and in part no doubt because of the academic propensity to think in terms of rigorous validation. Grossman, in contrast, embeds his definition in a sentence in which he castigated the media because "[the] economics of political information . . . do not encourage its widespread distribution in the telecommunications marketplace."[14] He had sought mainly to underscore the dearth on television of public affairs forums that provide extended commentary on major political issues and to set out a terse definition of political information. However, Grossman and the political scientists converge in the basic demand for a hard currency in political reporting whereby the news is both factual and important to people's lives.

Both definitions have another similarity in raising the question of the competence and commitment of the primary producers of political information and commentary—the media organizations and owners and the professional print and television journalists. At issue are both the commitment of the owners to provide the hard political information demanded by the two definitions and the journalists' technical capability and professional integrity in determining and using valid data. The latter group's task is complicated by the pressures from media owners who stress profitability over journalistic standards and reward quick, sensational coverage based on unverified information and aggressive assertions that pass for analysis. This bottom-line–driven environment has become a formidable barrier to a high level of professionalism. By the end of the 1990s, journalism's failure to maintain standards and credibility had become a central problem in the industry. Although there are still journalists with impeccable standards and credible print and television sources such as the

New York Times, Wall Street Journal, Washington Post, and CNN, a kind of Gresham's Law now rules whereby bad information drives out the good.

There are remarkable similarities between the experience of the media and that of social policy analysts and their mainly Washington-based institutions since the 1960s. Analysts in federal agencies initially sought to develop sound policy data and analyses employing accepted methodological procedures applied appropriately and without partisan bias. These professional norms of "neutral competence" envisioned analysts trying to develop the best numbers they could and giving their political masters the unvarnished findings without a partisan spin that tailored answers to conform to the predilections of their bosses. *Speaking Truth to Power,* the title of political scientist Aaron Wildavsky's influential book on policy analysis, captured the essence of the code of expected conduct.[15]

In practice, of course, these social policy analysts often fell short of the mark, but the norms they developed had real force in shaping the analytic product. That situation changed as some analysts began to massage information to produce the answers wanted by their superiors on the basis of the premise that improperly developed numbers and slanted analyses are professionally acceptable when they further the desired political agenda. Like so many of the media organizations, those at the top of the federal executive branch—presidents and their inner circle and cabinet and subcabinet members—came to value the partisan-driven information and analysis over the product of neutral competence.

The decline of analytic norms among a number of governmental practitioners and members of partisan think tanks led me to argue in 1998: "Honest numbers and honest analysts are now more central to reasoned public policy making and to American democracy itself than at anytime in the postwar era. . . . The critical issue is whether or not neutral competence can actually be practiced successfully in the federal government generally and in the executive branch specifically."[16] The two sentences could be easily be modified by substituting "journalists" for "analysts" in the first one and recasting the second to read: "The critical issue is whether or not the professional norms of journalism can be followed in this new era dominated by a highly diverse mass media that mixes together the cultures of entertainment, the tabloid press, and mainstream organizations and by the increasingly large media conglomerates that focus relentlessly on the bottom line."

Those of us who emphasize the crucial place of information and analysis in the American political system may be naive or myopic in stressing the importance of mere numbers in the political equation. Or the standard for accuracy and adequacy may be set too high, in that voters may be able to make reasonable political choices with much more limited information. The aggrandizement of the role of policy numbers and analyses may well reflect the narrowness and arrogance of information professions. However, I keep coming back to the vexing question of how citizens can make sensible political choices if they do not understand policy problems or their implications. Without good information, how can people determine what is in their own best interests or figure out if their representatives in Congress are serving their needs rather those of corporate America or other special interests? The nation's unique form of representative democracy continues to rest upon Madison's requirement, as recast: Citizens "must arm themselves with the power" sound political knowledge provides if they "mean to be their own Governors." That is from the Father of the Constitution—straight from the horse's mouth—not from some number-cruncher, policy wonk, or arrogant policy analyst.

The Political System and the Economy

The economy and the political system are inseparably intertwined in an ongoing dynamic process, as are political and economic equality. In the reign of Reaganism, no joint product of economic and political factors may have been more important in the deterioration of the federal institutions of governance than the phenomenal growth of the maldistribution of income and wealth. Although the two distributions are key macroeconomic variables, they are usually not perceived as critical political factors. However, the interaction of the economy and the political system together allocate the economic pie among the nation's citizens. Although the economy is the more dominant factor, who gets what each year—ranging from wages to health care to stock options to federal income maintenance payments—depends on the interplay of the economy and the political system.

At any point in time, the economy's underlying technological dimensions will determine the mix of human and physical resources required to maximize gross domestic product. An unregulated free-market economy, however, does not necessarily move toward an equitable distribution of income and wealth. Ronald Reagan's economic policies and political philosophy, driven by market fundamentalism, yielded a staggering decline in the share of total after-tax income for the great bulk of the American people and an even worse drop in their share of wealth. The biggest winners were large corporations and the top 1 percent of the income distribution, whose gains fueled the huge increase in campaign contributions. As Kevin Phillips observed: "The new crux was the vast, relentless takeover of U.S. politics and policymaking by large donors to federal campaigns and propaganda organs. . . . Politics was finance and finance was politics, just as the men with diamond stick pins had said a century earlier."[17] Reaganism had returned the United States to the Gilded Age—the Darwinian belief in the survival of the fittest dominated political thinking; modern-day corporate tycoons controlled the political system.

The first nation to embrace the egalitarian ethos had come to have the most unequal distribution of income and wealth among the capitalist democracies. These widening gaps had made a mockery both of the principle of political equality for everyone eligible to vote and the basic concept of equality of economic opportunity for all. The world of Reaganism looked nothing like the quarter-century after World War II, during which the nation had produced a rapid increase in the number of middle-class families who could realistically believe in fulfilling the American Dream. Here the United States went beyond the other wealthy democracies in extending this status. These years, when democracy and capitalism moved in step, were part of a longer period running from the New Deal into the early 1970s—"years that remain the zenith of twentieth-century American egalitarianism."[18]

Since 1981, the nation has moved in the opposite direction. During his 2000 presidential campaign, former senator Bill Bradley pointed out that the danger of "'a failure to understand that democracy and capitalism are separate parts of the American dream, and that keeping that dream alive depends on keeping one from corrupting the other.'"[19]

Reaganism's unregulated free-market capitalism begot the political dominance by big-money interests, which in turn carried the nation to higher and higher levels of political and economic inequality. The increasing maldistribution of income and wealth, by harming the middle class, undermined representative democracy, which must have this broad group significantly involved in governance.

The Golden Years

It is instructive to see two strikingly different cases of income and wealth distribution by considering the first decades after the end of World War II in comparison with the 1980s and 1990s. After the nation demobilized, the tremendous industrial capacity created in wartime was shifted relatively quickly from the all-out production of a host of military items to turning out a vast array of products for the civilians.

In the postwar years, the potent combination of an unfulfilled desire for goods and services, ample funds to buy them, the resourcefulness of the most entrepreneurial of nations, and by far the mightiest industrial capacity in the world generated a strikingly long period of high-productivity prosperity. Periods of recession came and went, but the mighty economy continued its remarkable productivity rate until 1973. Brown University history professor James Patterson pointed out in his book *Grand Expectations*, which covers the period 1945–74: "No comparable period of United States history witnessed so much economic and civic progress."[20]

Most important of all, the benefits of the economy spread much further down the income distribution to create a burgeoning middle class. The early postwar years, which produced an amazing period of broad personal income growth and a clear decrease in income inequality, remain the golden era of high wages for relatively uneducated blue-collar workers, such as those who staffed the vast automobile assembly lines. Equality of opportunity for all American families willing to strive for it began to look like a realistic objective and took on the more ambitious postwar version of that notion in seeing the fulfillment of the American Dream for increasing numbers of families. The new version of an egalitarian nation promised continuing economic gains that would allow parents themselves to do better and better and their children to surpass them.

From 1947 to 1969, the bottom fifth of income earners (the lowest quintile), which can be labeled the "working class," experienced the biggest percentage increase among the five quintiles in its share of total income.[21] The next three quintiles, basically the broad middle class, also ended up with higher shares of income. Only the top 20 percent had a decline in their share, and within that quintile, the top 5 percent suffered the largest decline. At the same time, the sum of these changes in the shares of income of the five quintiles only yielded a modest increase in distributional equity, not a dramatic leveling of income. The top 5 percent's share of total income at the beginning of the period slightly exceeded that of the bottom 40 percent and by 1969 had dropped a little below the income share of the bottom two quintiles.

Postwar U.S. economic growth, in which those in the top fifth of the income distribution prospered and the remaining 80 percent did even better, made prosperity a reality for millions of people. Depression-era families saw their incomes and the value of their assets (especially homes) rise far beyond their expectations in the grim 1930s. Their children could go to college and become esteemed professionals. The gains were widespread, with financial security coming to families where the main earners had limited skills. Greater equality of opportunity did not promise equality of results, nor did the American people believe it should. But it did make the chance of reaching solid middle-class status much higher for large numbers of the nation's citizens.

However, when we look back over the entire postwar era, only in these first twenty-five years after World War II did the United States clearly move toward fulfilling its basic promise of increasing equality of economic opportunity for its lower- and middle-income families. Better opportunities and results created a large, prospering middle class, whose families were optimistic about their futures and those of their children. In fulfilling the American Dream for so many families, the first twenty-five years after the war truly transformed the nation.

Maldistribution under Reaganism

Isaac Shapiro, Robert Greenstein, and Wendell Primus of the Center on Budget and Policy Priorities (CBPP) have drawn on the Congressional Budget Office study *Historical Effective Tax Rates, 1979–1997* to develop a strikingly sharp analysis of income disparities in the United States.[22] Three points need to be made about the Internal Revenue Service (IRS) data set, which is built up from individual tax returns (without identifying particular taxpayers). First, IRS data provide the soundest detailed information on those at the top of the income distribution, including their yearly reported capital gains. Second, the IRS income information offers the most useful base for the analysis of disparities, because the much more widely used census data do not permit breaking out the income of those at the top and do not take account of the reported capital gains that were so critical in 1979–97. Third, these data show the widening income gap with such unambiguous clarity that the upcoming treatment requires only a limited presentation to provide an accurate portrayal of the changes since 1979.

The CBPP study divided all U.S. households into quintiles (with the highest fifth further disaggregated) on the basis of their real after-tax yearly income (in 1997 dollars) during the period 1979–97 and indicated the average incomes for each group. The first thing to note is that the higher the quintile, the greater the percentage gain in average income. Those in the highest quintile were by far the biggest gainers, and the top 1 percent had astounding increases in dollar and percentage terms.[23] The lowest fifth's average after-tax income fell from $10,900 to $10,800; the middle fifth had their income go up from a little under $34,000 to just above $37,000, or 10 percent for the eighteen years. In contrast, the top 1 percent on average experienced an after-tax income rise from $263,700 to $677, 900—an increase of $414,200, or 157 percent. Astonishingly, the bottom 20 percent of households actually lost $100 in income during the eighteen years, while those at the very top gained more than $414,000 dollars. During the eighteen years, the top 1 percent's six-figure gain of $414,200 was 122 times greater than the middle quintile's gain of $3,400!

Another way to compare changes during the period is to consider the shares of total after-tax income going to the top and the bottom. At the start of the eighteen-year period, the top 1 percent had 7.5 percent of national after-tax income and the lowest two quintiles (the bottom 40 percent) had 18.5 percent, or roughly two and a half times as great a share as the former. At the end of the eighteen-year period, the top 1 percent had gained 6.1 percent more of total after-tax income to reach 13.6 percent; the bottom two quintiles had suffered a loss of 3.5 percent to fall to a 15.0 percent share of national after-tax income. By 1997, almost 14 cents out of every dollar of national income went to the top 1 percent, whereas the entire 40 percent at the bottom of the distribution received 15 cents. In the eighteen years under Reaganism, the bottom 40 percent started with a significantly larger share of total after-tax income than the top 1 percent, but the two ended the period nearly equal. It was a change healthy neither for egalitarianism nor democracy.

Wealth is far more unevenly distributed than income. In 1998, the bottom 90 percent had 59 percent of household before-tax income compared with roughly 41 percent for the top 10 percent. In sharp contrast, the top 1 percent owned 48 percent of all common stock, whereas the remainder of the top 10 percent owned 38 percent.[24] In the case of financial wealth generally and common stock particularly, the income gap appears minute compared with the vast chasm that divides the those at the top from the great bulk of the U.S. population. The top 10 percent of all U.S. households owned 86 percent of all common stocks, and the highest quintile had 96 percent. That left the bottom 80 percent with a grand total of 4 percent of all common stock. In light of these percentages, far too much has been made about the increasing number of people owning what are mainly quite small amounts of common stock. The fact that roughly 50 percent of households now own common stock either directly or indirectly through pension plans should certainly not be seen at this point as a major move toward egalitarianism.

Americans historically have been comfortable with greater income inequality than the other wealthy democracies, particularly those in Western Europe; but greater and greater economic inequality can threat political equality and the foundation of capitalism. The long period from the mid-1930s to well into the 1970s were the high ground of egalitarianism in the twentieth century, a time when capitalism and democracy seemed in harmony. However, the growing maldistribution of income and wealth during the era of Reaganism became a political tornado sweeping away Madisonian representative democracy and full political citizenship as defined by it and battering the federal institutions of governance so badly that the most pressing domestic policy needs were ignored and new policies frequently made matters worse. An even closer look is needed at the Reagan administration and Reaganism to further investigate the power of the economy and economic thought in shaping the political system of the most capitalistic nation in the world.

three

Reagan and Reaganism

Ronald Reagan dominated policy, politics, and governance and changed America as no other president since Franklin Delano Roosevelt. Reagan was not just the president; he appeared to think like the average man (not woman) and yet strode tall and heroic across the wide screen. He embodied Americanism in its most pristine, mythical form. Of all presidents, Reagan is the only one warranting an "ism" attached to his name. Reaganism—his political philosophy with its virulent antigovernmentism and its confident vision of America as the most powerful and just of nations destined to lead the world—not only dominated the last two decades of the twentieth century but also will be a major factor in at least the early years of the next one. Jimmy Carter, George H. W. Bush, and Bill Clinton measured much lower on the presidential Richter scale than did Ronald Reagan. Like Franklin Roosevelt, he had the remarkable power to go beyond institutions to the people and change how Americans thought and acted.

President Reagan's extraordinary political leadership drove Congress and the public in the wrong direction. Although his political philosophy and policies were closely linked, the former likely has had the greater impact. His words and music were not new but echoed the same song as the Gilded Age and the 1920s that deified unfettered free-market capitalism and individual self-interest. Like the words in the songs of the earlier eras, his lyrics led down a path of widespread business corruption, disproportionate corporate influence, and the increasing maldistribution of income and wealth. A straight line can be traced from President Reagan to Enron, from greed and excessive deregulation to corporate corruption.

Ronald Reagan differed markedly in four ways from all the other men who have been the U.S. chief executive during the modern presidency. First, he detested government and saw himself outside of it, even as president. Second, he mainly ignored information and analysis, and he understood little about how government operated generally and less about how the large-scale federal bureaucratic agencies performed specifically. Third, he seemingly did not pay attention to, and therefore often did not comprehend, major policy issues. Fourth, he was surprisingly passive in his relationship with most of his subordinates as well as unbelievably detached from the presidency itself. His speechwriter Peggy Noonan, his most ardent admirer among the many White House staff members who have written insider books on the Reagan administration, observed: "There were times when I would see the earnest young people in the middle levels of the administration trying to get somebody to listen to their thoughts ... and see the sunny president who did not seem to know or notice, and I would think to myself (if I was tired enough, frustrated enough) that the battle for the mind of Ronald Reagan was like the trench warfare of World War I: Never have so many fought so hard for such barren terrain."[1] The point is not that President Reagan lacked intelligence or that he did not believe fervently in his basic principles but that he lacked knowledge of or interest in most policy and administrative issues.

The Reagan years brought to national leadership the most remarkable president of the postwar era. In some ways, his story is straight out of the heroic Hollywood when he was a star. Many questioned his capabilities, but he had the good fortune of having the perfect act to follow in the Carter presidency, which had imploded in its last two years. President Reagan also made his entrance just at the time that the dominant political philosophy of the previous fifty years—Franklin Roosevelt's New Deal activism—was on its last legs. Reagan's leadership style meshed perfectly with the deep concerns of the American people, who had lost faith in the nation as an economic superstar. His eternal optimism, his unreserved belief in and commitment to his basic principles, his striking ability to reach and convince people, and his black-or-white way of thinking gave his new antigovernment, antitax, probusiness, pro-deregulation, pro-states'-rights way of thinking particular force and credibility.

Reagan turned out to be the most dangerous of leaders, not because he was evil or warped, but because his overconfidence and lack of knowledge combined with his leadership capabilities both to sell his deleterious message and to convince the public that it had led to great success. When he left office after two terms, Reaganism continued through the presidencies of George H. W. Bush; Bill Clinton, who validated it; and George W. Bush, who revivified it. Although readers may disagree with my negative assessment of the Reagan administration and Reaganism, one conclusion appears uncontroversial: The Reagan presidency had a huge impact on U.S. domestic policy and political thinking that still continues. It needs noting that "domestic policy" as used here includes economic policy but excludes international security and national defense.

Reaganism

Reaganism's antecedents go all the way back to the eighteenth century and the Anti-Federalists who did battle with the Federalists over the Constitution in a losing fight to create a weak national government subservient to the states. Reagan's political philosophy also can be traced back to the market fundamentalism that flourished in the Gilded Age and the 1920s and emphasized unregulated capitalism and individual self-interest. In these two earlier periods, America succumbed to plutocratic governance with big business dominance over governments that seemed delighted to take their cues from corporate America. Although the tenets of Reaganism are not new, the current conceptualization mirrors the stream of political thought that emerged in the late 1960s and fueled the virulent antigovernmentism that now dominates American political thought.

A Convergence of Forces

Once the golden years of prosperity ended in 1973 and the economy slowed down, liberals and conservatives, Democrats and Republicans, and mainstream thinkers and extremists alike all questioned the direction of the federal government and many cast it as a menace to individual freedom and entrepreneurial success. A theory of minimal government gained respectability. Robert Nozick's 1974 volume *Anarchy, the State, and Utopia* set out the libertarian rationale for a government whose main functions would be to provide security at home and abroad and to protect the sanctity of contract and private property.[2] Another libertarian thinker, Murray Rothbard, put the case against government most starkly: "'If you wish to know how libertarians regard the State and any of its acts, simply think of the state as a criminal band, and all of the libertarian attitudes will logically fall into place.'"[3] Few went as far as the libertarians with their disproportionate concern with individual freedom that would throw out all federal efforts to distribute or redistribute income, even the Social Security program. President Reagan himself called for a safety net for truly poor people and quickly retreated from any attacks on Social Security. At the same time, strong supporters of proactive federal domestic policy were hard to locate anywhere and almost disappeared among national politicians.

Brilliant, impeccably logical arguments could be developed and refined on the basis of the assumption that no government existed or else that government could easily be dismantled. This assumption in effect buried the sticky real-world problems of implementation. It made the federal government with all its flaws the raw meat for university classes, doctoral dissertations, and the making of academic reputations for professors who could articulate the elegant abstract logic, while ignoring the vast array of existing popular federal government programs that protected millions of Americans. Social Security had become the primary source of income for most retired Americans. The Food and Drug Administration, which touched the lives of nearly all Americans, was estimated to be involved with products that accounted for 20 to 25 cents of every dollar spent by consumers. Federal funds mainly financed President Dwight D. Eisenhower's Interstate Highway System.

Although citizens castigated government in the abstract, efforts to reduce or eliminate programs that benefited them directly elicited their vehement opposition. The minimalist theory had not confronted this mundane reality. Despite the appeal of the philosophy in selling the abstract idea of a much smaller, quite limited federal government, the theory did not confront the towering barriers to going from the "here" of the current reality to the "there" of the desired outcome. The fervent embrace of the theory by politicians and the public never actually threatened a revolution that would sweep government away because the draconian implementation problems were ignored in mindless tirades against Washington and its bureaucrats. Nevertheless, the proponents' attacks inflicted significant costs in diminishing the federal government's credibility and ultimately its capacity.

Key elements of libertarian theory had been around a long time. The difference in the 1970s came from the general support for less federal domestic government. It was no longer restricted to Republicans and conservatives or to new groups such as the neoconservatives and the new left, but came also from liberal Democrats. Although there were clear differences in political direction among the groups (e.g., whether or not to reduce federal grants to states and localities), we need not consider them because they all moved away from a strong activist federal domestic government. Richard Nixon had pushed a New Federalism that gave state and local governments much more control over federal grants-in-aid. Less restrictive block grants replaced some of the tightly specified categorical federal grants. The notion of devolution to subnational governments with a far lighter federal hand gained currency across much of the political spectrum. Many liberals who did not favor cutbacks in federal grants-in-aid often wanted fewer program restrictions on state and local governments. This striking sea change in political thought both provided philosophical underpinnings for Reaganism's virulent antigovernmentism and made the theme acceptable.

Although the theory of a minimalist national government provided an intellectual framework for attacking the liberal themes that had produced big government, the double-digit inflation of the 1970s that particularly hurt the middle class drove the dramatic shift toward antigovernmentism. As Theodore White, the doyen of the presidential election writers, observed: "There were many themes to the Reagan campaign. . . . But underlying all was the appeal to the *Untermensch* of politics: The government is cheating you, inflation is stealing from you the value of your dollars."[4] With the coming of the frightening inflation, all forces converged. The stage had been set for the charismatic Reagan's message. Reagan himself had fired his shots at the federal government on the national stage since 1964, when his speech supporting Barry Goldwater's nomination as Republican candidate for president electrified conservatives. Then his performance appealed mainly to the right wing of the Republican Party. From the perspective of the political center of that time, which was much to the left of that of the 1980s, the message appeared as extreme. But a decade and a half made a tremendous difference in American political thought. The political center had shifted so dramatically to the right that open season was declared for shooting at the federal government. President Reagan became the foremost hunter as he finally killed the already dying Rooseveltian liberalism and replaced it with Reaganism.

The Man and the Message

Reaganism is not an overarching ideology like Marxism. It is a blend of the man and his message that centers on a handful of principles he held as unchallengeable. The message itself—that is, Reaganism—can be set out simply: The United States is and can continue to be the dominant nation in the world in economic, geopolitical, and moral terms without citizen sacrifice if it is not held back by the dead hand of government. Controlling the federal government is the heart of Reaganism—cut taxes, regulations, and bureaucratic power deeply to create more incentives to work, save, and invest. Unleash the mighty American entrepreneurial spirit, and "It's Morning Again in America," the latter being a central theme of Reagan's 1984 presidential campaign. In the president's cosmology, unregulated capitalism occupied a premier place as the only creator of wealth and hence the elemental force of American economic strength. At the center of Reagan's world is the individual—not the community. If individuals are unchained from the debilitating burden of the welfare state, they can produce the best of all possible Americas by acting solely in their own self interest.

Just as so many other Americans, Ronald Reagan himself believed wholeheartedly in a shining nation that never was. Noonan, a self-described true believer in Reaganism, closed her book on the Reagan presidency with this sentence. "[America] is the fairest place that ever was, it's wide open, and no one has cause for bitterness."[5] Blacks, Native Americans, Hispanics—it is as if they do not exist, or if they do, racism was never a problem. In its fullest flower, Reaganism is the purest vision of a righteous America. President Reagan's message was precisely what Americans yearned to hear after the particularly discouraging years of the late 1960s and the 1970s, when they had begun to lose faith in the nation's destiny. Reaganism became the high road of American politics. The message needed President Reagan for its successful launching; however, once in the air, it took on a life beyond him.

Reagan honed a consistent message in his years as spokesman for General Electric (essentially, this message was stated in his 1964 speech at the Republican National Convention that brought him national recognition as a conservative spokesperson) and used it year in and year out during the quarter-century ending on January 20, 1989. It can be said that he had two careers. In the first one, he became a competent and successful actor, but not one having outstanding talent or the box office appeal to make him a major star. His second career as salesman of the message succeeded beyond all expectations. Although it clearly drew on his acting skills and carried him to sixteen years of elected office, he should not be seen either as just an actor or as a conventional politician. He is best classed as a prophet of an America restored—the classic figure pointing out a current path of doom and a new one to national salvation and rebirth. As General Electric spokesman, as California governor, and as president, Reagan spread the secular religion of the American nation.

The fact remained that neither consistency nor deep belief in the message were enough. Hedley Donovan wrote early in the first Reagan term: "For all the coherence of purpose, all the communicating skills, all the charm and normality of Ronald Reagan, there had to be a receptive country 'out there.' Ronald Reagan reading the cue cards for a Ted Kennedy speech would not generate any more support than the Senator has."[6] As Murray Edelman has pointed out in discussing moving messages such as "The only thing we have to fear is fear itself," President Roosevelt's message of hope in his first inaugural address on March 4, 1933: "It is not creativity that wins an audience in such cases, but rather telling people what they want to hear in a context that makes the message credible."[7]

Edelman saw credibility—actually, "believability," in the terms of this book—as central in such messages. So it is; but the acceptance well may flow from the fact that the claim knowingly or unknowingly distorts a reality that is too hard to face. "Fear" did not stand as the only problem of the Great Depression, as Roosevelt well knew, but it was a heartening message to a downcast nation. Reagan's message, so often at odds with basic facts, still convinced people. The country was ready for a prophet preaching virulent antigovernmentism. But at this stage, it had needed a strong leader to sell the message. After that, the accepted message could flow out of the mouths of ordinary leaders, although they might give it more punch by wrapping it in the name of the prophet.

The right message, however, is not sufficient to produce strong leaders. The second need is a heroic bearer—a bigger-than-life hero. The shaping event for Reagan was the assassination attempt on his life on March 30, 1981, just a bit over two months after he became president. Though he was seriously wounded, his calm, joking behavior gave him a special quality. In real life, Ronald Reagan took on John Wayne's Hollywood image of the archetypal American hero. In a similar vein, Franklin Delano Roosevelt, as president-elect, escaped unharmed from an assassination attempt nearly a half-century before President Reagan and showed exemplary courage. With Reagan, the hero had again stepped to center stage.

At the beginning of the 1980s, Americans questioned the country's postwar preeminence as the economic, geopolitical, and moral leader of the free world. What stood out among the many ills that plagued the nation were double-digit interest rates and inflation and a "failed" president's audacity in trying to blame the American people for the country's troubles. The final straw came just at the end of the tainted Carter presidency as the nation suffered through the wrenching Iranian hostage crisis, which included an embarrassingly bungled helicopter rescue attempt as President Carter tried vainly to free the American prisoners.

President Reagan changed that dark mood by calling forth the nation's deepest values and myths that he himself held to unreservedly. Garry Wills, in a penetrating passage—which pointed out how Mark Twain used the myth of an unblemished America of happy small towns as cultural satire—caught the central element of the Reagan cosmology: "He is the sincerest claimant to a heritage that never existed, a perfect blend of an authentic America he grew up in and of America's own fables of its past."[8] He did not preach the distorted image of reality as a politician intent on tricking the public, but instead he was the truest of true believers resurrecting a shining but unreal America that he and millions of others so fervently wanted to come again. Paul Erickson observed: "Reagan's rhetoric has appealed to and encouraged one of [America's] worst habits, the desire to believe which goes beyond even gullibility."[9] This dream of America unbounded, based on the nation's most cherished myths, became the foundation for Reagan's politics of unreality.

The Reagan Phenomenon

Reagan as president embraced an unrealistic worldview formed in the Hollywood of bold heroes and dastardly villains during the prewar and early postwar years when patriotism and fantasy were unashamedly blended together. Reagan never escaped that world. Lou Cannon, who watched Reagan closely during his political career and had long been a Reagan admirer, observed:

> [Reagan] made sense of foreign policy through his long-developed habit of devising dramatic, all-purpose stories with moralistic messages, forceful plots and well-developed heroes and villains. . . . The more Reagan repeated a story, the more he believed it and the more he resisted information that undermined its premises. . . . Ronald Reagan's subordinates often despaired of him because he seemed to inhabit a fantasy world where cinematic events competed for attention with reality.[10]

The Reality Deficit

A final set of ingredients rounded out the product. At the core of Reagan's unreality was a strange mixture of detachment, ignorance, and a highly positive, ever optimistic image of himself. Schieffer and Gates captured this detachment succinctly in observing that "Reagan's people came to see him more as an abstract idea than as a flesh-and-blood leader. . . . Reagan's disengaged style . . . [is] the most striking characteristic of his presidency."[11] Just as striking is Reagan's ignorance, using that term in its literal sense of lacking in knowledge, training, and/or information. Although intelligent, Reagan seldom used his mental skills on organizational or policy issues. Thus, his passivity and lack of curiosity combined with his ignorance to produce a president who did not know and had no interest in knowing.

This detachment and disinterest could at times make President Reagan's lack of information incomprehensible. For example, in a meeting with Senators Sam Nunn and Barry Goldwater on the budget, the president admitted that he had been an active supporter of the recently passed Gramm-Rudman legislation but had not been told about its absolutely critical requirement that made budget cuts mandatory if Congress did not meet the specified budget reduction goals. In a comment that also shows another critical side of Reagan, Schieffer and Gates observed: "[Gramm-Rudman] had been one of the most highly publicized and fiercely debated bills in recent congressional history. Yet Reagan, who had signed the legislation into law, was unabashedly taking the position that he did not understand its purpose. Reagan showed no sign that he had shared in creating the problem. As was so often the case, the problem had to be someone else's fault."[12]

In Ronald Reagan's unreal world, his idealized self shielded him against any disconcerting reality. Nowhere is this more vivid, and more poignant, than in the case of the Iranian hostages. The Iran-Contra hearings in mid-1987 made painfully clear that the United States had engaged in an arms-for-hostages effort with Iran in part because of President Reagan's great concern for the American hostages, particularly Central Intelligence Agency agent William Buckley. At that time, even the president appeared to accept that the dealings with Iran had degenerated into an arms–hostage swap. But such a notion simply would not stay in his mind. In his December 3, 1987, television interview with four network newscasters, the president said that the Iran-Contra affair had not been a scandal and argued that at no time did he see his administration's efforts as trading weapons for hostages. In his image, Reagan would not, and could not, engage in such objectionable behavior. It followed in his own mind that he had done no such thing. His statement was not a lie in the sense of being *knowingly* false.

Reagan's denial of failure also had another facet, which Frances FitzGerald observed in her review of several books on Reagan: "After his [Reagan's] operation for cancer of the colon the previous summer, he had told a reporter, 'I didn't have cancer. I had something inside me that had cancer in it, and it was removed.' To admit to failure would have been to admit that his luck had given out—that his magic had gone for good."[13] The nation's civic religion in its purest form stood proclaimed by a shaman who brought his magic to Americans who wanted, as did he, to believe fully in the myths of nationhood. The politics of unreality remained real to Reagan no matter how much it clashed with hard facts.

Reagan and Roosevelt

No president save Roosevelt challenged Reagan as the magician of the modern presidency. In his provocative brief history of the New Deal, Paul Conkin wrote of Roosevelt: "It was the magic of a man, based as much on illusion as on reality. . . . As all successful artists, he was able to effect many of his designs, even when they were poor ones. Persuasion was his brush and chisel."[14] Roosevelt and Reagan both came to the presidency at times of crisis—one of near economic collapse, the other of a loss of faith in an America in decline. Both crises demanded a restoration of confidence. Each man had striking success. Although Roosevelt in his first two terms could not bring the American economy back to its pre-Depression level, he did raise the spirits of the nation during the suffering of the 1930s "by the force of his own personality and behavior."[15] Reagan faced a lesser economic challenge, with the United States suffering through a minor recession—albeit experiencing double-digit inflation. But that meant greater danger in the case of confidence. The latter is like so many factors, of which the "right" amount is desirable but too little or too much is harmful. Too little confidence can keep a person or a country from performing at the highest levels of capacity, whereas the other extreme of overconfidence can be equally damaging. The American people's movement from too little to too much confidence is a central aspect of the Reagan presidency. That overconfidence had two deleterious aspects. First, it led to a massive consumer buying binge, encouraged greed, justified unprecedented levels of public debt, and underinvestment in public infrastructure. Second, it led to a denial of the basic problems confronting the United States.

Reagan's years as a motion picture actor are important for understanding both the Reagan style and his success as the messenger of antigovernmentism. He had had direction from his Hollywood days on, and he long had been completely comfortable with being told where to stand, what to say, and how to say it. The perfect president for the "Age of Television" could be adroitly packaged by superb White House political managers who made the most of him striding tall, handsome, and optimistic on the presidential stage. Cannon titled his massive study of the Reagan years *President Reagan: The Role of a Lifetime* to indicate that Reagan was first and foremost a professional actor who took each real-life part as a movie role and did not (and by 1981 probably could not) himself distinguish the difference.[16] At the same time, President Reagan's power did not come from mere acting. Paul Newman or Robert Redford—both of whom had far more distinguished movie careers than Reagan—would not be convincing presidents *off* the screen, unless they had the intangible political leadership qualities of Reagan and Roosevelt.

If "acting" means playing a part for effect or saying what the speaker really does not believe, Franklin Roosevelt, the supreme pragmatist, acted in terms of that definition far more often than Reagan the ideologue. James MacGregor Burns underscored President Roosevelt's theatrical poses and touches and stressed his acting skills.[17] Seeing Roosevelt appear to be walking when he could not use his polio-damaged legs or entertaining the press with a look that said "you know I'm putting on an act, but you still swallow it whole" reveals a master performer with more theatrical skills than many professional actors. That the powerful political leader may at times be acting should not cause us to think that such leadership can be faked. President Reagan's basic message, which he fully believed, amplified by his extraordinary political leadership, became one of the most—if not *the* most—important shaping factors of the mood and tone of the final two decades of the twentieth century. Particularly in the case of Reagan the true believer, the fact that his acting skills, including his ability to take direction from his packagers, became powerful means of reaching his goal of creating a more conservative, antigovernment, probusiness, individualistic, optimistic America in no way implies that he was only "acting" in the theatrical sense.

Everyman and Superman

The hero image that each had fully earned undergirded the political leadership of both Franklin Roosevelt and Reagan. Michael Kammen has argued: "Americans expect their heroes to be Everyman and Superman simultaneously."[18] No president in memory fits that bill better than Reagan. He is the quintessential Everyman. Yet Reagan achieved what the typical man could do only in his daydreams. One of Reagan's favorite expressions, "Make my day," symbolized strength and toughness. It represented the ordinary man's Walter Mitty dream in purest form—the Superman side of the Kammen duality. This hero image with its bigger-than-life dimension is a crucial similarity between Reagan and Roosevelt. Roosevelt, who was not wounded in the preinaugural assassination attempt, "did not twitch a muscle or show any sign of shock, and the descriptions of his courage and calm in the face of danger called forth great acclaim from the press and public."[19] Reagan, by joking in the hospital emergency room and saying to his wife Nancy, "Honey, I forgot to duck," brought the same kind of public and press praise. This bravery in the face of death exemplifies a set of characteristics that reinforces the Superman image. Like Roosevelt, Reagan came across as supremely confident, the master of his own moods and of his environment. Not only did others believe in these two presidents; the heroes believed in themselves.

Besides their heroic behavior after the assassination attempts, both Roosevelt and Reagan took early action that showed their power to control events. On March 9, 1933, five days after taking office (before the Twentieth Amendment, presidents were inaugurated on March 4), Roosevelt called a special session of Congress to consider emergency banking legislation as the United States faced the collapse of its financial structure. Burns's account makes vivid the Roosevelt magic: "Completed by the President and his advisers at two o'clock that morning [March 9], the bill was still in rough form. But even during the meager forty minutes allotted to the debate, shouts of 'Vote! Vote!' echoed from the floor.... The House promptly passed the bill without a record vote; the Senate approved it a few hours later; the President signed it by nine o'clock."[20] With that job done in a breathtaking eighteen hours, Roosevelt sent a surprise message the next day on the grim state of the economy to Congress. Here, vividly, is the hero in action.

President Reagan faced no such draconian crisis as the potential collapse of the financial system. His early tests were the pushing of his landmark legislation through Congress with a thin Republican majority in the Senate and a heavily Democratic House and his firing of the members of the Professional Air Traffic Controllers Organization (PATCO) after the union started a nationwide walkout on August 3, 1981. In his confrontation with PATCO, Reagan never flinched in crushing the strike and driving PATCO into bankruptcy. The 1981 victory of his budget and tax package in Congress stands as far more important and much more impressive in power and persuasiveness, but the battle with PATCO played out more dramatically as the confrontational, valiant victory of the hero.

Like Roosevelt, only a few months after the attempt on his life, Reagan acted decisively, triumphed, and further validated his bigger-than-life image.[21] The contrast between the images of Carter burdened under presidential care, almost shrinking in size before our eyes, and of Johnson and Nixon agonizing in office, with Reagan's carefree confidence greatly enhanced his Superman image. During the deepest recession in the postwar period, when the overwhelming majority of economists (including his Council of Economic Advisers chair) were predicting a tepid economic recovery, Reagan assured everyone that a dramatic boom would come. It did. With Reagan, a combination of general optimism and specific faith in a few principles brought an inner serenity, a calmness under pressure and uncertainty that few possess. He was Everyman and Superman.

Virulent Antigovernmentism

All Reagan policies, it can be argued, flowed from his unrelenting distaste for big government. Nowhere were its dangers clearer than in communism. Whatever Marxist theory said about the eventual withering away of the state, in practice communism was statism at its monolithic worst. The Soviet Union offered the ultimate case of evil government, combining the deadening hand of central planning and dictatorial oppression. Hence, the national security area became the exception in the attack on active government, with money poured into esoteric weapons systems. For Reagan, big, bad government meant federal domestic government. He attacked it relentlessly during his presidency, not only with rhetoric but also with policies that degraded the federal government and undermined both its capacity and its credibility. That rhetoric—which later was delivered by harsher voices—formed the base for their attacks against the national government.

Reagan as Outsider

In Reagan's sixteen years as governor and as president, he did not ever see himself or his top aides as part of the government. They were citizens against big government, struggling to unchain businesses and individuals from oppressive taxes and regulation. Reagan embodied the basic American view of government in which there was a marked distinction between the pride in the nation itself and in being an American and the antipathy toward the government of that nation. "I love my country; I hate my government" is a distinctly American theme. The nineteenth-century poet and essayist Ralph Waldo Emerson set out how Americans feel when he wrote nearly 150 years ago that "the less government we have, the better—the fewer laws, and the less confined power." Reagan carried his view of government a stage further to the myth of the absence of the federal government in creating a great nation. Cannon captured this central false belief:

He imagined that the American nation had been carved from wilderness by pioneers unrestrained by the forces of nature or the power of the state.... Reagan never noticed that it was the government that had protected these frontier heroes, set aside land for homes and schools, built telegraph lines and underwritten construction of an intercontinental railway system.... America was "we" to Ronald Reagan, a "we" of heroic individuals, while government was always "they."[22]

Reagan's belief in the absolute evil of big government was fundamentally different from that of earlier presidents. Nixon and Carter had seen the political power of rhetorical antigovernmentism. Attacking a bumbling federal government—particularly the inefficient, overpaid, oppressive "bureaucrats"—became the surest ground of presidential politics, a sturdy weapon for winning the presidency. But neither Nixon nor Carter conceived of themselves as apart from government. After being elected president, the task was to gain control of government from the career civil servants who made up the permanent government that was in place when a president arrived and when he left. Nixon's and Carter's mistreatment and misuse of career civil servants may have been misguided, but both had the goal of mastering government so as to make it more responsive, efficient, and effective in pursuing presidential objectives. Reagan's "they" became "my government," with both men accepting the basic responsibility of presidential governance.

Nixon and Carter had spent most of their adult lives in government service. Once the former returned from World War II, he won a seat in the U.S. House of Representatives, moved to the U.S. Senate, and then served eight years as President Eisenhower's vice president. President Nixon could hardly cast himself as an outsider, as a citizen president. Carter before his political career had graduated from the Naval Academy and served as a career military officer—a bureaucrat in the ultimate bureaucracy, the armed forces. Carter's political career in Georgia culminated in his governorship, of which he saw as a major achievement his reorganization of the state government. Carter campaigned as an antigovernment outsider, but he envisioned making the federal government more efficient, not bludgeoning it. Both Nixon and Carter saw themselves as experienced government executives who could master the machinery of government and use federal agencies to further the new programs they sought. Both employed antigovernment rhetoric in *winning* the presidency; however, each saw a competent government as a central tool in *governing*.

Having come to government just before his fifty-fifth birthday, Reagan was not a man of government and never became one. Government, for Reagan, remained a black box that he never cared to open in his sixteen years as California governor and as president. A White House reporter who covered Governor Reagan (not Cannon, I note), in response to my questions in an off-the-record interview as to how ignorant Reagan was about government, said immediately that clearly such ignorance was the case when Reagan became California's governor, and then reflected for a moment to add it was still true during Reagan's presidency. President Reagan seldom sought policy options or queried his staff about policy issues during his two terms. In the case of the national security advisers who reported directly to Reagan and who had responsibility in the White House for keeping the president well informed on foreign and defense policy, Cannon argued that "Reagan really did not know what a national security adviser was supposed to do" and quoted Robert C. (Bud) McFarlane, one of the two national security advisers heavily involved in Iran-Contra, as observing: "'The president doesn't even remember my name.'"[23]

The mix of President Reagan's ideology and limited knowledge of how the federal government operated led him to attack it without seeing that a wounded government in any way constrained his administration's governance of the nation. As president, Reagan continued to think as an outsider, combining citizens' prejudices, inconsistencies, and lack of knowledge about the federal government. Linda Bennett and Stephen Bennett's analysis of public opinion data on how citizens perceived the government in Washington led them to argue: "Cranky about taxes, even in the face of a huge cut in the national income tax [during the Reagan administration], citizens still have a 'wish list' they want the national government to spend on, particularly domestic programs. Convinced that government wastes too much and that increased efficiency (and honesty) would pay for their policy preferences, they do not see that their attitudes are in any way inconsistent."[24] What escaped Reagan and the public was that reducing waste, fraud, and abuse in the federal government and increasing its efficiency demanded a highly skilled workforce and that low pay and public castigation of the federal workforce led in the wrong direction. Reagan's antigovernmentism and lack of knowledge about government somehow combined comfortably in his mind to justify an all-out attack by its chief executive on the domestic government.

President Reagan, like so many citizens, venerated the Constitution as an almost sacred document, without knowing all that much about it. Not surprisingly, his failure to perceive the constitutional consequences of his acts led him to do basic harm to the document he revered in the abstract. In the Iran-Contra affair, his administration created a secret government. The administration's top officials hid from Congress and the public its illegal acts in pursuit of its basic foreign policy goals. Thus, by knowingly misleading and lying to Congress, the administration subverted the basic process of governance. The framers of the Constitution foresaw Congress and the president as honorable adversaries—not as lying to each other and thereby damaging the internal credibility that is the foundation of democratic governance.

In *Turmoil and Triumph,* his account of his years as Reagan's secretary of state, George Shultz's critique of the Iran-Contra scandal praised as "on the mark" Karen Elliott House's *Wall Street Journal* column of November 13, 1985, which observed: "'If some malicious Merlin were trying to concoct a scheme that, with one stroke of a wizard's wand, would undermine American principles, policies, people, interests and allies, it would be hard to conjure up anything more hurtful and humiliating than secretly shipping supplies of American weaponry to the world's primary terrorist state in exchange for a handful of hostages.'"[25] Rather than Iran-Contra being an aberration, this contempt for the letter and the spirit of the law went to the top of the Reagan administration. The belief that the law of the land, if it conflicted with President Reagan's highest objectives, did not need to be upheld and could even be subverted ultimately struck at the very foundation of the Constitution, whose guiding principle is adherence to the rule of law, not of men. Contempt for the letter and the spirit of the law stood out in the Reagan presidency.

Reaganism: The Twenty-Year Economic Record

The first two decades of Reaganism stretched from the despair of double-digit inflation to the powerful economic boom at the end of the millennium, an outcome that some claim should be credited to Reagan's presidency. University of Houston political scientist John Sloan, in his

1999 book *The Reagan Effect,* concluded with this judgment: "Reagan's tax cuts for both individuals and corporations stimulated the prosperity that, except for a short, mild recession in 1990–1991, has continued into the 1990s."[26] Proponents of a highly positive Reagan effect claim that his policies and political philosophy became the key drivers of the subsequent prosperity, and particularly of the 1995–2000 boom. The present inquiry into the validity of this argument begins by looking broadly at the Reagan economic legacy during the twenty years that ended with the close of Bill Clinton's presidency.

This analysis of the Reagan economic record is the first of three interrelated sections, the other two treating his managerial style and competence and his political thought with the consideration of Reagan policies interspersed among the them. Although the three discussions clearly overlap (e.g., political philosophy drove his policy choices) and lack well-delineated boundaries, important differences make the separation useful for the purposes of discussion. The question of responsibility is a good example. In the case of the economy, presidents rush to take full credit for strong economic outcomes and blame weak ones on Congress or some other institution, or on uncontrollable economic factors. The fact remains that a president often is only a bystander watching powerful forces over which he has no control make or break his presidency. President Carter, for example, did not cause the 1979 price increases by the Organization of the Petroleum Exporting Countries (OPEC) that bedeviled him.

In contrast, a president does bear responsibility for his policies. President Reagan, in pushing through the largest income tax cut in American history, deserved praise or censure depending on the various outcomes flowing from that policy. Also important are presidential decisions not to act. For example, President George H. W. Bush's early promise that under no circumstances would he raise income taxes to lower the gigantic yearly budget deficits likely cost him the presidency when he finally abandoned his pledge. Political style and thought also belong to a president, being in one case part of his persona and in the other his underlying political principles. The two can drive decisions, help sell them, and influence how they are executed. They are separated from specific policy and administrative choices because style and thought are often much broader in setting the overall tone and direction that can shape numerous choices made by an administration. For example, President Reagan's antigovernmentism dominated the decisions his administration made in managing the executive branch.

The Reagan Administration's Economic Performance

Two diametrically opposite interpretations of President Reagan's own eight-year record are important in the analysis of the economic record of the two decades of Reaganism. This is so even though few would disagree that the eight-year macroeconomic (aggregate) results during the Reagan years are below average when assessed against earlier postwar presidencies on the traditional measures of inflation-adjusted growth in gross domestic product (GDP), unemployment rates, inflation levels, and size of budget deficits. During the years 1947–72, the nation's output grew at an average annual rate of 3.9 percent, the unemployment rate registered 4.7 percent a year, and inflation increased at 2.2 percent a year, while budget deficits were generally low and some years showed a surplus.[27] Except on the measure of changes in inflation, the macroeconomic performance of the earlier quarter-century was vastly superior to that of the Reagan years.

To put President Reagan's own record in a much more favorable light, his supporters blamed the huge problems left by an inept Carter administration for Reagan's initial two years of near-zero GDP growth, disassociated Reagan from the slow growth and record deficits of the subsequent George H. W. Bush years, and finally maintained that Reagan's policies during his presidency had laid the foundation for the strong economy that began in 1995. A brief critique of the overall economic performance of Reagan, his predecessor, and his successor provides some perspective on the Reagan administration's record.[28] Carter's full four years and Reagan's entire two terms both had roughly the same average annual GDP growth rate of a little more than 3 percent, not a strong performance. Looking to other macroeconomic measures, the worst recession and the highest unemployment rates in the postwar period occurred during Reagan's first term. New jobs per year grew faster during the Carter administration. Carter's average annual unemployment rate stood at 6.5 percent, a point below Reagan's average of 7.5 percent—both relatively high rates.

The huge Reagan tax cuts and massive increases in defense spending produced eight years of deficits that went far beyond anything ever experienced in peacetime. In three of the years, the deficit was above $200 billion, and all eight years exceeded Carter's previous postwar record of roughly $74 billion. However, the double-digit inflation and interest rates, which frightened the American people and crushed Carter's presidency, fell dramatically during Reagan's administration. As for President George H. W. Bush, the Reagan boom lasted through his first year, but the Bush presidency ended up having the lowest rate of economic growth among the elected postwar administrations. Budget deficits soared to record levels and annually averaged materially higher than those of the Reagan years.

The final six years of Reagan's presidency form the base for his supporters' argument for the outstanding economic performance that got the United States rolling again, a claim generally believed by the public at the time. To start with, Reagan's defenders point out that he inherited a sick economy from Carter with a small negative growth rate, a tax system that discouraged investment and savings, and a debilitating double-digit inflation rate. Reagan first had to slay the inflation dragon, which his strongest admirers maintain stands as his epic achievement and became the platform for a high-growth economy. Only after that could he produce the 1983–88 boom and a strong annual GDP growth rate of a little above 4 percent. In the election year of 1984, the growth rate reached a spectacular 7.3 percent, the highest since 1959, and helped propel Reagan's landslide reelection. Thus the blame for the weak growth rate in the 1981–82 period can be placed squarely on Carter's shoulders.

The same type of argument can be used to explain why the Reagan administration's 7.5 percent average annual unemployment rate exceeded that of Carter's term. The needed corrections for the poor economic performance before the Reagan presidency did bring the 1982 unemployment rate to 9.7 percent, the highest rate for a single year during the postwar era. However, the annual rate declined every year thereafter, finally reaching 5.5 percent by 1988, well below the 7.1 percent of Carter's final year. Reagan left office with a strong and extended economic boom featuring sustained growth and a dropping unemployment rate well below the one at the start of his administration. His supporters blame his inept successor for failing to exert the needed stewardship to keep Reagan's buoyant economy on course and thus hold George H. W. Bush responsible for the stagnant economy and burgeoning deficits during his single term.

The drastically reduced marginal tax rates of the first Reagan budget went far beyond any of the previous tax reductions in American history.

The 1986 Tax Reform Act, which ranks as the high point of domestic policy in Reagan's second term, simplified that system and made major reductions in tax loopholes. Reagan reluctantly raised taxes several times, but these in total were still much less than the first-year reduction. His initial budget also had the largest defense buildup during peacetime in American history and significant cutbacks in social programs.

However, neither the budget reductions nor the tax increases prevented record deficits. Concomitantly, the gross federal debt nearly tripled, rising from $909 to $2,600 billion during the eight Reagan years. The yearly deficits and rapidly rising national debt had three major consequences. First, the deficits helped bring what at the time was the longest period of economic growth during peacetime in American history, but they also contributed to the serious declines in net national savings and investment. Second, the deficit-driven boom quickly made interest on the debt one of the largest outlays in the yearly budget. Third, the deficits put a damper on domestic spending, with underinvestment in human resources and public infrastructure being particularly serious.

Although Republicans and Democrats alike condemned the budget deficits, Reagan supporters sought to exonerate him of blame by arguing that the president had tried without success to induce the Democratic Congress to balance the budget. The main claim made was that Congress simply would not make the major reductions in domestic programs needed to balance the budget. In his advocates' story of the Reagan triumph, Carter, Congress, and George H. W. Bush are revealed to be the big culprits. These three are alleged to have caused the overall low growth and astronomical deficits from the early 1980s to the late 1990s. It is a wonderful tale, making President Reagan and Reaganism the real heroes of the high-growth economy. The only problem is that Reagan advocates make numerous overblown and invalid claims.

Take the six strong growth years. To start with, pruning off the initial two years of the Reagan presidency from the growth calculation does appear reasonable in light of the much-needed attack on double-digit inflation. At the same time, the truncated period without the weak growth years did not rank as one of outstanding GDP growth rate performance. In the period 1962–66, annual GDP growth exceeded 6 percent in three of the years and averaged 5.8 percent growth for the five years.

Why then did the Reagan growth record strike people as such an over-powering achievement at the time? There were four main reasons. First, the highest prices and interest rates in the postwar era made people highly apprehensive, so the low inflation and increased growth together took on great importance. Second, the bad economic years, which started in 1973 and ended the long early postwar prosperity, had crushed the high expectations of that period and brought deep gloom that contributed to the excessively high assessment of the Reagan recovery. Third, the president's own ability to sell himself as the hero who conquered inflation had been pivotal in establishing an image of success. Fourth, the president's personal faith in the nation's greatness and his 1984 pitch of "It's Morning Again in America," in which there could be no mistaking that "again" referred to the early postwar years, strongly reinforced the positive assessment of the Reagan record.

Once his administration had started the flood of record deficits, Reagan refused to increase taxes enough to stop the hemorrhaging and came to believe the deficits were beneficial in blocking Democratic spending efforts. In light of both the record peacetime defense increases and the domestic program reductions in his first year, it is small wonder the Democrats did not respond favorably to Reagan's recommendations to balance the budget by massive domestic cuts. The Reagan proposals for deep domestic program decreases—which would have thrown many Republican members of Congress into panic because voters would have been furious at reductions in some of their favored programs—were a subterfuge employed in the false claim that the Democratic Congress bore full responsibility for not balancing the budget. We can leave to others the debate as to whether the president plotted from the beginning to use the deficits to hold back domestic program spending. The main point is that Reagan, who dominated the weak Democratic Congress, bears most of the responsibility for the eight years of massive deficits during his presidency.

To go on with the demythologization of President Reagan, his admirers' argument that he brought about the striking reductions in inflation and interest rates has no validity whatsoever. The Federal Reserve Board's stringent monetary policy became the national government's main weapon in bringing prices and interest rates down to acceptable levels. The effort began late in the Carter presidency; and once inflation had declined, monetary policy continued to hold it in check despite the huge budget deficits brought about by the Reagan administration's tax cuts and inadequate tax increases.

Furthermore, the OPEC price increase in 1979 was but one of the calamities that befell the star-crossed Carter presidency, whereas the OPEC price collapse blessed Reagan by providing him with a platform for claiming to have saved America by restoring low inflation and interest rates. But both of the price movements were what economists call "exogenous changes" that were external to the system (in this case, the government) and were beyond the control of the actors within it. For a president, exogenous changes are the luck of the draw—figuratively being dealt a deuce or an ace, as in the respective cases of Carter and Reagan. The simple fact is that neither president actually had much to do with either the oil-price-induced inflation or the oil-price–induced deflation.

Then–Federal Reserve Board chair Paul Volcker, who steadfastly held to the Fed's tight monetary policy, became the real individual hero in stamping out inflation during the Reagan administration. Sloan noted:

> The self-serving conservative narrative is that Volcker's policies caused the recession, and Reagan's policies brought about noninflationary economic growth. [I suggest instead] that Reagan deserves credit for not attacking Volcker during the dark days of the 1981–1982 recession and for reappointing him in 1983, but Volcker was clearly the architect of the anti-inflationary strategy that has proved to be so essential for promoting a prolonged economic expansion.[29]

The final irony is that the president who appointed Volcker was Carter, not Reagan. There is no good evidence to substantiate his supporters' claim that Reagan made the signal contribution to conquering high inflation that is so central in his deification.

Reagan and the Mighty Boom of the 1990s

Reagan supporters have make a good case that the president's strong probusiness efforts helped create a better climate for corporate rejuvenation. But in taking the next step to give Reagan so much of the credit for the outstanding 1995–2000 economic performance, the strongest since the 1960s, his admirers have leapt far beyond the evidence to where faith

dominates facts. Among the policy efforts during the Reagan administration and in the dozen years thereafter that appear to have contributed
to the economic boom during the Clinton years, a number were aimed
at correcting policy errors made by the Reagan administration. The first
factors to be considered are the policies of the key federal actors and their
institutions. George H. W. Bush and Clinton courageously pushed
through large tax increases that cost them dearly in trying to halt the out-
of-control deficits wrought by Reagan tax cuts. The first lost the presidency; the second, his control of Congress.

Also important were the budget spending limits enacted by Congress
in 1990 and extended in 1993 and 1997. Robert Reischauer, a former director of the Congressional Budget Office now with the Urban Institute,
has written: "Enforceable spending caps . . . have helped transform the
large deficits of the past into today's surpluses. Between 1990 and 1998,
discretionary spending, adjusted for inflation, was cut 11 percent."[30]
Though it is not possible to assess the individual contributions of the tax
increases and the budget caps in laying the base for the coming of a strong
economy, they were part of a serious effort that ended the long period
of big yearly budget deficits running from early in the Reagan administration into Clinton's second term.

Although Federal Reserve chair Paul Volcker and his successor Alan
Greenspan were certainly the stars in taming and controlling inflation in
the last two decades of the twentieth century, Robert Rubin made important contributions to financial stability, both as the top White House
economic adviser during Clinton's first term and as secretary of the treasury during part of his second term. During Rubin's tenure as treasury secretary, he emerged as the second central player, admittedly well below
Greenspan in the battle against inflation. Moreover, as the president sank
into the morass of scandal, Rubin, formerly a highly successful Wall Street
investment banker, and his top Department of the Treasury staff seemed
to detach from the administration and become more a part of the Federal
Reserve–led financial team that kept the economy on the right path, insulated from the political sideshow. This Fed–Treasury team effort stands
out both as a surprising example of organizational cooperation amid the
institutional conflict of the 1990s and as an important factor in the low
inflation that contributed to the strength of the "new economy" in the
late 1990s.

President Reagan did contribute to the recovery of American industry through his administration's concerted deregulation efforts. These changes were helpful both in eliminating restrictions and red tape and in signaling to business and agency regulators that the Reagan administration favored loose reins by the federal government. At the same time, Reagan advocates have accorded deregulation a higher place in the business recovery than it deserves. Businesses generally decry the severity of government regulations and do so most vociferously as an excuse when their performance is poor. Regulations do hurt, but corporations usually adjust to them as a part of doing business and well may find the increased cost negligible. This in no way denies either that regulatory requirements can raise costs significantly for American corporations and decrease their competitiveness or that the Reagan deregulation reduced firms' regulatory outlays and further encouraged business by signaling a new hands-off approach by Washington. However, difficult internal institutional changes that the corporations had been putting off for years look to be the main factors in the transformation to lean and mean U.S. firms.

The highest barriers to international competitiveness were within the corporations themselves, erected by their own shortsightedness over the years, not by the actions of such external institutions as the federal government. A distinguished group of researchers at the Massachusetts Institute of Technology (MIT) argued in 1989 that the biggest blockages to international competitiveness came from internal "organizational patterns and attitudes."[31] For years, overconfident, complacent corporations were their own worst enemies. Finally, large numbers of corporations—frightened by the sharp 1981–82 recession, falling profits, and declining international competitiveness—accepted that their main problems were self-inflicted. This painful recognition propelled badly needed organizational changes, including downsizing, better strategic planning, greater use of ideas from front-line staff in product development and production, more emphasis on worker incentives, and a basic restructuring and streamlining to create flatter, more flexible firms.

This strikingly rapid internal transformation by American businesses appears to have been the most important factor generating the strong increase in sales and profits that underlay the United States's capacity to gain or regain the lead in cutting-edge industries in a relatively short period of time. Later chapters will consider the corporate corruption in which a number of firms used accounting trickery to grossly overstate their profits and thus push up the price of their stocks. This dark side of deregulation under Reaganism that let corporations cook their books created fictitious rapid growth in the reported profits of a number of large firms, and the corruption ultimately put a damper on the stock market and likely on economic growth. At the same time, these later dishonest acts in no way negate the signal contribution made to strengthening the U.S. economy through the difficult internal changes in organizational structure undertaken by the nation's businesses.

Among the drivers of the economic boom, none received so much attention as the extensive business investment in new technology. *New York Times* reporter Richard Stevenson, writing in 1999 on Federal Reserve chair Alan Greenspan's testimony before a congressional committee, summarized Greenspan's "favorite theme" over the last few years: "Huge investments in technology are yielding substantial gains in productivity, or output for every hour worked, a fundamental and far-reaching improvement in the way the economy functions. . . . Technology has been perhaps the dominant force in the economy in recent years, fostering widespread changes in the way businesses operate and contributing tremendously to the vibrancy and durability of the expansion, which is now in its ninth year."[32] By the early twenty-first century, a precipitous decline in the stock market value of technology firms raised questions about this sector's future contribution to productivity and profits. Technology companies, apparently caught up in the belief that they were recession proof, overexpanded their capacity and suffered the consequences when the stock market bubble burst. The earlier strong business investment, however, still appears to have been an important factor in the economic boom.

The United States, in reestablishing a level of world economic hegemony similar to that of the early postwar years, benefited much from the weakness of its major rivals, which were already rapidly going downhill just as it began experiencing higher growth. Japan, the biggest U.S. economic rival and often predicted to leave America in its wake, collapsed from long-neglected internal problems (e.g., highly inefficient sectors, including food distribution, with its "mom and pop" stores, and the huge banking industry) into a seemingly endless period of stagnant growth. West Germany, the second biggest rival, began an extremely costly reunification with communist East Germany after the fall of the Soviet Union, and much like Japan found itself unable to jump back on a high-growth path. In visualizing how America opened up a wide lead over Japan and Germany so rapidly, think of the final mile of a marathon race led by three runners, two of whom tire and slow down to a crawl while the third one speeds up. In addition, much of the rest of the world fell into economic decline—often, as in the case of the rapidly growing East Asian countries, from deep internal problems such as cronyism and outdated financial systems. These global economic doldrums had the additional effect of helping keep down the cost of goods and services in the United States.

Another key factor in the rapid recovery of corporate profitability came from workers' reluctance to press for large wage increases. As the U.S. boom lengthened and created labor shortages of skilled American workers, the fear of a continuing supply of relatively cheap, highly skilled foreign workers tended to make U.S. jobholders leery of pushing hard for higher wages. Workers knew that their corporations could seek to import workers, subcontract with foreign firms, or relocate to another country. Going just across the Mexican border offers the best example. Employees also were believed to be concerned about trying to engage in hard wage bargaining because corporate efforts in the early 1990s, such as the downsizing that included higher-paying white collar jobs, truly frightened employees about job insecurity. In the highly competitive international marketplace, workers did not necessarily see American corporations as ruthless but rather as players forced to hold wage costs down to compete successfully. These worker concerns dissipated to some extent as clear labor shortages developed in the late 1990s, but they had already made a real contribution to keeping inflation low.

The sharp rise of the average annual productivity growth rate in the period 1995–2000 to 3.1 percent, compared with less than one-half that annual rate in the previous two decades, argues against the claim that Reagan policies were critical in this powerful economic boom.[33] Output per worker or labor productivity is so important because of its impact on growth. The MIT economist Frank Levy observed: "In the long run, the level of output per worker sets limits on a worker's income . . . so the growth of incomes depends on the growth of productivity."[34] The average yearly productivity growth rate averaged close to 3 percent in the period 1948–73, a time of remarkable income growth for workers from the top to the bottom of the income distribution; that rate had dropped to around

1.1 percent in the 1980s. The 2001 *Economic Report of the President* presented a trend line indicating a 1.4 percent annual productivity growth rate for the period 1973–95. Reagan administration policies had little or no impact on the trend of average annual productivity growth before 1995. The argument that Reagan's policies contributed materially to the jump to more than 3 percent in the 1995–2000 period is another claim that does not hold up. There are some indications that the 3 percent growth rate may be overstated, but even if that is the case, it does not alter the basic point made in the last sentence.

The available evidence leads me to conclude that both the strong economy of 1995–2000 and the nation's return to a level of world economic hegemony not seen since the early postwar years owe little to Reagan's economic policy. Rather, several other factors were important in the strong performance of the 1990s: the internal corporate changes that restored American business competitiveness; the Federal Reserve Board's monetary management under Volcker and Greenspan, including the Fed's effort that crushed inflation in the early 1980s; the Bush and Clinton tax increases, coupled with the enforceable budget spending caps; and the international economic collapse. Reagan supporters, however, have not backed down. The continuing mythology that Reagan's policies and philosophy restored the U.S. economy and ought to be the basis for future domestic policy stands as one of the highest barriers to needed institutional and economic policy reform.

Managerial Style and Competence

Ronald Reagan was sui generis in combining superior leadership skills, an incredible lack of knowledge about how institutions worked and no interest in learning more, a disdain for policy information and analysis, and immutable ideological beliefs that colored managerial choices.[35] Both the title and subtitle of my 1990 book *Mismanaging America: The Rise of the Anti-Analytic Presidency* were meant to characterize the Reagan years. The book's discussion of President Reagan as manager distinguishes that function from that of leader, with the latter as the motivational, persuasive role and the former as the organization-running job. Reagan ranks as the top leader in the capacity to motivate change (be it good or bad) and as the worst managerial president of the postwar era. The apt image is of Reagan working out with weights much of his life, but only doing so with his right arm and always posing so that the mighty right limb of political leadership can be seen and the helpless left arm of managerial incompetence is kept behind his back.

Inferior information and incompetent ideological appointees reflected Reagan's managerial deficit. Presidents Kennedy and Johnson had established strong policy analysis staffs to advise top agency political executives and had made sound policy information and analyses a regular part of the agency policymaking process. President Reagan so decimated the analytic structure and processes that highly questionable information and shaky analyses became a mark of his administration's decision making—the anti-analytic presidency. The president's managerial deficiencies led to the appointment of numerous managers who were hard-right ideologues, often possessing limited knowledge of how government worked and/or adhering to principles impervious to facts or both. Reagan and the political executives—driven by their rigid ideological beliefs—both engaged in unremitting attacks on the federal government generally and on professional civil servants specifically in a concerted effort to denigrate their skills and also pursued a dangerously simplistic regulatory approach. The latter offers a clear case of an ideological principle leading to wrongheaded policies, to which the Reagan true believers clung without adjustment.

President Reagan's antigovernmentism had embedded in it the firm belief in the power of unregulated free-market capitalism and, concomitantly, the unparalleled excellence of American corporations when not held back by the federal government. His administration saw correctly that excessive regulation harmed business and set out on a policy of massive deregulation to increase business profitability. But its simplistic deregulation policy that favored American industry led to private-sector fraud and financial excesses and to inadequate federal regulatory control. Reagan incorrectly believed that deregulation meant no government controls, which translated into decimating the federal monitoring effort. As we will see, the lack of enough competent monitors during the Reagan administration led to horrendous loses by the federal government, as exemplified by the savings and loan scandal. The dysfunctional Reagan regulatory approach, which still has great political appeal, underlay the federal government's failure to prevent the blatant business dishonesty that yielded several corporate bankruptcies (led by Enron) and numerous overstatements of profits by businesses that were abetted by their accounting firms.

By the end of his two terms, Reagan had reduced the institutional competence of the presidency and, even more broadly, that of the domestic policy side of the whole government, making the government less capable than earlier in the postwar years of efficiently carrying out the nation's laws. The Reagan presidency is the ultimate case of divergence between a president's absolute organizational competence and the public's perception of his organizational mastery of the federal government. Although Reagan ranked well below other postwar presidents in his institutional competence, both the American people and a number of presidential critics perceived him as a master manager. This perception lasted well into Reagan's second term, when his ineptitude during Iran-Contra stripped away the image his staff had created of a tall-in-the-saddle manager able to delegate but stay in control. Moreover, Reaganism's hands-off managerial approach to business continued to thrive—as the terrorist attacks of September 11, 2001, and the Enron scandal frighteningly revealed.

Inspection staffs over the years had been reduced to levels below that needed to carry out their responsibilities, often because corporate America pressured the White House and Congress to cut monitors so businesses could cut corners. Federal staffs were reduced, whether their responsibility had been to inspect food to find out if it was safe to eat or to monitor corporations to determine if they were producing accurate and adequate financial data for use by the public, businesses, and governments. Given the direction of the administrative effort early in President Reagan's first term, it was not hard to foresee a level of mismanagement distinctly worse than that of any previous postwar government. But the fact that Reagan's misguided approach to management continued in vogue long after he left office is startling and underscores the lack of institutional capability in the executive branch since Eisenhower.

Political Philosophy

President Reagan's impact on the American public's mood, beliefs, and behavior far surpassed that of the other presidents in the postwar era. It is his political philosophy that has so changed the United States in the years since his inauguration in 1981. His way of thinking rested on five interrelated beliefs, which can best be summarized by setting out a short description of each in its strongest explicit form—that is, without the hidden meanings or different translations used when others over time employed these original tenets of Reaganism:

- *Antigovernmentism:* The federal government is the problem, never the solution, and must be cut back until it supports only a small number legitimate functions, mainly those involving national security and the protection of life and property. Other needed government activities should, if possible, be carried out by state and local governments.
- *Boundless optimism:* America can again be a land of milk and honey. Removing the dead hand of the federal government from citizens and corporations so as to eliminate the highest income tax rates and excessive regulations and monitoring will allow all to thrive without personal sacrifice.
- *Unregulated capitalism:* Through powerful market forces, the unfettered private sector will sufficiently protect the public against business abuses, with little or no government intervention being needed.
- *Individualism:* Individuals, once freed from government restrictions, can act solely in their own self-interest and that of their families to produce the highest economic growth and the best of all possible Americas.
- *Self-reliance:* People who fail to take advantage of the available opportunities do not deserve government support. Society's hard-working winners have no obligation to aid those who do not act on their own initiative.

Several comments about President Reagan's fundamental beliefs are needed. First, the five tenets are intended to fairly reflect the core ideology of Reaganism. Second, the president, the truest of the true believers in Reaganism, did not accept that the Reagan message as he delivered it had explicit negative aspects or could become a destructive force. For example, the repeated charge that he was a racist always hurt Reagan and struck him as unfair and probably malicious. Nor does it appear he realized that a tenet, such as the one labeled "self-reliance," in the hands of others could be packaged in coded language sanctioning derogatory racial and ethnic stereotypes. The most striking aspect of Reagan's Reaganism is that his lack of insight, his unquestioning belief in the goodness of his ideology, and his seemingly so unthreatening "Great Communicator's" unswerving optimism and modulated style of presentation combined to make his message more acceptable, more powerful, and more harmful.

Third, the message as delivered by Reagan himself needs to be distinguished from its interpretations by later Republican leaders. Representative Newt Gingrich crafted by far the most important translation after becoming speaker of the House in January 1995. Gingrich lacked Reagan's soothing political style, which gave his words a sugary covering. Gingrich, in contrast, brought to that message his unbelievable physical and emotional energy, a harsher judgment than Reagan of America and its people, and his hard, sometimes vindictive operating style. This combustible mixture produced a "mean" version of Reaganism that differed markedly in tone from the earlier one. The Gingrich version and those of later Republican hardcore ideologues set out the ideas in starker terms and in a more combative style, which increased political polarization and battered Congress's institutional structure. This mean Reaganism, however, did not visibly distort the basic themes; it only stripped away the protective covering of the Reagan style to reveal an underlying divisiveness and destructiveness that had been there all along—even though Reagan himself may not have recognized, and certainly did not admit, the potential for harm.

Fourth, the exponents of mean Reaganism, with its overt social Darwinism, sought to put the harsher aspects of Reagan's message into practice with far more intensity and attention to detail than did the often passive president. Reagan had a favorite story about a "Chicago welfare queen" who bilked the federal government. This tale, as so often was the case with Reagan, greatly embellished the facts. He dramatized the story to the point that it became an overarching myth of welfare recipients leading the good life at the expense of hardworking taxpayers. Yet though he told it frequently and no doubt created a memorable image of a welfare cheater, he did not use this powerful base by following through in the legislative arena. It would be Gingrich, who drew on his unfailing energy and tenacity and his disdain for "losers," to employ the Reagan theme as the vehicle for forcing through the welfare changes of 1996. These changes, which undercut the safety net for poor women and their children, finally struck down the mythical welfare queen.

Fifth, President Reagan's great capacity for political leadership, derived in part from his beliefs, made it possible to push through his policies and administrative changes. Once in place, their force, made still more powerful by the beliefs, often materially increased the level of the outcomes far beyond what less charismatic presidents could have produced. Moreover, the Reagan message in its later and harsher translation continues both to have tremendous appeal to the public and also to shape what citizens believe and how they behave—with deleterious consequences for individuals, the political system, and the economy. The extraordinary power of Reagan's public leadership, which has given his message its continuing power, is central to the question of relative culpability for what has happened under Reaganism.

For example, take the Democratic Congress during Reagan's presidency. That body passed the legislation that put Reagan's policies in place, including the critical 1981 budget and tax package, and it sanctioned the Reagan administrative practices, at least to the extent of not blocking them. Congress, then, can rightly be charged as an accomplice both through action and inaction. But recognizing that Congress also stands at the docket guilty of the bad policies and administrative practices is not to argue equal culpability. Reagan dominated Congress on most of the new policies, particularly the earlier ones, and almost all of the changes in administrative practices during his presidency. Both inflicted damage. However, Reagan's impact far outweighed that of the weak Congress. Reagan's ideas overrode political opponents and constitutional barriers far more than had those of any other president since Franklin Roosevelt's powerful leadership brought forth the New Deal (which also underwent subsequent translations).

The arguments that Reagan and Roosevelt before him have had a much greater impact on the nation's political thinking than any of the other presidents since 1933 and that Reaganism has been harmful to the American political system are not meant to imply that leaders dominate history. The current prevailing view is that exogenous factors—defined as those beyond the control of a nation's policymakers, such as a natural disaster or an oil price increase in the international market—generally are much more powerful than the actions of governments, whatever the leadership capability of their leaders and the strength of their institutions. For instance, the Great Depression that swept from country to country

crushed Herbert Hoover's presidency and held down the American economy until World War II, regardless of what President Roosevelt tried to
do. Exogenous factors sometimes are totally dominant. At other times,
leadership can alter outcomes, even if the impact is secondary compared
with that of exogenous forces.

It is also the case that both scholars and citizens are not likely to be
comfortable with the argument that elected officials, including presidents,
have little or no control over what happens. Paul Kennedy has paraphrased
the nineteenth-century German chancellor Otto von Bismarck by arguing that the major nations such as the United States and Japan are travel-
ing on "'the stream of Time,' which they can 'neither create nor direct,'
but upon which they can 'steer with more or less skill and experience.'"[36]
Kennedy wrote his book a few years before Japan's terrible economic
problems, and it certainly appears that the country since then has been
led by those with a painful lack of steering capability. The next chapters,
on the key institutions of federal governance and on citizens, will add a
number of dimensions to the argument that Reaganism has done untold
damage to the U.S. steering mechanism—that is, to its institutions of governance. Its leaders, whether determined to use the tenets of Reaganism
(George W. Bush) or afraid not to stay with the dominant political philosophy (Bill Clinton), have carried the United States on a course that has
been devastating to political equality and economic opportunity and security, even if it has not brought the macroeconomic damage that has be-
fallen Japan.

four

Governing in the American Republic

The United States created the first representative democracy by granting a majority of white males political equality in electing those who would serve them in Congress. The striking boldness of this step can be seen from the fact that by the 1870s, only two European countries had joined America in granting broad manhood suffrage; and roughly fifty years after that at the end of World War I, only twenty nations had representative assemblies chosen by the bulk of their adult male citizens. Just as remarkable, in light of the uncharted terrain, the U.S. Constitution's institutional structure composed of separate executive, legislative, and judicial branches has changed little in its underlying specifications since the late eighteenth century. Even the Seventeenth Amendment in 1913, which required senators to be chosen directly by the people instead of being selected by the state legislatures, had no real impact on the Senate's long-established institutional relationships with the presidency and the House of Representatives.

Although the Founders had developed a government structure based on their wide reading and experience, the framers knew that their effort was the first experiment in representative democracy and that what had been crafted suffered from critical compromises made to increase agreement, not efficiency. Had the framers been interviewed and asked to speculate about the future, I suspect that few if any would have expected the constitutional structure to have survived with such limited changes for more than 200 years or to have become a "national icon."[1] Yet as the distinguished Pulitzer Prize–winning historian Gordon Wood of Brown University observed in his 2002 overview of the American Revolution: "As the Federalists of the 1790s eventually discovered to their dismay, this democracy . . . was no longer a simple form of government that could be skeptically challenged and contested as it had been since the ancient Greeks. Instead, it became the civic faith of the United States to which all Americans must unquestionably adhere."[2]

Scholars still grapple with the implications of this relatively unchanged eighteenth-century document, which is a secular bible in the eyes of the American people—whose knowledge of what the Constitution says is limited and often wrong. It should not be surprising, then, that the various compromises reached at the Constitutional Convention as well as the underlying institutional structure of governance set out in the original Constitution still materially affect key issues examined in this book. Moreover, the long struggle between the Federalists, who supported a strong, efficient federal government, and the Anti-Federalists, who favored the states and distrusted the national government, is important for understanding the shift from Franklin Roosevelt's New Deal philosophy to Reaganism.

A Unique System

No other nation has adopted the American model of governance. As the historian James McGregor Burns has observed: "Decade after decade foreign leaders and publics rejected the American presidential–congressional–judicial checks-and-balance system in favor of the unified Cabinet–parliamentary system."[3] New democracies found the separation of the three branches in the U.S. political system cumbersome and susceptible to unwanted blockages. Moreover, American scholars who have studied the nation's unique governmental structure over the years—including a political science professor and future president, Woodrow Wilson—often both questioned its capacity to operate efficiently and criticized the difficulty of affixing responsibility under it. Many an American academic who studied in the United Kingdom came to extol the efficiency of that nation's parliamentary model as the means for curing this country's institutional blockages and rendering national politicians accountable.

In the American system, the veto power of the separate (independent) branches of government over each other can bring gridlock. This is the case even when one political party holds the presidency and controls Congress because the parties often lack the power to punish members who defy them. The system also is susceptible to the potential blockages under divided government when a president has to deal with one or both houses of Congress under the control of the political party in opposition. In sharp contrast, the British system combines the executive and legislative functions, and the parties have powerful sanctions that keep their members of Parliament in line when a party vote is demanded.

The U.S. separated government also complicates accountability as compared with the British parliamentary structure. In the latter, the government in power can be blamed for a failed policy without being able to claim that the opposition party had a hand in the results. In contrast, Congress may escape accountability by pointing out with some legitimacy that the president performed poorly in executing sound legislation. Alternatively, a president may be able to argue with merit that Congress passed a wrongheaded law over his veto or interfered with the executive branch's effort at implementation. Or both can blame the Supreme Court. The American system offers an admirable means of passing the buck and leaving the public unclear about the responsibility for policy failure.

The criticism turned to fulsome praise in the early post–World War II era, when the United States achieved world economic and geopolitical hegemony and attained an exceptional degree of social and political calm at home. Then, the mounting socioeconomic problems that erupted in the 1960s rekindled the issue of whether the U.S. institutional structure was unworkable. As Burns wrote in 1984: "The Framers have simply been too shrewd for us. They have outwitted us. They designed separate institutions that cannot be unified by mechanical linkages, frail bridges, tinkering. If we are to 'turn the Founders upside down'—to put together what they put asunder—we must directly confront the constitutional structure they erected."[4]

Others were far harsher. In an all-out attack in his 1996 book *The Frozen Republic: How the Constitution Is Paralyzing Democracy,* Daniel Lazare claimed that the framers' document fit the needs of their society in 1787 but soon proved wanting. Particularly critical was the decision at the Constitutional Convention by the delegates from the nonslaveholding states to placate the South so as to keep its delegates from refusing to join the proposed union. The provision that the slaves in each state were to be counted as three-fifths of a person for the purpose of apportioning House members inevitably led to the Civil War. Abraham Lincoln succinctly spelled out the fatal flaw in observing that "this government cannot endure permanently half slave and half free."

Seven decades after its ratification, the Constitution's accommodation to slavery brought four years of strife in the bloody Civil War. Although constitutional amendments ended slavery and granted the vote to black males, Lazare still viewed the Constitution as badly flawed: "For approximately the next three-quarters of a century, it proved to be a straight-jacket, in which even the mildest social reform was prohibited . . . then, following a brief golden age after World War II, it has resulted in crippling gridlock and paralysis. The Constitution has performed this way not despite the Founders, but because of them."[5]

The Constitution's separated institutions are not without their defenders. In *The Presidency in a Separated System,* political scientist Charles Jones wrote: "I come away from this study quite in awe of the American national government . . . [and] conclude that it is more important to make the separated system work well than to change systems."[6] Jones sought to refute those who claimed that the system had become hopelessly gridlocked through divided government. His argument placed much emphasis on structural balance and institutional competence. As to the former, he argued: "The test in a separated system . . . [is] one of achievement by the system, with the president and members of Congress inextricably bonded. . . . Solo triumphs for presidents in the separated system are, and should be, rare."[7] In his view, presidents should not operate as if Congress is subordinate, but instead should seek realistic give-and-take to reach sensible compromises acceptable to both of the legitimate participants in the policymaking process. He also stressed the need for a president to be able communicate with the executive branch agencies so that their secretaries would have a clear understanding of the administration's goals and could do a good job in carrying out their policy and legislative tasks.[8]

A dramatic change occurred after *The Presidency in a Separated System* was published in 1994. When Newt Gingrich became speaker of the House, political polarization increased geometrically. In this harsh political environment, reasoned compromise has become almost impossible on critical domestic policy issues. The separated system has not mitigated, and well may have added to, the polarization. Since 1994, the laws enacted have not been responsive to critical domestic policy problems and in some cases have made them worse. The overriding issue is whether or not the two-centuries-old model for governance still fosters sufficient institutional competence and credibility in the federal executive and legislative branches to support the reasoned deliberations and compromise needed for realistic policymaking. Has the framers' carefully crafted institutional solution to solve the problems of their own time become hopelessly obsolete for the twenty-first century—an albatross weighing down the American political system?

The War between the Federalists and the Anti-Federalists

During the Constitutional Convention and the ratification effort, the fierce debate between the Federalists and the Anti-Federalists concerned the degree of control by citizens over their elected members of Congress in a representative democracy. Garry Wills pointed out that the Anti-Federalists wanted a sufficiently large number of elected officials to represent the various views within each congressional district; a legislature made up of persons with values and skills like those of their constituents; and the members of Congress to be in close proximity to their constituents so that the latter could watch their representatives carefully in open proceedings, give them explicit instructions on how to vote, and recall them for failing to follow citizens' instructions.[9] The Anti-Federalists' ideal conceptualization of representative democracy held that the number of representatives should be *sufficiently large* so they could be mirror images of their *small* number of constituents, and that there be little separation between the people and their elected officials. By reducing the discretion of the elected members of a legislature to a minimum, the Anti-Federalist model of representation would have diminished the value of deliberations because opinions dictated by the constituents would be unlikely to be changed.

James Madison attacked the Anti-Federalist argument in *The Federalist* No. 10:

> [Deliberations] refine and enlarge the public views by passing them through the medium of a chosen body of citizens, whose wisdom may best discern the true interest of their country and whose patriotism and love of justice will be least likely to sacrifice it to temporary or partial considerations. . . . It may well happen that the public voice, pronounced

by representatives of the people, will be more consonant to the public good than if pronounced by the people themselves, convened for the purpose.[10]

Congress's need for representatives of competence and integrity led Madison to ask in *The Federalist* No. 10 "whether small or extensive republics are most favorable to the election of proper guardians of the public weal," and to answer that the larger setting is superior because "the suffrages of the people being more free, will be more likely to center on men who possess the most attractive merit and the most diffusive and established characters."[11] Such thinking rationalized the provision in Article I indicating that the number of representatives would not exceed 1 for every 30,000 persons (except that each state would have at least a single representative). In Madison's judgment, this structural requirement of a large, diverse voting base would both help to cancel out the impact of factions and aid voters in distinguishing corrupt candidates from those of well-established merit.

The clash of the Federalists and the Anti-Federalists pitted the revolutionary concepts of 1776 against those of 1787—state sovereignty against nationalism. As Wood observed: "Given America's experience with central power, it is easy to see how the erection of a national government represented a political revolution as great as the revolution of a decade earlier, when the British monarchy had been overthrown and new state governments formed. . . . [The 1787 Philadelphia Convention] was indeed a more desperate revolution, bred from despair and from the sense of impending failure of the earlier revolution."[12] In 1776, the fear of an overly powerful central government like that of King George III and the British Parliament led to the creation of a weak Continental Congress that was dependent on the states, where the people were closer to their elected officials. It was a states-dominated representative democracy that rejected a ruling elite in the national government.

Both Madison and Alexander Hamilton were in general agreement that the states must be clearly subordinate to the national government and subject to national oversight. The Anti-Federalists took the opposite position in continuing to support power centered in the states and held by ordinary citizens and in rejecting the Federalist notion of a natural aristocracy. It was the goal of the Anti-Federalists to have elected officials who would be like the people electing them. If this shift occurred, the Federalist James Otis warned in 1776, "'When the pot boils, the scum will rise.'"[13] Otis's prediction came to pass at the state level in the years immediately after the Declaration of Independence. The new men, whom the Federalists came to see as unfit, uncouth, and without scruples, did push aside the natural aristocracy the Federalists saw as possessing the high status, great knowledge, and proper temperament for enlightened governance.

The Anti-Federalists, who held fast to the tenets of the 1776 Revolution, continued to reject a ruling elite similar to the aristocrats in the British government the colonists had challenged and defeated by force of arms. Wood wrote: "Both sides fully appreciated the central issue the Constitution posed and grappled with it throughout the debates: whether a professedly popular government should actually be in the hands of, rather than simply derived from, common ordinary people."[14] The central issue came down to the kind of people who should represent their constituents in the national government and the nature of the relationship between the two—that is, to matters of institutional structure and process and of individual competence and integrity. In the latter case, several state constitutions had sought to address the question of the desirable qualities of legislators by declaring that senators and representatives must be able and virtuous. These stipulations about desirable individual characteristics, however, had not prevented far too many unqualified, greedy, and dishonest state representatives from holding office.

The Founders had created the first great republican democracy based on the notion that the large body of voters could behave responsibly. Madison, addressing the Virginia ratifying convention, best set out the faith and the fear in relying on the people:

> But I go on this great republican principle, that the people will have the virtue and intelligence to select men of wisdom and virtue. Is there no virtue among us? If there be not, we are in a wretched situation. No theoretical checks, no form of government, can render us secure. To suppose that any form of government will secure liberty or happiness without any virtue in the people is a chimerical idea.[15]

'Twas a risky leap of faith. As Wood pointed out: "Noah Webster raised the critical question. It was commendable, he wrote, that only wise and honest men be elected to office. 'But how can a constitution ensure the choice of such men? *A constitution that leaves the choice entirely with the people?*"[16]

Today the issue of voter capability needs to be cast in terms of the vast, diverse array of eligible voters who must cope with a polarized environment in which political information and ideas abound but hard facts and sound analysis are difficult to determine when the latest techniques are employed by the candidates and their parties and big-money interests to manipulate the electorate. Be that as it may, no change has been made in the charge to the electorate, nor has a wondrous structural fix been found to transform ordinary citizens into intelligent and virtuous voters. Are the people up to the challenge of choosing men and women of competence and integrity to serve them in the Senate and the House of Representatives? The questions raised by Madison and Webster are at least as salient today as in the 1780s. Only a competent, committed electorate can restore the U.S. political system to a level of efficiency sufficient to cope with the long-untreated policy problems threatening citizens' economic security and political equality.

The Madisonian Model of Representative Democracy

It needs to be clear that there is no model of Madisonian representative democracy explicitly written down by the Father of the Constitution. Rather, I have set out its basic features on the nature of the relationship between eligible voters and representatives and of the role of the latter in Congress based primarily on *The Federalist Papers*. During the time when the question of the ratification of the Constitution held sway, Madison offered a relatively explicit, quite straightforward approach to structuring the two relationships and to establishing responsibilities for citizens and representatives. Hamilton provided insights into the role and responsibilities of members of the House of Representatives. Dahl pointed out that the Federalists and Anti-Federalists "were of one mind about the need for representative government."[17] The battle came over the key relationships and responsibilities of the people and their elected representatives.

Madison in *The Federalist* No. 10 asked much of those chosen as the representatives of the people: The members of the House were to serve as the guardians of their constituents' best interests and seek the public good through their deliberations. Although the Madisonian model incorporated a significant degree of freedom for each representative so as to enhance congressional debate, the House members were still the people's agents, who would be shirking their most basic responsibility if they failed to serve the best interests of those in their congressional district. Moreover, as Hamilton had written in *The Federalist* No. 71: "It is a just observation that the people commonly intend the PUBLIC GOOD. This often applies to their very errors."[18] Hence, freeing up representatives to engage in deliberations was not meant to weaken the link between citizens and representatives but rather to improve the chances of attaining the public good that both sought.

It was unclear then and remains so now as to how the appropriate institutions should proceed in operational terms for the key relationships to come out as desired. The degree of separation between citizens and their representatives in particular continues to be a vexing problem because what is needed for efficient performance is not easily specified with any precision. The distance the Anti-Federalists wanted between citizens and their representatives certainly appeared inadequate—a noose around the neck of the representatives that could easily be pulled by their constituents to inhibit the give-and-take of extended debate. However, not only is it exceedingly difficult to determine prospectively when that new distance will be widened too far; the appropriate degree of separation may vary over time with changing circumstances. This latter problem appears far more critical today where big-money interests can establish a degree of separation so great that those charged with being the people's agents may come to answer to major campaign contributors and their highly paid lobbyists. But such considerations jump ahead of the story.

In the Madisonian model, the citizens' choices of the politicians who would represent them stood out as the most critical single step in the entire process. If voters had the capacity to make a sound choice, their main task would be accomplished. Once chosen, wise, virtuous representatives could deliberate on the public good without tight control by their constituents and still serve them well. Michael Schudson observed: "The knowledge that citizens of the 1790s were expected to have was local knowledge—not of laws or principles, but of men. Voters were expected to be familiar with the character of the candidates for office."[19] These voters of yore, the male property owners who almost certainly included the area's leading citizens, would likely be acquainted with the candidates personally or else know others whom they trusted who knew the candidates. In the late eighteenth century, the assumption appeared to be a realistic one that the distance between the voters and the candidates would be small at the point of selecting representatives.

Madison envisioned voters selecting "men who possess the most attractive merit and the most diffusive and established characters."[20] Hamilton also rejected the Anti-Federalists' notion that elected officials should simply reflect whatever the community wanted and maintained that the people's chosen representatives had the duty to protect their constituents' interests even when they incurred the people's anger by telling them when they erred. In *The Federalist* No. 71, Hamilton blended a concept of service that demanded courage and integrity with realism about political practices:

> The republican principle demands that the deliberative sense of community should govern the conduct of those they intrust the management of their affairs; but it does not require unqualified complaisance ... to every transient impulse which the people may receive from the arts of men, who flatter their prejudices to betray their interests. ... It is the duty of the persons whom they have appointed to be the guardians of those interests to withstand the temporary delusion in order to give them time and opportunity for more cool and sedate reflection.[21]

This statement combined the high-mindedness of a man with both exceptional public integrity ("Propriety was Hamilton's lodestar," wrote his biographer, Forrest McDonald) and a profound understanding of the potential dangers of national politics as practiced near the end of the eighteenth century.[22]

In *The Federalist* No. 71, Hamilton—as I see it—had laid out a daunting set of operational principles for the people's representatives:

- First, the objective of the governmental process is not simply the compliance with the people's wishes but the promotion of the public's well-being.
- Second, the people want the public good but may assess it incorrectly.

- Third, those elected to manage the people's affairs should seek the sense of the community they serve, but to do so does not mean slavish compliance.
- Fourth, the members of Congress must determine if the people may have been misled, and reject those views based on prejudice and misleading or wrong-headed ideas, however strongly held by the people and however angry at them their constituents might become.

It well may be that the combination of capability, integrity, and courage demanded were too great for the representatives and also asked too much from the voters in being able to discern these qualities in those selected as agents.

The question also arose as to how well the Madisonian institutional structure facilitated the search for such exemplary representatives, encouraged representatives to serve their constituents' best interests, and stimulated the needed deliberations. The first point to make is that no matter how good the structure and processes were on paper, the model had not been tested. Hard evidence was in short supply. In addition, the institutional structure was not the best one that could have been devised on the basis of the available information but rather the one that made it through the Constitutional Convention, where the compromises needed to win ratification left much to be desired.

Stanford University historian Jack Rakove, in his Pulitzer Prize–winning study of the development of the Constitution, pointed out that (1) Hamilton was quite skeptical that the electoral process would produce superior lawmakers, and in the case of the more confident Madison, his "innate skepticism" kept him from thinking that his predictions were well grounded in evidence; (2) Madison never spelled out structural processes that would lead toward the election of wise and virtuous senators with a broad national vision that would move that body toward reasoned deliberations; and (3) the Constitution did not set high qualifications for those seeking office or indicate how to conduct national elections and permitted much discretion for state legislatures in establishing the rules for voting.[23]

The various institutional defects came about in part from the framers' inability to craft precise structural and procedural arrangements and in part from the politics of the Constitutional Convention that necessitated less than satisfactory choices from a system-building perspective so as to have the Constitution be accepted at Philadelphia. That even the Founders, unquestionably an extraordinary group led by towering figures, could not solve some of the institutional problems is hardly surprising in light of what we now know about the profound difficulty of crafting structural fixes. That the play of politics yielded a framework for governance that had institutional weaknesses recognizable at the outset is less surprising yet. At the same time, Madison's and Hamilton's visions of representative democracy clearly set out the needed relationships between the citizens and their representatives and among their representatives when interacting with their colleagues in the House and with persons or organizations not from the representatives' districts (i.e., special interests, in the current political vernacular). How these relationships are holding up at any point in time remains a crucial measure of the political health of the American Republic.

Political Equality

The American Republic stood on two pillars: (1) a set of critical institutional relationships between voters and their elected representatives and among the latter, and (2) an electorate in which all citizens had equal political status. Wood wrote of the special place of equality in the nation's history: "The noblest ideas and aspirations of Americans—their commitments to freedom, constitutionalism, the well-being of ordinary people, and equality, especially equality—came out of the Revolutionary era."[24] Both equality of opportunity and political equality were primary objectives. As to the former, Wood noted that "republican equality did not mean the elimination of all distinctions" because natural differences in ability and experience were well recognized.[25]

Political equality, however, embraced a single status for all who were eligible to vote. Robert Dahl of Yale University, the distinguished political scientist and scholar of democracy, made the critical point:

> Let me . . . view democracy as, ideally at least, a political system designed for citizens of a state who are willing to treat one another, for political purposes, as *political* equals. If we believe that all human beings are cre-

ated equal, that they are endowed with certain inalienable rights, that among them are life, liberty, and the pursuit of happiness, that to secure these rights governments are instituted among a people, deriving their just powers from the consent of the governed, then we are obligated to support the goal of political equality. Political equality requires democratic political institutions. [26]

Political equality and Madisonian representative democracy were indelibly linked in the new American Republic. One constituted the needed institutional relationships between representatives and their constituents and among the former when in session. The other indicated the political status required for all eligible voters in choosing their representatives. Although neither speaks to all aspects of the U.S. political system, the two address core elements of the American Republic.

In the formative period between 1776 and 1787, an entirely different kind of nation emerged in which ordinary people, not titled aristocrats, would choose their leaders. Wood called equality "the most powerful idea in all of American history."[27] Equality of economic opportunity did not demand the same final results for each person or, realistically, that everyone start from the same point. It did require that when children were born, they had a fair chance at economic success. Nor could one imagine true political equality for everyone (e.g., knowledge is a factor). Yet the range of inequality needed to be narrower on the political side than on the economic one. That is why the growth of the maldistribution of income and wealth has been so destructive in the political arena, destroying both Madisonian representative democracy and political equality in three different periods from the late nineteenth century through the late twentieth century and producing a plutocratic form of government in the United States.

A Necessary Evil or a Necessary Good?

In *A Necessary Evil,* in which Pulitzer Prize–winning historian Garry Wills attacked a number of myths and misperceptions in the Constitution, he rejected "one of the most astounding assumptions of our political life, the belief that government should be inefficient."[28] The Founders did not so fear federal power that they *purposely* created and embedded a number of checks and balances to serve as *permanent* barriers that inhibited the key institutions from operating efficiently. If Madison and Hamilton in *The Federalist Papers* had sought inefficiency to keep the beast of central government at bay, the national government could well merit the title of "a necessary evil," a status that would justify antigovernmentism and distrust of federal government action. If not, the federal government appears to be "a necessary good" that warrants major efforts to strengthen the national institutions crafted in the Constitution or, if necessary, replace them to restore the needed efficiency.

Wills's thesis is that checks and balances to block efficient governance were anathema to the key drafters, including the foremost interpreter of the original Constitution, James Madison, who still stands wrongly accused of paternity for this bastard concept. The drafters sought a clean separation of the legislative, executive, and judicial functions and a distribution of power that facilitated the three branches in doing their own jobs so as to enhance overall efficiency.

The separation of powers had been only a minor concept during much of the eighteenth century; but Wood noted that "the constitutional reformers in the years after 1776 exploited it with a sweeping intensity and eventually magnified it into the dominant principle of the American political system."[29] The Continental Congress, which had been weak from its inception because of its lack of power in its relationship with the states, had become even less efficient in trying to carry out the executive, legislative, and judicial functions. At the same time, the leading Federalist thinkers feared that lodging all three powers in a single strong entity could lead to tyranny. This danger could be avoided, Madison argued in *The Federalist* No. 51, "by so contriving the interior structure of the government as that its several constituent parts may, by their mutual relations, be the means of keeping each other in their proper places."[30]

Wood indicated that the major writers on government during the 1780s agreed that the functions had to be kept separate so the three branches "'may, uninterrupted by one another, exercise their several powers.'"[31] Wills pointed out: "[The branches] of government may, *precisely in the name of efficiency,* have to fight off encroachment of those functions. Should the executive try to legislate, or the legislature try to execute, they would be returning to the inefficient confusion of functions that the Articles [of Confederation] created. They check each other in this sense. But opposition is not encouraged for its own sake."[32] The concept of the separation of powers, as spelled out in the Constitution, represented the end product of the thinking of the best minds among the Federalists as the mechanism for producing a well-constituted government while avoiding either tyranny or powerlessness.

However compelling the concept of the separation of powers seemed in theory, it would not necessarily be simple to put into practice. As Wood observed in his seminal analysis of the thesis: "It was an imposing conception—a kinetic theory of politics—[where] . . . out of the clashing and checking . . . Madison believed the public will, the true perfection of the whole, would somehow arise."[33] Once the process had been set in motion, checking to maintain just the right balance could demand great skill in that the new government structure crafted by the framers would not be self-adjusting. Neither the concept of the separation of powers nor the Constitution's original institutional structure was inherently flawed, but at the outset of the new Republic and still today an active effort is needed to maintain a reasonable balance among the functions.

Once governance became increasingly complex during the 1960s, specialized competence emerged as a central component of institutional efficiency. Wills argued that the voters, who are amateurs in political matters, ought to choose representatives having their basic values yet should not take the next step by selecting persons like themselves in possessing only their limited political skills. Nobody wants inefficient doctors to treat them or incompetent lawyers to counsel them. Why then would voters pick inept members of Congress who waste tax dollars or prefer incompetent government statisticians who provide inaccurate or incomplete information that will be used in major decisions? It would be the equivalent of a business organization hiring unqualified staff so that permanent ineptitude could always block profits.

The notion of federal government inefficiency as the safeguard against too much centralized power goes back to deliberations at the Constitutional Convention in the summer of 1787 and the extended debate in the states over ratification. Their designations notwithstanding, the Anti-Federalists fervently embraced states' rights and an unrelenting antigovernmentism that sought to minimize power at the center, while the Federalists favored an efficient national system with far more control over the states than had been the case under the Articles of Confederation. Not only did their arguments for a strong central government win the day, *The Federalist Papers* came to be seen as the foremost work in political thought ever written in the United States—"the one product of the American mind that is rightly counted among the classics of political theory."[34] After having long been scattered about and difficult to find, the writings and speeches of the Anti-Federalists were brought together by University of Chicago political scientist Herbert Storing in his monumental seven-volume work *The Complete Anti-Federalist* (published four years after his death in 1977). His conclusion was that the Anti-Federalists had the weaker argument in the constitutional debate but that "their concerns and principles continue to play an important part in the dialogue over the life of the American polity."[35] His insight foreshadowed the coming shift in political thinking as the Anti-Federalists' antigovernmentism became the central plank of Reaganism.

Wills wrote that late–twentieth-century conservatives inappropriately blended together the contradictory notions of the two eighteenth-century protagonists: "The modern enthusiasts for what they take to be federalism cannot bring themselves to admit . . . that *The Federalist,* under the cover of some sweet phrases thrown to the states, argued in fact for national sovereignty . . . [so they concocted] what they obviously considered the best of both worlds—a government adopted for anti-government reasons, what *The Federalist* itself called a 'monster.'"[36] For example, in *The Federalist* No. 44, Madison had caustically ridiculed the Anti-Federalists' state supremacy thesis: "The world would have seen, for the first time, a system of government founded on an inversion of the fundamental principles of all government; it would have seen the authority of the whole society everywhere subordinate to the authority of its parts; it would have seen a monster, in which the head was under the direction of its members."[37]

The Federalists were advocates of clear federal supremacy over the states, and, as Wills added: "The modern cult of checks [to be used as an offensive weapon] as the primary virtue of the Constitution was not shared by the framers."[38] Given that the leading Federalists, including George Washington, held strongly that the states needed to be kept subordinate to the national government, it is the sheerest perversion for the hardcore Republican right to claim that the Constitution's checks were intended to render the national government inefficient as a means of protecting states' rights.

Despite the historical record, the proponents of Reaganism have hailed the checks and balances, which they attribute to Madison's genius, as the supreme achievement in protecting the states from the federal government. The great irony is the degree to which Anti-Federalist thinking has won out by standing the Federalists' unrelenting quest for efficiency in their eighteenth-century model on its head and claiming that institutional ineptitude had been the original intent in order to protect the rights of the states from any federal incursion. The Federalists' model for the national government, which rested on their firm belief that it was a necessary good had been hijacked and recast in the Anti-Federalist image of a faulty vehicle cleverly constructed to perform so poorly that it would constrain the necessary evil of a national government.

Implementation Success and the Strength of the Model

Two aspects of the Constitution are particularly striking. First, there had been phenomenal success in implementing the original structural design and its division of institutional functions. Second, the model was amazingly robust, as reflected in the adherence to the Founders' concept of governance during the 170 years from George Washington through Dwight Eisenhower. Implementation is the place to start.

However brilliant the Founders' design on the drawing board, the Constitution was at the time a theory or hypothesis about accomplishing a specific outcome. In testing a theory, it is necessary to distinguish between an idea that was put in place properly and did not work and an idea that was not tested because it was not implemented properly. The former is theory failure; the latter, implementation failure. It seems safe to rule out the latter for the Constitution. First, an implementation may fail because the program designers lack experience in operating major government systems and provide the implementers with an unrealistic model. Second, separate designers and implementers can create tensions, with the latter feeling little responsibility for a strong implementation effort because they had no involvement in the design. Experience and motivation were not obstacles in 1789. Several Founders had served in earlier governments, were important in the design of the institutional structure, and became central actors during implementation.

Two exceptional leaders—President Washington and Secretary of the Treasury Hamilton—guided the implementation over time. The former likely was the only American with the stature to command sufficient respect to settle disputes and enforce his choices. The latter, probably the most effective cabinet member in American history, combined the compelling vision and administrative capacity to put in place the governmental foundation needed for the United States to become a great nation. He was a man far ahead of his peers. Paul Van Riper called Hamilton the "guiding genius" who kept the new government afloat and acclaimed him the "founder of the American administrative state"; Jerry McCaffery argued that "Hamilton's role in debt management, securing the currency, and providing and defending a stable revenue base mark him as a Founding Father of the American budget system."[39]

The new American institutional structure demanded what the students of implementation call a "fixer," an implementer who can handle the administrative problems that are bound to emerge during the usually extended period required to put a complex design of this type in place. In Hamilton, the new nation had the ultimate fixer who could see beyond the design while still staying true to the basic intent and could successfully confront the major difficulties the theorists almost certainly could not have foreseen. Putting that new government in place still represents an extraordinary implementation success, but such success only meant that the theory would have a fair test.

Once in place, that model of governance proved to be robust in maintaining the original structure and functional relationships among the branches. Although there have been several adjustments, including restricting presidents to two terms, the one noteworthy change for the original institutions, as was noted above, came through the Seventeenth Amendment providing for the direct election of senators. For all its importance in giving the people the direct vote to elect senators, the 1913 change still left the basic power relationships among the institutional entities undisturbed. In addition, the direct election of senators tended to move that body more into line with the framers' conceptualization of it as the premier deliberative body, where the excesses of the House could be controlled. Even the addition of numerous federal agencies and departments and their growth to great size as the United States went from a new, small country to the mightiest of nations did not alter the appointment process for federal executives or the formal institutional relationship among the agencies, the president, and Congress.

For roughly seventeen decades, with some possible exceptions (e.g., the Great Depression years), the branches of government generally did not unduly usurp each other's prerogatives. On occasion, Congress itself allowed for needed adjustments to respond to changes in the political or economic environment. For instance, it recognized the need for much greater peacetime presidential power in foreign policy after World War II as the nation became a world leader enmeshed in international affairs. Congress also sought to strengthen economic policy capability by establishing the independent Federal Reserve System in 1913 and the Council of Economic Advisers in 1946. As to the former, Congress actually delegated primary power over monetary policy to a completely new independent institution. The 1946 legislation provided presidents with a competent professional staff that could offer sophisticated advice and analysis on economic policy issues, and this new capacity did focus presidents more on macroeconomic policymaking.

However, at the end of the 1950s, the chairman of the Federal Reserve Board was far from being the "second most powerful player in the national government," as Fed chair Alan Greenspan came to be called during much of the Clinton administration. Nor had presidents yet tried to dominate fiscal policy from the Oval Office, as would soon be the case starting with John F. Kennedy's brief presidency. When President Eisenhower left office on January 20, 1961, the framers' basic structure seemed to have been modified sufficiently to face up to the massive new federal responsibilities in foreign and international security affairs and monetary and fiscal policy.

The First Twenty-Five Years after World War II

Daniel Lazare wrote of "a brief golden age after World War II," during which the Constitution seemed to work to perfection. Without necessarily accepting his further judgment of poor performance during much if not all of the rest of the time, those early postwar years were a golden period in economic and political affairs. The eight years of the Eisenhower administration came at the apex of political system's health, when economic resources, the political structure, and public confidence in the federal government were most in harmony in the postwar era.

These eight years provide the best comparative baseline for considering the impact of the several major changes starting in the 1960s that challenged the viability of the Constitution's institutional structure. The period came after the Harry Truman administration, during which there had been considerable political and social strain resulting from its feisty, unpopular leader's actions and the immense effort to integrate 10 million World War II veterans into the peacetime economy. Although President Eisenhower's prestige, won through his achievements as the victorious supreme commander of Allied forces in Europe, contributed to political harmony, its high level flowed mainly from an exceptional domestic policy and political setting. The milieu, not the man, brought this period of strong bipartisanship and domestic placidity after the fall of the right-wing Wisconsin senator Joseph McCarthy, who had claimed that there were numerous communist sympathizers in the federal government.

These years offer a calm environment against which to consider ten critical, interrelated political system changes that generated the current high political barriers to efficient federal governance: (1) the overcentralization of the White House, which has brought a dramatic shift of power from the executive agencies to the president and his staff in the Executive Office of the President; (2) the loss of institutional competence and internal credibility in Congress; (3) the decline of federal agencies' managerial competence, both from the rising complexity of the new social and environmental policies under shared governance and from the increased power of agency political executives over career civil servants; (4) the much-reduced influence of political parties in selecting candidates and managing their campaigns; (5) the emergence of professional politicians who mainly operate on their own, with only limited political party control; (6) the rise of the media as the primary systemic vehicle providing political information, opinion, and discourse; (7) the decline of that entity's capacity for sound, meaningful reporting as the media became increasingly oriented toward scandal and dominated by the profit imperative; (8) the influence of moneyed interests in the political process generally and in the national election campaigns specifically; (9) the decline in citizens' sense of obligation and commitment to the political process; and (10) the relative decline in the public's capacity to understand the complex policies being debated in the harsh, highly partisan political environment in which officeholders, candidates, and the parties fought by distorting the issues through the use of misleading information and commentary.

The next several chapters will focus on these growing political barriers to efficient and effective federal government. We begin in the calm of the Eisenhower years, which offers a useful comparative marker—the lull before the storm.

The Eisenhower Years

The historian John Patrick Diggins found the United States in the Eisenhower years to be "more complacent than compassionate"; its citizens pursued private pleasures and profits "and remained almost indifferent to public responsibilities."[40] The federal government at that time faced severe challenges, but they were seen as coming almost exclusively in the areas of international diplomacy and security.

President Eisenhower considered his main tasks to be diminishing nuclear threats and conventional wars and raising the institutional capability of a badly organized and outdated national security structure. In the area of domestic policy, except for the Interstate Highway system and higher education grants, both justified as national defense needs, little was done. The national government and the subnational entities continued to operate their programs with little or no overlap. This dual federalism with everyone on their own turf escaped the controversies that arose from the shared governance of the 1960s and 1970s. With rare exceptions, the big issues of civil rights, poverty, and the environment lay buried below the surface, so the minimal domestic policy demands on the national government were well within the competence levels of the federal institutions during the Eisenhower years.

President Eisenhower himself made a real contribution as the last elected president to perceive both the need for strong cabinet ministers with the mandate and flexibility to efficiently manage their huge federal agencies and also the dangers of a too-powerful White House staff usurping the cabinet members' power.[41] At the other end of Pennsylvania

Avenue, a handful of committee chairs tightly controlled Congress. During part of the Eisenhower period, Speaker of the House Sam Rayburn and Senate Majority Leader Lyndon Johnson, both Texas Democrats, dominated their respective chambers. In particular, the majority leader had made the Senate, long notorious for blocking change, operate with a level of efficiency seldom, if ever, seen before. Despite divided government, a striking congruity marked presidential, executive agency, and congressional relationships.

Other factors made the political environment of the Eisenhower years much more tranquil than today. Instead of primaries determining candidate selection, senior political party members in the 1950s chose their presidential candidates at the national conventions. This meant that the candidates' political peers generally had seen them over a period of years in local, state, and national elected positions. Newspapers still dominated television as a political force. The federal government still retained its image of accomplishment from the war years, and citizens had a strong sense of obligation that had been fostered during World War II. In the earlier period, career service in the federal government offered a relatively prestigious job, in part because the careerists were important factors in the decision-making process in the Executive Office of the President and the executive agencies. During the Eisenhower years, the constitutional model crafted in the eighteenth century looked as viable as it ever had and appeared to affirm the infallibility of the Founders and the agelessness of the Constitution.

The Challenge after the Eisenhower Presidency

Neither the politicians nor the public realized that the limited demands placed on the political system during the Eisenhower presidency had masked large cracks in the aging structure. Although the rot had occurred, it remained unseen or else exposed but viewed as harmless. Think of an old bridge with serious defects. During the time that single automobiles were driven across it, its problems may have remained hidden and it could have been deemed safe. But once a large number of heavy trucks began to cross it, its defects were quickly revealed. Before the early 1960s, the relative tranquility covered over the inadequate support structure. Then, during the next four decades, deleterious changes in the political system made it far more difficult to successfully develop and implement the kinds of domestic policies the nation needs.

The massive postwar threat to the framers' governance structure came from an array of new social and environmental programs, starting with the antipoverty efforts mandated by the Economic Opportunity Act of 1964. These new programs were funded by grants-in-aid to states and localities and operated by these governments. Problems arose because the use of federal funds by subnational governments required more active management, which could involve considerable federal oversight. In comparison with the social programs of the Great Depression, their successors came during a time of great prosperity and mainly targeted poor and disadvantaged people because so many middle-class families had begun to live the American Dream.

The new domestic programs were fundamentally different from the ongoing policy efforts in their degree of political impact on states and localities. Although subnational governments were deeply concerned as to where defense contracts would be awarded and military bases located, the military-industrial complex had been able to spread around the huge defense outlays in ways that did not ruffle feathers too much among military contractors, congressional barons, and state and local political interests. Macroeconomic decisions (e.g., the Federal Reserve Board's efforts to influence the level of interest rates) also could have major repercussions for state and local economies, but such policies were aimed at the entire country, not differentially at particular subnational governments.

Shared governance in the domestic policy arena brought overlapping responsibilities and the occasional intense confrontation between federal officials and those from state and local government that would escalate to the White House and Congress. The Office of Economic Opportunity, the flagship agency of President Lyndon Johnson's new War on Poverty, exploded without much warning on the states and cities as it immediately funded controversial, untried programs. For instance, residential Job Corps centers in rural areas that sought to provide work skills mainly to urban black youths from northern and midwestern environments often provoked culture clashes overlaid with racism. Community Action Agencies (CAAs) fought the concentrated poverty of the urban ghettoes and rural backwaters in hundreds of localities. The CAAs often began as nonprofit organizations that saw themselves as taking on entrenched state and

local governments. Lawful efforts by CAAs disturbed state and local officials all across the country. Moreover, in a handful of cases, these new organizations or groups that appeared to be associated with them engaged
in violent actions.

The conflicts between federal civil servants and their state and local
counterparts and elected officials could spark high levels of involvement
by both the White House and Congress that spilled into each other's do-
main and went far beyond anything previously experienced. State and
local officials had been comfortable in a domestic policy environment
they fully controlled before the inception of federal social grants-in-aid
programs in the 1960s. Although these officials in general welcomed the
increased federal funding, they rushed to protect themselves both from
grants going directly to nongovernmental community organizations hostile to state and local governments and from the much-increased federal
agency management efforts. The best defense turned out to be seeking
help from their congressional representatives, whose responsiveness to
states and localities begot White House and agency responsiveness. Congress became increasingly involved with the grants-in-aid programs, not
only through significantly more oversight but also in extensive micromanagement efforts that put it squarely into the executive branch's main
function.

Executive branch domestic policy agencies employed tens of thousands
of program specialists, many of whom interacted with state and local political officials and career staffs. Congress and the Executive Office of the
President added large professional staffs, which responded to complaints
from the field and often clashed with each other in ways that further in-
termingled the once separate functions. The calm of the 1950s gave no
hint of the changes starting in the 1960s that would sharply challenge the
workability of the Constitution. Then, the shared governance of domestic policy pushed the institutional structure of U.S. federalism to the
breaking point as the boundaries of the separate functions vanished not
only within the federal government but also in federal relationships with
states and localities. More than 200 years ago, the framers understood the
need for efficient federal governance; however, their specific institutional
model, whatever its strength in earlier times, may be unworkable today.

five

The Presidency and Congress in Decline

This analysis of the deteriorating American political system under Reaganism will consider several of its key institutions in some detail: the presidency and Congress to start with, the federal executive agencies, and the political parties and the media. Each must perform well if the political system is to work. Also receiving in-depth scrutiny are the American people, whose intelligent participation is a necessary element of sound governance just as is the performance of institutions. Centering discussion on these specific institutions and the electorate does not exclude the treatment of other key actors, such as the K Street lobbyists (the name coming from the Washington street where these people are most likely to have an office), but simply brings them in when they interact with the specified institutions.

Two other general comments pertaining to the remainder of the book are needed. First, three dominant questions guide the book: How extensive is institutional damage to the national institutions since Ronald Reagan became president? What is the evidence to support my claim that Reaganism has been a major factor in the institutional deterioration? Can Humpty-Dumpty be put back together again in the hostile political environment with the constitutional model left the nation by the Founding Fathers? Second, the grim picture I paint of the U.S. political system may be badly overblown—another misdirected academic jeremiad. It could be that the genius of American democracy drawn from the wisdom of the Founders as set down in the Constitution and the underlying strength of the nation's people will confound the critics by working in mysterious ways to right the system when it is threatened. The burden of making the case against the seemingly inherent resiliency of the U.S. political system falls on those who would claim the contrary.

The Executive Branch

The treatment of the presidency in this chapter will be restricted mainly to organizational issues and the practice of "spinning." Further discussions of presidents and their staffs will be found throughout the book, with their placement reflecting a judgment as to where they best fit and how they may be employed to avoid duplication. Presidential organizational capability is singled out because it is too often an overlooked issue when presidents are being critiqued. This is so even though the Constitution originally cast the president as both the chief or political leader and the executive or managerial leader and continues to do so. Sound presidential policy leadership requires both political and organizational mastery.

The practice of spinning, whereby politicians, generally supported by a strong staff, engage in concerted efforts to distort and manipulate the public and the media, took on its present form during Bill Clinton's presidency, when lying became an art form. Bill Kovach and Tom Rosenstiel, both respected critics of journalism, pointed out that politicians had made "lying . . . respectable by calling it *spin*" and then quoted Benjamin Bradlee, one of the *Washington Post* heroes of Watergate, on a key difference between the mid-1970s and the Clinton years: "'People lie now in a way that they never lied before—and the ease with which they lie, the total ease. . . . People expect no consequences. . . . This word *spinning* . . . is a nice uptown way of saying lying.'"[1] Except for untrue statements about sexual activities, political spinning may not call forth negative sanctions or damage the politician's reputation. A clear case in point is George W. Bush's plethora of distortions in selling his tax cut proposals, which elicited no public outrage.

Presidential Power

Political mastery has to do with a president's capacity to exert influence over his party, Congress, other politicians, the media, and the public. Organizational mastery concerns a president's ability to exercise managerial influence over the Executive Office of the President (EOP) and the political executives leading the agencies responsible for the administration or operation of the programs funded by the federal government. President Dwight D. Eisenhower remains the only organizational virtuoso of the postwar era. None of those who followed had strong managerial skills on entering office, and they generally did not understand why the skills they lacked were important for sound policymaking. Organizational skills do not in and of themselves make a president successful, but the lack of managerial capability can block a president with strong political skills from signal achievements.

Organizational mastery—a critical element of institutional competence—declined markedly during John F. Kennedy's presidency. Richard Reeves, in his 1993 mainly unfavorable book on the Kennedy presidency, portrayed him as uninterested in organizational structure and process and himself "careless and dangerously disorganized."[2] As leader, Kennedy wanted to be the central focus of all efforts. He began almost immediately to strengthen the power of White House staff vis-à-vis the cabinet. Garry Wills wrote: "In his 1963 book on Kennedy, Hugh Sidney celebrated the escape from Eisenhower: 'John Kennedy . . . recaptured all of the power and more which Dwight Eisenhower ladled out to his Cabinet officers. In fact, Kennedy in the first week nearly put the Cabinet on the shelf as far as being a force in policy matters, and he rarely bothered to dust it off.'"[3] Kennedy had remarkable political skills, but he did not achieve much substantively in his short presidency. There is no way of knowing how much his limited organizational skills contributed to his lack of achievement as compared with his shortness of time in office.

What does seem most likely is that Kennedy's aura of success led later presidents to follow his example in exerting strong control over the cabinet secretaries. The shift may have had little impact during President Kennedy's three years in office, but the domination over the cabinet secretaries has had a pernicious effect on the institutional performance of the executive branch in administrations that followed. The greater control over time by the increasingly powerful presidency has made the agencies far more difficult to manage efficiently because it strips cabinet and sub-cabinet members of needed power and flexibility and further complicates the delicate balance among the president, the agencies, and Congress. Moreover, as presidents have drawn more power into the White House, Congress has protected its historic role vis-à-vis the agencies by further diluting agency authority through increased micromanagement of agency activities.

Reaganism has been singled out for its deleterious impact on the federal institutions of governance, but there had been damage to the U.S. political system in the two decades between the end of the Eisenhower presidency and the start of the Reagan administration. At the same time, Reagan's relentless attack on the federal government and its institutions of governance during his entire presidency went far beyond those of his immediate predecessors. As candidates, presidents Richard Nixon and Jimmy Carter employed harmful antigovernment rhetoric; once in office, however, they saw themselves as the chief executives of "their" governments. President Reagan, who never stopped viewing himself and his key staff as outsiders attacking the federal government, diminished its institutional competence far more than any of the other postwar presidents.

The added complexity of the federal government's new social programs in the 1960s and its environmental efforts in the 1970s increased greatly the demands on presidential and agency managerial competence. Although subsequent presidents fled managerial responsibility, they sought more and more political control over agency managers by enlarging and strengthening White House staffs. It turned out to be a most debilitating combination that struck at the organizational capabilities of the entire executive branch. The decrease in managerial competence of the elected presidents after Eisenhower had a deleterious impact. First, presidents tended to appoint more political executives at the top of the domestic agencies who had limited managerial skills. Second, they weakened agency authority and flexibility by taking power from cabinet secretaries and giving it to White House personnel whose main concern was controlling the agency executives so they did not cause political problems that embarrassed the White House.

A president's disinterest or institutional incompetence in managing the executive branch can severely harm domestic policies and programs throughout the federal government. His poor choices of key White House advisers and cabinet secretaries, like a pebble thrown in a pond, can spread forth to yield incompetent political executives in the entire executive branch. Recent presidents have often viewed the executive agencies as threats to their political power and made organizational and staffing decisions to maximize presidential political control, not policy performance, thereby lowering managerial capacity in the executive branch. The Constitution at the outset linked presidential political control to agency managerial capacity by making the president the federal government's chief executive with the fundamental power to appoint the top staff persons and managers in the executive branch. Although the Senate must confirm such political appointments, few are really challenged, particularly at the start of a new administration, when the Senate feels an incoming president should be able to name his closest White House aides and his agency leaders. Moreover, many of those in the White House closest to the president, including his chief of staff, do not require Senate confirmation.

Picking the key White house aides and cabinet members remains a new president's most important managerial task by far. Because that group is actually quite small—fifty people at the most, probably closer to thirty—this should be a doable task for a president who understands organizational demands. Unfortunately, these early key personnel choices can misshape the presidency. Pick wrong and the entire executive branch will have major management problems. These will be compounded for the executive agencies if the president chooses to put key White House staff between himself and his cabinet secretaries. The hard organizational reality is that presidents can exert political control over the agencies from the White House and the EOP, but they cannot take over ongoing agency management from above. As to the former, White House staff can demand public adherence by cabinet and subcabinet members to the president's position with a high likelihood of success or, if necessary, do a good job of muzzling them. Further, the iron-fisted style of Office of Management and Budget (OMB) directors David Stockman in President Reagan's first term and Richard Darman in the George H. W. Bush years, demonstrated clearly that OMB can take full control of the big budget choices and leave only small ones to the agencies. Even this level of control demands a sizeable presidential staff, but not one even remotely large enough to manage the agencies' vast array of programs that operate in states and localities.

However presidential policy decisions are made, the direct federal responsibility for their implementation in the field rests with agency staffs. If they are not heavily involved in developing the policies that the agency will implement, White House policymakers cut themselves off from agency knowledge about implementation problems that will arise in the field. Moreover, agencies excluded from policymaking for programs that will fall under their mandate may limit their implementation effort because they have little investment in the policy. The president's appointment of a member of an agency subcabinet as his enforcer on the spot to strengthen presidential political control can be equally debilitating for sound policymaking. The president's "people" in an agency can have credibility problems with other agency political executives, including the secretary, or else undermine the latter's control over his subcabinet.

Since Eisenhower, presidents have sought greater political control and spurned his approach of creating capable agencies and giving them the institutional freedom to manage their agencies efficiently. It could be that the Eisenhower approach no longer makes political sense in the current harsh, polarized environment. If political control continues to dominate presidential thinking, however, competent executive branch management may be possible only if a constitutional amendment both takes away a president's power to appoint the executive agencies' top managers and gives these managers real independence from the president and his staff. That all recent presidents would be horrified by such an amendment goes a long way toward explaining why the federal government is so poorly managed.

The Reagan–Bush Years and the Anti-Analytic Presidency

The dozen years of the Reagan–Bush presidential management efforts can be summarized in a sentence: President Reagan succeeded in a massive attack that materially reduced the federal government's organizational, information development, and analytic capacity to support policymaking; his successor did little to restore the damaged managerial capability.[4] The institutional decline in policy information and analysis will be considered now, and the discussion of managerial deterioration will be taken up primarily in the next chapter. As the first anti-analytic president of the modern era, Reagan's distaste for expert policy information, analysis, and advice underlay the severe damage in his administration to much of the institutional analytic capacity that had been built up in the executive branch in the postwar era. From the outset of the Reagan administration, most of the strong domestic policy analytic offices, such as those at the Departments of Health and Human Services and Labor, lost status, staff, and funds. In addition, the Reagan administration also cut back the central statistical agencies such as the Census Bureau, thereby damaging the basic economic and social data widely used in the public and private sectors for analysis and decision making.

During the Reagan–Bush years, secrecy reigned, with the White House decision-making process being limited to a handful of people. It was as if a further high wall had been erected within the presidential branch itself that separated the president and the handful of his top advisers, who had frequent access to him, from the EOP institutional structure with its cadre of competent careerists. From its outset, the Reagan presidency cut back analytic strength in the EOP by downgrading the status and reducing the analytic staffs of White House domestic policy offices such as the Office of Policy Development, which as the Domestic Policy Staff had been a major analytic factor in the Carter administration. OMB—by far the biggest analytic staff in the EOP, and the only one with large numbers of competent career civil servants who could not be fired at a change of administration—gained great power. However, its director, David Stockman, often did not draw heavily on the information skills of the competent OMB analytic staff in major policy decisions because he believed that he needed no one to help him develop his big ideas. Stockman's lone-operator style had large repercussions, including his first-year budget plan that began the long period of huge yearly deficits.

Although President George H. W. Bush had a more benign view of government than his predecessor, his obsession with secrecy drove him beyond President Reagan in restricting the number of his advisers. The isolation at the top meant that the two presidents and their advisers, particularly in domestic policymaking, often were flying blind, making decisions based on ideology or hunches with little or no well-prepared information and analysis debated by key actors during the policymaking process. President Reagan attacked a presidential policymaking structure that had visible flaws and further twisted and distorted it to a point where it threatened the American constitutional process that linked together the president, the executive branch, Congress, and the public. He acted long before Bush had any real involvement and deserves most of the blame, but the latter too is culpable, mainly for acts of omission.

The Presidential Spin Machine

President Bill Clinton created, in the words of *Washington Post* media reporter Howard Kurtz, a "well-oiled propaganda machine—arguably the most successful team of White House spin doctors in history."[5] It served him well in defending his policies and in protecting or enhancing his reputation. In Clinton's case, a House of Representatives led by right-wing true believers was bent on destroying him by attacking on a variety of fronts, including the Monica Lewinsky affair, Whitewater, and using the Lincoln Bedroom either to pay off or attract big campaign contributors. Spinning in this hostile environment went for the jugular. Defense dominated the Clinton game plan.

Because the Republicans were ever relentless and sometimes rash, they would be punished on occasion by a deft offensive thrust. This was made easier because the staff had an exceptional performer in President Clinton, so skilled that he could be successful despite his self-inflicted wounds. He combined a folksy style, tremendous intellectual firepower that made him a master of manipulation and subterfuge, and such comfort with distortion and lying that morality never inhibited his presentation. Drawing on these skills, Clinton and his supporting staff molded spinning into an institutional weapon that in capable hands could be devastatingly effective. But it was a performance that had routinized lying in the White House and that had used lying in trying to cover up behavior that much diminished the internal and external credibility of the presidency.

In sharp contrast, President George W. Bush used distortions in 2001 to sell the most important tax legislation in twenty years. Deceptive propaganda and budget chicanery were at the top of the list of egregious behavior utilized in passing the tax act. Moreover, the president himself served as the point man in his travels around the country making face-to-face presentations. Princeton University economics professor and *New York Times* columnist Paul Krugman observed: "I can't think of any precedent in the history of American economic policy . . . [where an administration was] quite this shameless about misrepresenting the actual content of its own economic plan."[6]

President Bush's gross distortions might be described as "sophisticated lies." Such technically true or seemingly reasonable claims by politicians employ deception to cover over the real intentions of the propagandists. For example, President Bush said on February 27: "In my plan, no one is targeted in or targeted out; everyone who pays income taxes will get relief."[7] Although his statement appears to say that the huge tax cut benefits those at the bottom of the income distribution, the fact is that only *income taxpayers* need apply.

The power of such a claim from the point of view of those seeking to hide the underlying truth is that the statement is technically correct. In this case, President Bush covered over the fact that the nation's neediest 12 million families with 24 million children would receive nothing while a disproportionate share of the tax cuts would go to a relatively small number of families with the largest incomes. Even though many of the families left out had payroll taxes deducted from their wages that took a significant percentage of their income because they did not pay income taxes meant these families were excluded from the Bush income tax cut of $1.35 trillion.

In my view, Bush's gross deception in selling his proposed tax policy violated his institutional responsibility to "faithfully execute the office of the President of the United States" and fundamentally degraded the presidency. When a president speaks to Congress and the public to spell out a policy proposal, surely faithful execution demands that his statements specify clearly and accurately what he plans so that listeners are likely to understand his objectives and the means of attaining them. That is, the oath of office set out in Article II, Section 1, of the Constitution appears to require transparency, not a bundle of distortions. It is a particularly egregious abuse of institutional responsibility for the president to deceive Congress and the American people on national television when introducing the most important tax legislation in at least two decades—legislation that will shape people's lives for years to come.

William Gale, Samara Porter, and Emily Tang of the Brookings Institution charged that the administration effort produced "a debate riddled with misinformation and a tax bill that sets new lows in budget gimmicks."[8] Despite repeated warnings before the passage of the tax plan about the extreme danger of locking the total ten-year surplus projection into law, the president misled the public by stressing the safety of what was in fact a reckless commitment of so much of the projected surplus to a tax cut. Before the tax cut proposal, the Congressional Budget Office had projected a surplus of $5.6 trillion for the ten years from 2002 through 2011, but several months later it projected a surplus of only $336 billion for the same period. Thus, the decline in the 2001 surplus projection looked like that of a dot-com stock in falling roughly 94 percent. What is so amazing is how quickly the change validated the wisdom of the warnings not to spend dollars based on budget projections of future surpluses until the money is in hand.

The aggregate data on the February 27, 2001, tax plan show that the tax reductions would further increase the maldistribution of income. Income statistics presented in chapter 2 showed that in the period 1979–97, the top 1 percent of the population had increased its share of total national income from 7.5 to 13.6 percent while others had their share of income decline, particularly the bottom quintiles. Despite this, the Bush plan moved in the same direction. The top 1 percent that paid a fourth of all federal income taxes would receive at least one-third of the total reduction; the bottom 60 percent of taxpayers, less than 15 percent.[9] That is, the Bush plan proposed that the top 1 percent of taxpayers receive more than twice as much from the total amount of tax reductions as the bottom 60 percent. This large segment of the population—84 million families and nearly 150 million people, making up a considerable portion of the middle class—was put in much greater economic jeopardy by the Bush tax plan. In addition, many of those in the next quintile (61–80 percent) likely faced an increased risk of reductions in their economic security and in the availability of public goods and services. The deleterious economic impact of presidential distortion could well harm the great majority of Americans.

Why did the institutionalized effort to mislead ordinary citizens work so well? Krugman, whose *New York Times* op-ed column provided an extended, penetrating critique of Bush's tax plan, proposed a disconcerting answer: "The Bush team's Orwellian propensities have long been apparent to anyone following his pronouncements on economics. . . . Once an administration believes that it can get away with insisting that black is white and up is down—and everything in the administration's history suggests that it believes just that—it's hard to see where the process stops. A habit of ignoring inconvenient reality, and presuming that the docile media will go along, soon infects all aspects of policy."[10]

Spinning had been routinized in the presidency to market the president's products. Orwellian language became part of the institutionalized weaponry used to mislead the people whose lack of political information and knowledge could bring them to accept false claims, especially if they meshed with the people's cherished myths and strongly held prejudices. A high-powered presidential propaganda machine seeks to package the product so that the message strikes the right notes, whether or not the underlying facts actually support the claims.

A key piece has been purposely passed over thus far in considering the political success of the tax cut: the ineptitude and cowardice of the Democrats. Fearing that opposition to a tax cut could cost them in the 2002 election where control of both the House and the Senate could change, the Democrats succumbed to the reelection imperative. They chose to hold back in the face of strong evidence that the misguided tax policy could eliminate the expected surplus and block needed increases in domestic programs during the coming decade—better to be reelected than go all out to defeat a blockbuster bill that likely would cost the nation dearly.

The passing of the 2001 tax package, even if less spectacular than the terrorist attack, was just as revealing of the massive meltdown of the institutions of governance created by the Constitution. It showed that the president and Congress had failed miserably in meeting the most critical domestic needs of the nation. The tax bill—in juxtaposing high levels of incompetence and internal distrust within damaged national political institutions and the enactment of an unjust, highly dangerous piece of legislation—gives credence to the proposition that institutional inefficiency is likely to bring institutional ineffectiveness. This paragraph offers a lead-in to what may be the most inefficient of the major players in the U.S. political system.

Congress in Decline

President Reagan contributed to the decline of Congress, but we need to be clear at the outset that members of Congress themselves inflicted the bulk of the damage to the institution's competence and credibility during his two terms. He only greased the skids in front of an already slipping Congress. What a ride down it has been since the 1970s, with its greatest damage inflicted on the integrity and the capacity of the institution. The 1994 election, which restored Republican control in Congress for the first time since the Eisenhower administration, brought a critical twist in the story of Ronald Reagan and Congress. The unexpected victory reshaped the House of Representatives with the election of seventy-three Republican freshmen, a huge gain numbering only two less than the new Democrats elected after Watergate two decades earlier. The

Washington political critic Elizabeth Drew saw the seventy-three freshmen as institutional enemies within, and she wrote: "The class of 1994 ... contained a large proportion of inexperienced ideologues. Nearly a third of the Republican freshman had no political background at all. ... [They] have had little respect for the institution itself or for making it work."[11] Led by the new speaker of the House, Newt Gingrich, the class of 1994 became the phalanx that pushed Mean Reaganism to new heights of harshness. The ensuing polarization dealt a destructive blow that rendered Congress almost unworkable. Mean Reaganism in the 1990s much surpassed both President Reagan and Reaganism in the 1980s in its deleterious impact on Congress.

A Period of Rapid Change

Congress, since the 1970s, has became less efficient in its capacity to treat the major problems facing the nation. Moreover, the fall came despite two signal improvements that should have strengthened the institution. First, the analytic and policy competence of individual members rose significantly, particularly from the early 1970s until the 1994 election. Second, major changes were made that improved congressional support agencies' technical capacity to increase greatly the amount of sound, nonpartisan policy information, analysis, and advice available to the members and their personal and committee staffs. This rise in the underlying analytic competence of the support agencies, which do not work specifically for a single committee and are intended to provide nonpartisan service to the entire Congress, has been particularly striking since the 1974 legislation establishing the new congressional budget process.

By the late 1970s, Congressional Budget Office data, based on the staff's economic projections and costing out of proposed legislation, were considered "the best numbers in town" for the yearly budget process. The General Accounting Office had upgraded itself to perform evaluations and analyses that produced sound data on program and policy issues. The Congressional Research Service engaged in an extensive, confidential effort that increased members' access to and use of nonpartisan information, analysis, and advice. It is certainly disconcerting that Congress lost institutional credibility, competence, and capacity to compromise even though both the technical abilities of Congress's members and the underlying information base for decision making improved dramatically for at least two decades.

The problem is that the members too often do not use their own analytic capacity and the sound nonpartisan data and analyses from the congressional support agencies in their voting decisions but instead respond to the press of public opinion on highly visible issues, however misguided that opinion might be. Writing in 1992, just before the start of the Clinton presidency, political scientist Paul Quirk observed: "[Congress] is often compelled to adopt whatever perception of those interests—however simplistic or misinformed—prevails among the mass public. . . . Some of the most costly policy mistakes of recent years resulted from undue congressional deference to uninformed public opinion."[12]

This look at Congress across twenty-five years involves the emergence of two dramatically different types of members. In his 1991 book *The United States of Ambition,* Alan Ehrenhalt, the former political editor of *Congressional Quarterly,* analyzed the emergence of a highly committed new breed of professional politicians who gained their political and policy skills in working their way up to higher and higher political jobs and were far more competent than their predecessors.[13] When Elizabeth Drew focused on the Republican class of 1994 in her 1999 book *The Corruption of American Politics,* she saw a Congress suffering a fall in quality—an accelerating incompetence.[14] In sorting out what has actually happened, the dates and circumstances of the descriptions and assessments of members of Congress and the institution itself need to be distinguished clearly.

The new breed that began entering Congress in the 1970s had, as their critical mark, the early choice of a political career. They possessed a number of desirable skills and values, being in general more committed, more knowledgeable about the policy agenda, and more policy oriented than the typical predecessor. In contrast to rank-and-file members in the Eisenhower years, these more policy-oriented professional politicians had sufficient intelligence, techniques, and information to engage fruitfully in the policy process as individual actors. At the same time, Oregon Democratic senator Ron Wyden (then a representative) argued that "'the reelection issue is omnipresent.'"[15] The fear of defeat hung over the new breed from their start in local or state politics because it could mean an end to the professional politicians' careers as members of a legislative body or as an executive branch political leader. Although losing often had the consolation prize of lucrative lobbying jobs paying far more than the members earned in Congress, the chance of career advancement, such as becoming a committee chair or winning a still higher office, would be gone.

Despite the near certainty of incumbents' reelection, they usually remained hyperresponsive to constituents and ever concerned with the one big-issue vote such as abortion or gun control that they feared could unseat them. To prevent this abrupt ending, new-breed members of Congress would stay on an unceasing quest to fill their campaign coffers. They took on "debts" to their major contributors to pay for their never-ending pursuit of constituents and thereby ran the risk of ending up in hot water with both of them. Those who make large contributions to members of Congress watched closely to see that recipients voted the right way. The large campaign contributions in turn could lead constituents in their districts and states to fear that the members, despite their frequent flights home, did not really pay attention to them but only to the special-interest contributors.

The new breed's relationship with contributors and constituents became far more complex as the electronic revolution transformed the communication process by bringing both a geometric increase in the amount of rapidly available information and strikingly different ways of using and abusing it. Technical changes in the speed of communications increased the demand for funds as members of Congress sought help, both for offensive and defensive purposes, in obtaining, interpreting, and repackaging the rapid flow of often conflicting information. The concerns of the voters stayed constantly in the minds of senators and representatives. Leon Panetta, the former member of the House of Representatives and White House chief of staff in the Clinton administration, told the Center for Public Integrity: "'You need to hire your consultants and your pollsters and your focus groups.... [Members] now more than ever turn to these consultants and pollsters that basically tell them what the public wants, and that's what they do.'"[16]

Chapter 8 will consider whether politicians now pander more to their constituents or their major contributors, but it is useful here to lay out the short answer. First, politicians generally listen to the people when a large majority of them strongly support a particular issue. Second, few issues fall into this category, leaving big campaign contributors the leeway to exert pressure on much legislation that is of interest to them. Third, if a politician's position is well to the left or the right of his or her constituents' view, the elected official will seek to persuade them that this is not actually the case. This is why politicians are continuously seeking to learn what voters want and then to convince them that they are doing the constituents' bidding. This self-perpetuating system may be demeaning because politicians appear to cave in *both* to moneyed interests and to voters, but politicians raise enough funds to keep being reelected. The result is that Congress has lost its institutional competence, its capacity to compromise, and its internal and external credibility while its individual members have become increasingly insulated from defeat. They generally stay until the hectic pace of their always overcrowded schedule—which includes ceaseless money chasing, not their constituents—finally drives them from office.

Declining Institutional Credibility and Competence

The structural foundation that previously had supported a level of internal credibility sufficient for furthering reasoned bipartisan compromise has been ripped apart. *New York Times* reporter R. W. Apple Jr. quoted Republican senator John McCain of Arizona on the problem of declining bipartisan compromise: "'The lack of personal relationships makes legislating much more difficult. Legislative results involve compromise, compromise requires trust, and you develop trust for someone only after you've known him well for a while.'"[17] This decline in internal credibility arose in part because of the new demands on members of Congress that have left them ridiculously overscheduled with little or no time for getting to know and trust each other in such settings as late afternoon drinks together or extended discussions in the hall. The reelection imperative has gobbled up the free hours in two time-consuming, often conflicting efforts.

On the one hand, wooing big contributors consumes inordinate amounts of time, and makes Congress appear increasingly corrupt to the public On the other hand, as Ehrenhalt wrote of the new-breed members: "When it comes to hearing constituents' complaints, they are tuned in fifty-two weeks a year. . . . They may not be statesmen, but they have refined responsiveness to a fine art."[18] The new breed may have failed miserably at statesmanship, but they succeeded at two decidedly unseemly tasks as they figuratively, and sometimes literally, begged for money and votes. House incumbents campaign with roughly a fivefold advantage in contributions, and those who chose to stand for reelection in 1998 were nearly invincible, with an amazing 98 percent success rate (senators seeking reelection did only slightly worse in winning 90 percent of the time).[19] This simple political formula generally holds in Congress: Incumbency plus huge campaign coffers equals reelection.

Despite the dramatic increase in the policy and political skills of individual members and the technical competence of the analytic units from the mid-1970s to the mid-1980s, Congress lost institutional competence. Ehrenhalt pointed out: "By the mid–1980s members of Congress were beginning to talk openly about a sort of paradox of talent, in which the membership became more and more competent, and the institution became more and more inept."[20] It is an outcome like that of a major league baseball team that improves markedly on paper in the off-season by the signing several free agents with greater skills than the players they replace and yet finishes lower than it did the previous year. If we assume both that the team's opposition did not become appreciably stronger and that injuries did not decimate the team, the key problem is management on and off the field. Why were the superior skills not put together and employed to produce a winner? When the implementation perspective is employed in the analysis of Congress, the same type of question applies: Why did the coming of new-breed members with their strong policy orientation and greater analytic skills end up decreasing rather than increasing the institution's competence to confront the serious challenges facing the nation?

One reason is that improved "hard" skills do not generally substitute for the qualities needed to make the tough decisions that maintain institutional credibility and competence. A strong vision of what needs to be done and courage remain overriding factors when members of Congress decide what to do. The reelection imperative, with its relentless struggle to ensure electoral success, can sweep aside institutional concerns. The only real deterrent may be tough, fearless leadership that seeks to maintain institutional integrity. In the period under observation, the leadership imperative focused those at the top on maintaining or increasing their institutional positions of power. For the career politician, keeping one's seat of power may even outrank keeping one's seat, and that means playing it safe in the game of chasing money and votes. This seemingly contradictory combination of rising individual competence and falling institutional capacity continued until the arrival of the Republican class of 1994.

In her 1999 book *The Corruption of American Politics,* Drew argued: "Perhaps the most important change is that the quality of the politicians in Washington has declined during the past twenty-five years, and that rate of decline has accelerated. . . . In general, the newer politicians are less grounded on issues, and many have scant interest in governing. A growing number have had no experience in government."[21] Although her assessment and the earlier one by Ehrenhalt seem clearly to be contradictory, that does not appear to be the case. To start with, Drew's notion of "quality" is not defined but appears to quite broad, whereas Ehrenhalt focused mainly on information and analytic skills and policy knowledge.

Drew also used the Nixon and Clinton impeachments for dramatic effect by pivoting her story on Senator Fred Thompson's drastically different experiences, first as the thirty-year-old minority counsel on the Senate Watergate committee, when he rose to glory, and then as senator, when he suffered a brutal battering leading the inquiry into illegal contributions during the 1996 elections. Although her choice of the two Thompson episodes provided an interesting contrast, it meant that Drew had to stretch her comparison over twenty-five years. As her discussion clearly shows, her prototypical member for the later period actually came from the seventy-three freshmen.[22] Apparently, Drew did not consider the coming of the new breed in that there is no explicit mention of Ehrenhalt in the text (unfortunately, the Drew book lacks footnotes). Her comparison appears to be between the mid-1980s Congress with its many new-breed members and the late 1990s version marked by a rise in the number of true believers. If so, the Drew and Ehrenhalt assessments of decline are compatible. During the entire quarter-century, members of Congress's individual analytic skills, policy knowledge, and political experience rose from 1974 until the start of the 104th Congress in 1995 and fell thereafter.

The Class of 1994 and Institutional Inefficiency

The seventy-three incoming Republican freshmen in the 104th Congress coupled technical incompetence with ideological fervor to bring a quantum drop in institutional efficiency to a level appreciably lower than at any time in the postwar era. Institutional destructiveness became a key element in the decline. The House Republicans' kamikaze mentality in their budget and impeachment efforts "to get Clinton" drove them to excessive behavior that shook the institutional foundation. By the end of the twentieth century, Congress, and the House in particular, had degenerated to the point where that body had become the most formidable barrier to reasoned compromise among the national governing institutions.

Three statements need to be made about the first Republican majority since the Eisenhower years and its near-record seventy-three freshmen. First, the institutional decline started well before the 1994 election, a point that acknowledges the earlier discussion of rising inefficiency and requires no further comment. Second, the later decline in institutional competence, capacity to compromise, and internal credibility has come after the near disappearance of traditional Republican moderates like former Rhode Island senator John Chafee, who sought bipartisanship *and* the resignation by Speaker Gingrich under pressure from the new members and other true believers who could accept no compromise. The more mature representatives were able for a time to exert some control over the worst tendencies of the hard-liners, whose ranks had been increased by the Class of 1994. Three, the decline in Congress led by the Republican majority had accelerated by 2000 to a level at which the institution barely functioned.

Senator Chafee's death in October 1999 symbolized the precipitous decline in the Senate of the ranks of Republican moderates who saw reasoned bipartisanship as the essence of sound governance. Former senators—such as Mark Hatfield of Oregon, Nancy Kassenbaum Baker of Kansas, and John Danforth of Missouri—once had been able to offset the full impact of the narrow partisan tendencies in their party by working with moderate Democrats to find an acceptable common ground. The shrinking number of influential moderates both diminished Congress's institutional capacity to compromise and left it vulnerable to the takeover of the Republican House and Senate by narrow, inward-looking partisans.

The rapid rise and fall of Newt Gingrich, the architect of the 1994 Republican victory, had a critical place in the transformation of the Republican Party in Congress. Gingrich in opposition had been radical and rash in attacking the Democratic majority in the House and the primary force giving Reaganism its harder edge. At the same time, he was a brilliant analyst, a student of history, an internationalist, and an able political tactician. The Brookings Institution's top expert on Congress, Thomas Mann, saw Gingrich as bringing an "'instinctive, patriotic support to a president of the opposition party on the big international questions of trade and foreign policy. There aren't many like him around.'"[23] Much like that president, Speaker Gingrich combined great ability with massive flaws that together shaped the two men's sometimes inexplicable behavior.

Gingrich's rise to power and his precipitous fall can be likened to the fate of Dr. Frankenstein in that he created the Republican freshmen class and his monster destroyed him. Gingrich's massive ego led him to underestimate the explosiveness of the large group of true believers, who in the main were more conservative, less willing to compromise, and far less able than he. In October 1999, Thomas Friedman, the *New York Times* foreign policy columnist, summed up the loss of Gingrich for the conduct of international affairs in exceptionally caustic terms: "The fact is, [House majority whip Tom] DeLay & Co. have no adult supervision anymore. Republican internationalists like Bob Dole and Newt Gingrich are gone; Trent Lott and [speaker of the House] Dennis Hastert together don't add up to zero. . . . The G.O.P. is led by people with no sense of how important America is to the world, both as an example and as a stabilizer."[24] Friedman's colorful phraseology notwithstanding, the fall in the quality of Republican leadership had been striking, and House Republicans often did look like out-of-control adolescents in all policy areas, not just international affairs.

Nowhere did this tendency emerge more clearly than in the intensely partisan, unproductive 1999 budget process. The House Republicans were not the only culprits, with their behavior becoming increasingly harmful because of the "breathtakingly partisan White House."[25] Bill Clinton, with his Machiavellian maneuvering, contributed greatly to the level of mean-spirited partisanship by figuratively driving the Republicans to what can only be labeled as "politically insane acts" in response to the skillful goading of the most brilliant political tactician of his times. President Clinton became the red flag that enraged DeLay during the 1999 budget process and drove him to suicidal fights in which the Republicans ended up being seen by the public as responsible for budget gridlock. With Congress and the president engaged in no-holds-barred combat in which each side refused compromise and sought a humiliating unconditional surrender, the institutional destructiveness of the budget struggle may have been as great as that of the impeachment, albeit lacking the high drama of the latter.

The End of the Century

By the end of the Clinton years, bipartisanship qualified as an endangered species. Moderate Republicanism was threatened with extinction. Constructive institutional leadership also had almost vanished. Statesmanship had not been sighted in years. The fixation of individual members on re-election and the Democratic and Republican Parties on retaining or regaining control of Congress had played havoc with that institution's competence, capacity to compromise, and internal credibility. Brookings Institution political scientist Thomas Mann made this assessment of the political parties at the end of the century: "[They] are more evenly balanced and ideologically polarized than at any time in contemporary history. . . . Changes in the coalitional bases of the parties in the electorate have sharply reduced the ranks of centrists in Congress and shifted the median position in each party toward its ideological pole."[26] The highly regarded *New York Times* columnist Anthony Lewis concluded in late 1999: "There have been contemptible Congresses before, and historians can argue about which was worst. But I remember none in modern times as dismal as the one now sitting. It has set records in cynicism and hypocrisy."[27]

Ehrenhalt, writing almost a decade after *The United States of Ambition,* took a longer view of institutional decline: "Congress has done relatively little of importance in the last 10 years. Bluntly put, it has ceased to be the primary political instrument for resolving the difficulties of modern American capitalism."[28] Although that overstates the case in light of the Clinton tax increase and the welfare reform bill, Congress in President Clinton's second term did appear to flee from serious policy issues. Yet that body in early 2001 passed the Bush tax plan with its potentially devastating impact on both the economic health of the American people and the nation's political system. Seldom have either the importance of Congress or the consequences of institutional decline been so clear.

When we look back over the final years of the last century, the impact of Reaganism during the late 1990s appears to be even greater than in Reagan's own administration. During the self-serving, partisan encounters during the last five years of the century, the most destructive weapons used had been crafted from Reagan's antigovernment, antitax, antiregulation, anti–social program, promilitary, pro–big business political philosophy. Speaker Gingrich took the tenets and forged them into a Mean Reaganism that spun beyond his control. Mean Reaganism in the 1990s blocked enlightened compromises between Congress and the president to support democratic capitalism by offsetting the income and wealth inequalities it produced. The fractured national governance structure had become a key barrier to the objective of increasing the chances for all citizens to achieve political equality and fulfill the American Dream. Twenty years of Reaganism had moved both parties to the right, created a highly ideological Republican Party without strong moderates to leaven it, and helped shove the Democratic Party into the wilderness without the benefit of either strong leadership or firm principles.

Money and Politics

Money and politics have not been strangers in the United States as dollars have passed from those interested in gaining something of value, such as a lucrative contract or a favorable ruling, to the hands and later the pockets of public officials. Outright bribery of national politicians more or less died out in the postwar era, to be replaced by legal means for buying access to members of Congress and to the president or his top political appointees through contributions to finance political campaigns. And with the advent of the legalization of bribery by another name, Pandora's Box opened wide and money flowed out in sums beyond the wildest dreams of politicians taking payoffs under the table. As Drew argued: "Indisputably, the greatest change in Washington over the past twenty-five years . . . has been the preoccupation with money. . . . The culture of money dominates Washington as never before. . . . It has cut a deep gash, if not inflicted a mortal wound, in the concept of public service."[29]

The most insidious aspect of campaign financing is that legalizing the contributions of large amounts of money to political candidates led to the veritable explosion of dollars in the political arena. Although a small bribe often went a long way, financing an election became a bottomless pit after expensive television ads in primary markets emerged as the mainstay of major national campaigns. During the last part of the twentieth century, the increasing role of money in electoral politics became particularly destructive to representative democracy by undermining the relationship between voters and their members of Congress. Paradoxically, individual members of Congress have seldom if ever been so unsullied by personal dishonesty. Yet political dishonesty has risen to a record postwar level as Washington politicians overtly mislead the public and do the business of special interests at the expense of their constituents and the nation.

Vast amounts of legal campaign contributions from moneyed interests, particularly big business, have contaminated the American political system. To elaborate on the last point requires that we consider the purposefully arcane world of campaign financing. The starting place is the 1971 Federal Election Campaign Act (FECA) and its major 1974 amendments, enacted after the Watergate scandal, which were aimed at materially strengthening the 1971 act. These sweeping changes were an honest attempt to put strong restrictions on campaign finance practices. Over the years, however, FECA as amended has been twisted into a hollow shell as campaigns have become nastier and more costly. In 1995, Republican senator John McCain of Arizona and Democratic senator Russell D. Feingold of Wisconsin first introduced their legislation to reduce the disproportionate influence of big money on national elections. Congress finally passed the McCain-Feingold campaign finance legislation in 2002, after it had been thwarted over the years by Senate filibusters or Republican resistance in the House. A consideration of the reasons behind the failure of FECA to hold back the flood of campaign dollars helps in understanding why McCain-Feingold is unlikely to succeed.

The Federal Election Campaign Act

Critical to FECA was the distinction between hard and soft money. The act limited the amount of hard money to be given (e.g., to $1,000 per individual per election) and mandated that the funds go directly either to individual candidates or political parties. Soft money could be given only to political parties, not to individual candidates, and was only to be spent to support party building, including voter registration and get-out-the-vote efforts. The distinction between the two varieties of money became muddied after the Supreme Court ruling on free speech handed down on January 30, 1976, in *Buckley v. Valeo.* That decision "created the rationale for what has become a major circumvention of the law, the running of 'issue ads' to help or hurt a candidate."[30] Corporations and labor unions could pay for advertisements on issues as long as they did not explicitly advocate a candidate's election or defeat, even if such advocacy was clearly implicit in the "issue ad." The ruling opened campaign financing to massive issue ads paid for by soft money raised in large amounts. Jeffrey Birnbaum, Washington bureau chief of *Fortune* magazine, summed up the sorry story of the 1974 FECA Amendments succinctly: "Soft money has made a mockery of public financing at the presidential level. It and its many allied forms of legal cheating have rendered the entire effort to control campaign fund-raising a farce."[31]

The 2000 election saw a quantum jump in the level of funds spent, particularly in the case of soft money. The two political parties and the Senate and House candidates raised roughly $1 billion in 1996 as compared with $2.1 billion in 2000, while soft money jumped from $85 million to $488 million.[32] To raise such sums, candidates and parties constantly had to pursue large contributors who had a big stake in the political process and wanted access to key policymakers. A clear example comes from the start of the George W. Bush administration, when big contributors were anxious to visit with the new president and his cabinet. A *New York Times* editorial noted that President Bush had celebrated his first 100 days in office by claiming a new tone in Washington in comparison to the time period that included the Lewinsky affair and Clinton rewarding big donors with overnight stays in the Lincoln Bedroom. It then observed: "What caught our attention at the 100-day mark, though, wasn't so much a matter of tone as of smell: the smell—you might call it stink—of buying and selling access.... Should we be happy that the president, instead of renting out his residence, is renting out his Cabinet officers?"[33] The statement brings to mind the old joke about a good-old-boy politician who defends his honor by pointing out proudly that he is not for sale, but adds that he can be rented. In the Bush example, the transactions take place in the high-rent district.

The most striking aspect of the surge of campaign giving has been the growth in the dominance of corporate America. Big business rapidly increased its campaign finance contributions relative to organized labor. *The margin rose from 8 to 1 in 1994 to 15 to 1 in 2000.*[34] Overturning the Clinton regulations to increase workplace safety that had been ten years in the making provides a striking example, early in the Bush administration, of how contributions from corporate America helped shield businesses from additional expenditures that would protect workers. Raw power, not subtlety, marked the quick victory. Helen Dewar and Cindy Skrzycki of the *Washington Post* wrote: "Every day for a week, at 6 p.m., business lobbyists meet in the office of House Majority Whip Tom DeLay of Texas to discuss strategy, talk with lawmakers, and count votes. . . . In a blitzkrieg that lasted less than a week, corporate America scored one of its biggest victories in years."[35] The ergonomics struggle had the highest importance for firms all across the business spectrum so that those politicians opposing it could expect to pay a heavy price. Corporate America had a Coolidge-like administration in their corner, with the theme song of "The business of America is business" sung loudly by the Bush team and the Republican Congress.

A key question is how big money impinges on Washington policymaking. Two longtime Washington-watchers—Drew and Birnbaum—have maintained in recent books that the impact of big money is not on major legislation such as Social Security but on lesser issues about which the public generally knows little. Drew used as example the meat packers' and poultry producers' blocking legislation requiring them to pay fees for a better inspection system and to pay criminal fines for violations. She quoted a former member of Congress: "'By and large, it's in the secondary issues—the ones that may affect the public the most. These are the issues where members of Congress are less free because of the financing of campaigns.'"[36] Birnbaum found from his experience covering tax legislation that lobbyists were heavily involved in every aspect of a tax-writing effort and argued generally that these highly paid Washington insiders tended to operate "on the lucrative edges of legislation."[37] Influential lobbyists concentrate well below the noise level that would be likely to attract the attention of ordinary citizens.

In the bowels of Congress, lobbyists may induce the change of a few words, the addition of a clause, or the insertion of a provision that appears to apply generally but is worded so that it affects only a single firm or individual without, of course, disclosing the name of the beneficiary. John Judis submerged in a footnote the critical insight that "the real story of the post war era was not the rise of big government, but of K Street" where thousands upon thousands of lobbyists offer their services for hire.[38] Money talks, but competent K Street operatives are needed to work at the often tricky task of translating those words to fit with legislation or regulations or other administrative actions. The glorified image of highly paid lobbyists is of them flipping through their Rolodexes where they have the private telephone numbers of movers and shakers, making a few telephone calls or paying a visit to the key member of Congress, and producing the desired results as if by magic. These superlobbyists may open the right doors for their minions through their contacts, but at the next stage, the need is for technical competence and a store of specialized knowledge. The lobbyists will be down in the trenches working on arcane issues in the usually lengthy process whereby the necessary details of bills and regulations are painstakingly negotiated.

The payoff is high to corporations, with the cost being borne by the great bulk of the population through lost tax dollars that could have funded programs meeting pressing domestic policy needs. The work of one or more lobbyists representing a corporate client, which may generate fees in the tens or hundreds of thousands of dollars, can save that client from legislation that could cost in the tens or hundreds of millions of dollars. And there will be occasions where a lobbyist-induced addition to legislation or the successful blocking of a potentially adverse change can run into the billions of dollars over time for the fortunate client. In total, this corporate welfare constitutes a raid on the federal government that saves American business hundreds of billions of dollars over time in taxes not paid. It is likely that full public financing of all national elections would prove amazingly cost-effective if it took Congress out of campaign fundraising.

Care must be taken not to go too far in assessing the damage from the campaign contributions by moneyed interests. Big campaign contributions do not lead members of Congress to ignore their ordinary constituents. Contrary to what the latter often contend, members of Congress still listen carefully to ordinary people in their states and districts to find out whether they are upset with the performance of their senators and representatives and/or their policy positions. Moreover, citizens generally receive a high level of service when they complain to congressional offices. Staff members of senators and representatives will often go to great lengths to straighten out constituents' individual problems, such as those concerning Social Security and Medicare. The careful care and feeding of constituents who seek help from a member of Congress decrease the chance of being upset in an election. So ordinary constituents and the big-money players both may be well served in having their special needs met. The impact of the preoccupation with money is not clearly visible, as would be the case when a constituent receives poor service or a big contribution does not yield useful access or influence for the giver. The damage manifests itself at the macro level where there can be great harm to the nation.

McCain-Feingold

Republican senator John McCain of Arizona and Democratic senator Russell D. Feingold of Wisconsin first put forward legislation to reduce the influence of big money in national political elections in 1995. Year after year, filibusters in the Senate or strong Republican opposition in the House of Representatives sent the McCain-Feingold proposals down to defeat. This outcome likely would have been the same in 2002 if it had not been for the Enron scandal, which intensified the image of a bought Congress. Passing the 2002 bill did not mean that the opposition had disappeared, but only that its task was to produce a weak law rather than block any legislation at all. A strong law seriously confronting the problem of the dominance of moneyed interests in politics could not be expected unless McCain-Feingold moved to change the economics of national political campaigns. The point is not that the 2002 bill was pure window dressing, but that the hard reality of politics in the early twenty-first century gravely restricted what could be done.

The 2002 campaign finance bill's ban on soft money and the doubling of the hard-money limit are the heart of the legislation. In the brief discussion below, other changes, such as soft-money contributions to state parties or prohibitions on issue ads, will not be considered. This is because they complicate exposition yet do not alter this basic judgment: The legislation's deleterious consequences over time could come to outweigh the benefits, but even if the gains far exceed the losses, the overall improvement is unlikely to be consequential. McCain-Feingold attacked the rapid growth of soft money by barring the national parties from accepting and spending any funds from this category, thereby "[plugging] the gusher of soft money from corporations and wealthy donors that has become so vital to the political parties."[39] Hard money is increased, so that individuals can now contribute $2,000 directly to candidates in each election as opposed to $1,000 under FECA.

The new legislation shuffled the politics deck by eliminating soft-money contributions to the national parties but widening the hard-money spigot so more of this form of support can be used to fund the costly political campaigns. The trade-off meant that the large soft-money contributors, who had written checks in the tens or hundreds of thousands of dollars under FECA, would lose power to the "bundlers," who are a second category of the big-money types. Bundlers, who may not be wealthy and prominent like very rich soft-money contributors, need to have a large number of contacts and be adroit at persuading lots of them to contribute the individual hard-money limit. These $2,000 checks can be bundled together into a large total contribution while still meeting the McCain-Feingold hard-money limits.

Although the new law's switch to hard money had the purpose of increasing the chance for significant participation by ordinary citizens, these people almost never make more than token political contributions. Ellen S. Miller, a senior fellow at *The American Prospect* and former executive director of the Center for Responsive Politics, has written:

> Today, less than one-tenth of 1 percent of Americans make a contribution of $1000, but these 340,000 individuals accounted for fully $1 billion of the $2.9 billion in hard and soft money that politicians, PACs [political action committees], and parties banked in 2000. Most of this money comes in large bundles from the "economically interested"— executives and business associates who've been arm-twisted into supporting a corporation's electoral favorites.[40]

The result of the soft-money change is that the chairs have been rearranged for the big players, with the bundlers now having the front seats in the power equation.

There is a likely negative impact to the greater importance of hard money because these funds start coming long before the primaries, whereas soft money "is rarely spent until a general election."[41] Hard money at this early stage can quietly remove unwanted candidates from running in the primaries or at least marginalize them. Adam Lioz, a specialist in election issues at the U.S. Public Interest Research Group, pointed out "that grass-roots candidates are effectively locked out of the system."[42] So also may be much of the electorate in a quite meaningful sense. They can be deprived of good prospects with a reasonable chance of winning in the general election who may be eliminated as viable candidates before the primaries by the big-money players.

Loophole hunting is an extremely well-developed activity. Not only are loopholes likely to be found, they may twist the new system in such a way that it becomes more dangerous than the one being replaced. The search for new means of raising large quantities of soft money is a case in point. *Washington Post* political analyst Thomas Edsall wrote: "Political activists on both sides are frantically creating new groups to fill the [soft-money] gap, using provisions of the tax code that allow the creation of tax-exempt organizations that they say are not covered by the new law."[43] If they turn out to be right, Edsall noted: "Simon B. Rosenberg, president of the centrist New Democrat Network . . . and others contend that the flow of soft money that has gone to the parties will likely go to ideological and single-interest groups that take polarizing stands on guns, abortion, school prayer, unions and taxes, effectively driving the politicians receiving the money further to the right or the left."[44] But speculation about the details aside, one prediction seems to be a near certainty: A means will be found to obtain large campaign contributions. Never bet against the reelection imperative.

The discussion of defects, however, should not obscure an even deeper problem in that an appreciably stronger version of McCain-Feingold too would be likely to fail. The problem is that systems can reach a point where they are so badly broken that no repairs can fix them to work as desired. The only viable alternative for reaching the objective sought is to build a new structure and procedures distinctly different from the existing means. The national electoral system for selecting presidents and members of Congress is a perfect example of a vehicle that is broken beyond mere repair. McCain-Feingold simply does not address the fundamental flaw that national elections are extremely costly and candidates are going to find the money one way or another. They will find means to circumvent a bill far stronger than the 2002 legislation because professional politicians' careers are on the line.

Members of Congress, who have constantly chased campaign funds for years, know better than anyone that costly campaigns are an 800-pound gorilla. Patch up one loophole and a new opening will come as long as the large gorilla is alive and well. Yet building a completely new structure not only eliminates the incumbents' advantage of easy access to funds but also requires major changes that almost always carry unknown consequences that could explode and jeopardize careers. When the issue of a completely new vehicle to clean up the big-money problem comes up, the total public financing of national elections is often recommended. A discussion of whether it would work, however, is premature. The prior question is whether anything beyond tinkering with the hopelessly broken current process is possible politically.

Controlling the Federal Executive Branch

This section comes now rather than in the next chapter on federal agency management because it has to do mainly with the managerial problems arising from the White House exerting political control over the executive agencies. Presidents seek more control for three reasons: (1) to avoid political embarrassment by making the agencies march to the president's tune; (2) to have their own people, not career civil servants, make the major managerial decisions; and (3) to diminish the permanent government. Far too often, political control becomes an exercise in distrust where the president and his staff worry about the motives of political appointees and the latter suspect career staff of disloyalty. Over time, the ranks of politically appointed executives have greatly increased and now occupy more and more of the higher layers in the agency hierarchy. Senior career civil servants have been pushed so far down in the agency command structure that many of them no longer have a meaningful role in the major decisions about agency policy and management. The White

House also moved to exert greater political control over agency executives. As might be expected, this bare-knuckles game of political control plays hob with managerial efficiency.

The Complex Balance of Political Appointees and Career Staff

America historically has used more political appointees at the top of the government and accorded less status to civil servants than other major industrial nations. Even so, the federal government's top career civil servants generally were respected as highly professional and had a major role in the management of the executive agencies. This status changed quickly when the Republicans regained the presidency with Richard Nixon's victory in 1968 and engaged in an intensified effort to take power from the civil servants in the EOP and the executive agencies.[45] The shift arose mainly because (1) President Nixon wanted to remove or control the huge number of civil servants appointed by Democrats who had occupied the White House since Roosevelt's 1932 election, except for the Eisenhower years; and (2) the new president had an extreme level of distrust of all but his closest advisers and a specific distaste for the federal government that he had attacked in his presidential campaign. In the 1980s, President Reagan materially increased White House control over entire agencies by putting Reagan loyalists in key subcabinet positions. Because these appointees frequently either feared that civil servants would undermine their ideological agenda or saw them as hopelessly bureaucratic, they pushed the career staffs further from the policy process.

The usual argument for shifting to political appointees is that by putting in their own people at the top, a president and his cabinet members will have loyal executives in command who develop and execute the policies as desired by the administration. Whether the greater control moves the agency in the preferred direction, however, depends on the quality of the political appointees, particularly their institutional competence to manage the thousands of civil servants in their agencies efficiently. Sound management by the political appointees demands great skill in the actual operation of a vast, complex agency. The most critical problem has been to recruit competent political executives and keep them on the job long enough to have a positive impact on the workings of their organizations.

In recent years, just filling positions quickly has been an almost insurmountable hurdle. The *Washington Post's* Al Kamen reported in May 2001 that the Bush administration had only 11 percent of its key political executives in place and would do well to fill half of the top 500 positions by Labor Day.[46] The costs of the slow staffing at the top of the agencies can run high. A presidency most needs its political executives at the start because the first year is its time of greatest impact, but rapid staffing will not take place in the current political environment. The reasons for the slow process revolve around the excessive amount of information demanded for the political executives, which reflects in part some members of Congress wanting to embarrass the new administration, and the administration demanding more or different information to protect itself.

President Clinton saw two straight picks for attorney general drop out after the discovery that the two women had not paid the required Social Security taxes for household workers. Other discouraging barriers, however, can be skipped over to make a final point on getting political executives in place at the start of a new administration: The whole process seems at times to reduce down to eliminating potential embarrassments on a résumé rather than on having the person's background show the kind of track record indicating the needed knowledge and skills for the job at hand. It is a passingly strange way of choosing the men and women in the top positions in the agencies if the goal is efficiency and effectiveness.

Hiring political executives quickly is a task of striking difficulty; keeping them long enough to master their positions seems to be even harder. A 1994 General Accounting Office study found that political executives had an average tenure of roughly two years.[47] Unfortunately, the short service means that the top political executives have sufficient time to make costly mistakes but not necessarily enough time to use the lessons they may have learned to initiate improvements. The Volcker Commission argued that large numbers of political executives having brief stays "may undermine the President's ability to govern, insulating the Administration from needed dispassionate advice and institutional memory" and can drive out the most able career staff because they foresee little chance to advance to the top levels of agency decision making .[48] The latter have the high level of skills that afford them the best outside job market prospects, whereas those of lesser ability are more likely to stay with the federal government.

The problems of rapid turnover of political appointees and the driving out of the best and brightest civil servants because of limited advancement opportunities exist even when the political appointees are qualified by their skills and experience. The situation is made materially worse by unqualified and/or highly ideological political executives. On the basis of the National Academy of Public Administration study of nearly 1,300 top-level political appointees who had served in the federal government from 1964 through 1984, Brookings Institution political scientist Paul Light, a longtime student of federal agency staffing, observed of the high-level political executives:

> There is particularly strong evidence on the need for appointee expertise. . . . Preparation for the job, whether defined in terms of management experience, negotiating skills, congressional relations, or personal style, makes a difference. Skills do matter. Contrary to those who argue that the president should have his man or woman regardless of objective qualifications, appointees themselves strongly suggest that their preparation for office has a direct bearing on their ability to use the career service to an administration's advantage. Party and ideology aside, the career service appears to be most helpful . . . to presidential appointees who know what they want and how to obtain it.[49]

With technically unqualified political executives, who are also hostile to government generally and "bureaucrats" specifically, as was the case in the Reagan administration, not only is efficient management unlikely, the future challenge may be made greater if the best civil servants are driven out and able recruits are discouraged from career service in the federal government.

Reagan Era Culpability

Just before his premature death in 1988 at the age of forty-nine years, Charles Levine, professor of government and public administration at American University and perhaps the most insightful writer on the federal civil service of his generation, argued that in the fifty years before the Reagan administration: "The federal government built a reasonably strong administrative capacity and in some areas a remarkably successful workforce despite the fact that federal employees were never accorded the prestige of their European or U.S. corporate counterparts."[50] Levine rendered a qualified judgment not trying to cover over that the high political executive turnover and the lack of civil servant prestige in this country had diminished federal government capacity. Despite this, there were outstanding agencies such as the Social Security Administration doing an excellent job in executing the law of the land.

The Reagan administration caused massive damage to the federal agencies and their career staffs. First, Reagan attacked the federal service itself as either inept or closet Democrats or both. Second, and closely related, the Reagan administration appointed a goodly number of inept, highly ideological political executives who drove out or wasted the most valuable of resources, high-level human talent. I observed: "[The ideological appointees] especially detested the career 'bureaucrats' whose advice and analysis might counsel caution or a different approach.... [The appointees often failed] because they either understood little about how government worked or were so over-committed to rigid principles that they allowed no organizational deviation and accepted no contradictory information and analysis."[51]

The case of Secretary of State George Shultz illuminates the negative approach of President Reagan and his political executives to civil servants. Secretary Shultz would have been an outstanding manager in any administration and towered over Reagan's other, often mediocre, political executives. Coming into the administration as the second secretary of state after Alexander Haig's early departure, Shultz was told that the State Department civil servants, like those in other agencies, were all Democrats and would not cooperate with him. But as a competent manager, he believed he could motivate professional career staff and recognized the institutional danger if he cut himself off from the foreign service officers who "bring a fund of knowledge and institutional memory not available anywhere else."[52] Shultz later observed during the Iran-Contra hearings that the government "basically is full of people who are here because they want to help and they're honest.... I have never worked with more able and more dedicated people."[53]

Institutional deterioration in federal agencies and the career civil service occurred in the two decades between the end of the Eisenhower administration and the start of the Reagan presidency, but nothing like the massive damage inflicted during Reagan's two terms. His administration purposely attacked the government that he led with malice aforethought and appointed numerous people to key leadership positions who carried out that attack with greater energy and even more conviction of the rightness of their actions than the president himself. During the Reagan years, that administration went beyond seeking strong political control to emasculating the permanent government. It has never recovered. Ronald Reagan succeeded brilliantly in his goal of delivering a damaging blow to the federal government and hence to the underlying institutional competence of the executive branch in carrying out the laws of the nation.

six

Why Federal Agency Management Matters

In a survey taken during the last years of the twentieth century, about two-thirds of the people agreed with this statement: "When something is run by the government, it is usually inefficient and wasteful." But did the people surveyed envision "the government" as an undifferentiated abstraction, or did they think specifically of the president, Congress, the federal agencies, a nasty bureaucrat in the Internal Revenue Service, or various combinations of these? Did they understand how government actually operated, and how it differed from business? What yardstick did they apply to decide that the government did or, as in two out of three cases, did not work well? Such questions raise the general issues of how people conceptualize the federal government and, concomitantly, what standards they apply in assessing its efficiency.

Two points need to be made about the people's perception of government. First, we simply do not know the image of the federal government actually in the minds of those surveyed or how they arrived at their stated evaluation of operational performance. For some, a negative assessment may have merely affirmed their fundamental belief that the federal government never works right, whereas others may have in mind a particular incident. Second, the likelihood is that most of the people being surveyed knew little or nothing about government's ongoing operational activities, in part because they had never thought much about it. People may mouth the shibboleth that government ought to operate like a business, but they likely are unaware of the basic differences in trying to manage when the politicians who make key decisions about the agencies may know little about administering a complex organization and care less about the problems. The federal government appears to be a black box that the public does not care to open for inspection.

Management and Politics

This chapter centers on the issue of government operations and institutional efficiency. Under the spotlight is the managerial competence of the federal institutions that directly provide goods and services (e.g., parks, Social Security payments), administer grants-in-aid to states and localities, and engage in supervisory and regulatory activities. The central actors fall into two groups—the politicians and the career civil servants. The first category includes 537 elected officials (if the vice president is counted) and the top executive branch political appointees selected by the president or a cabinet member and approved by the Senate, as well as a few of the top presidential aides. The latter, including the White House chief of staff and others who may be in the chief executive's inner circle of closest advisers, are not subject to Senate scrutiny. In the organization charts, the Senate-approved agency political executives, who are served by a number of lower-level political appointees, have the top managerial positions and hence outrank all civil servants. Yet the highest levels of White House and agency officials are few in number, so the permanent staff will be many times larger. These careerists, who carry out the myriad jobs the U.S. government now performs, have critical institutional knowledge often lacked by their bosses. which can give these subordinates considerable power if there are organizational struggles with their political masters.

Three institutions dominate the development, enactment, and administration of the federal government's policies and programs: (1) the presidency, which starts with the man in the Oval Office and stretches through the Executive Office of the President; (2) Congress, which comprises the Senate and House of Representatives with their 535 elected members, a number of personal and committee political staffs, and a few independent agencies such as the Congressional Budget Office (CBO); and (3) the executive branch agencies, which dwarf the other two institutions in numbers of employees but are subordinate to them in the structural hierarchy. The Constitution casts the president as the chief executive of these agencies but gives Congress the purse strings, so the agencies must serve two masters who often will disagree on agency management and operations—usually on partisan, not organizational, grounds. Agency political executives, who on paper have organizational authority over thousands of civil servants and billions of dollars, may in actuality be only a pawn in the battle between a top White House aide and a senator, or more likely one of his or her staff. Successful agency managers can neither rely solely on the best organizational practices nor ignore them completely in responding to political demands.

An obvious, but nevertheless crucial, difference between political executives and career civil servants is that the former are short-timers, as noted above, lasting two years in the job on average. In the case of a change of administration where the new president is from a different party, basically all of the top political executives will leave, and the new administration appoints their successors. Staying in place are the civil servants and the physical resources—lands, buildings, laboratories, offices, and computers—which can be labeled "the machinery of government" or "the permanent government." These human and physical resources and structural and procedural configurations represent the nation's existing investment that can be utilized in operating the various federal policies and programs.

How politicians and career civil servants work together is central to efficient management. First, careerists, in serving many masters in the executive branch and Congress, can be dragged hither and yon by their relatively small number of leaders, thereby greatly complicating the task of governance and concomitantly the competence demanded for success. Second, civil servants have institutional knowledge and memory that political leaders must have to govern efficiently. An agency's permanent staff can be drawn on as advisers and lower-level managers to improve its governance if it has competent political leadership, but careerists also can defy agency leaders by employing their knowledge and memory to protect their preferred policies and organizational status.

Two issues of managerial competence stand out in the interaction of political leaders and the federal machinery of government as it plays out in the process of governance. The first is whether or not the federal government can be effective unless the machinery of government has the competence and the resources to meet the managerial needs of political leaders. The second issue involves the question of whether the president and his key appointments in the White House and top layers of the agencies will have the ability and the commitment to make appropriate use of that machinery in managing the federal government.

As these two interrelated issues indicate, the potential sources of mismanagement are a mixture of political and technical factors. Congress, the president, and his political appointees can misshape agency management efforts in a number of ways. For example, top officials may adhere to rigid ideological principles—"civil servants can never be trusted"—and misuse this resource, paying off political debts by appointing unqualified people to subcabinet positions or currying favor with big campaign funders by acts such as refusing to proceed against a powerful industry that is violating a law. Technical problems involve inadequate managerial methods, processes, and practices, such as failing to upgrade either a weak financial control system or a monitoring staff to meet the greater demands raised by a more complex program. The varied reasons for these problems can include political executives' unwillingness to devote time to a new system that will not be in place for years, long-term bureaucratic tactics of foot dragging, and even outright sabotage by career staff to avoid changes. But whatever the source of the problem, declining internal credibility in the relationships among political executives and careerists makes managerial inefficiency and damage to the machinery of government more likely.

One possible outcome of this embattled interaction in the domestic policy arena is such a low level of performance that a hollow, incompetent domestic government simply does not work, as was the case in Ronald Reagan's administration. To consider in greater depth what has happened to the machinery of government in the domestic policy area since the end of that administration, we need to indicate the dimensions of *hollowness* and *competence*. Hollow government involves the chronic underfunding and/or understaffing of agencies that limit the government's basic capacity to execute its legally mandated functions. Hollowness of government implies several possible deficiencies: too few staff overall, too few specialists, inadequate working conditions (e.g., inferior laboratories, crowded office space, or obsolete equipment of the Food and Drug Administration, or FDA), and weak information and analytic systems. Incompetence refers to the lack of experienced, capable staff. Hollowness is mainly a static concept of factors that can be assessed with a checklist—

such as the number of FDA microbiologists. Competence is more of a dynamic notion implying the ability of individuals to do particular jobs efficiently. For example, a competent and experienced FDA microbiologist would not only have the appropriate Ph.D. and five years of the kind of experience specified in the job description, but he or she would in fact be able to work at the high level required for acceptable performance. A key issue is the extent to which the federal machinery of government continued to be hollow and incompetent after the Reagan administration.

Among the many problems that arise from political executive–permanent staff interaction, two critical, related signs of management failure need emphasizing: the inadequate monitoring of programs, and the paucity of sound data needed to assess managerial and policy performance and inform decision making. Looking at management failure will be useful, however, only if considered in an appropriate political environment. The savings and loan (S&L) scandal during the Reagan administration still offers the most illuminating case of the interaction of political and technical factors that led to destructive, ideologically driven politics and gross mismanagement. The Enron scandal, considered in a later chapter, may yet challenge for first place, but much of what happened with Enron starting in the 1990s mirrored what had happened in the S&L case more than a decade earlier. When the latter scandal moved from the local and state arenas to Washington, as would be expected, the telltale inadequate monitoring and information were soon overshadowed by ideological fervor and venal political acts at the highest levels that ultimately cost the federal government more than $100 billion.

Although the S&L scandal revealed staggering institutional incompetence and corruption played out on a national scale, such high-visibility cases are the exception. Even more important is the deterioration in the everyday efforts of federal departments and agencies charged with responsibility for a variety of services and for protecting the health, welfare, and safety of the American people. This decay, which occurs beneath the surface and generally out of view from the public, is the "garden-variety" form of hollow, incompetent government. Like the dripping of water on stone, the impact of garden-variety deterioration does accumulate over time. However, Congress, the president, top agency political executives, and the media all are unlikely to show much interest unless a problem explodes to the surface.

A good example is the Justice Department's Immigration and Naturalization Service (INS), which had been understaffed and badly managed for years without much concern, at least before September 11, 2001. Many people preferred shoddy INS performance. Businesses including big farms desired cheap labor, and colleges and universities wanted the flow of foreign students to continue. A 2002 Justice Department report by its inspector general staff observed: "'The INS's foreign student program has been dysfunctional, and the INS has acknowledged for several years that it does not know how many foreign students are in the United States.... The INS's current paper-based tracking system is inefficient, inaccurate and unreliable.'"[1] A paper-based tracking system for hundreds of thousands of students is hard to imagine at the start of the twenty-first century. One pictures clerks sitting on high stools and wearing green eye shades. That the INS has been in the running for the worst-managed agency in the federal government year after year and had almost worthless data has hardly been a secret. In the agency power structure, the INS had no political clout and was left to rot away. Alas, disasters waiting to happen can occur with horrendous results beyond our imagination.

Both President Bill Clinton and Congress undertook serious efforts to improve government management and program effectiveness. These included the administration's much ballyhooed attempt to reinvent government—the National Performance Review—and Congress's Government Performance and Results Act of 1993, which was referred to as the Results Act, to emphasize that programs must produce a positive impact on participants' lives to fulfill the agencies' objectives. Both ran afoul of major barriers raised by those who feared they would lose status and/or turf if the organizational changes were implemented successfully. And most discouraging for those like the author who believe that government efficiency must be fueled by sound, relevant, timely data and analyses, the search for honest numbers proved as difficult as ever and did not yield a strong managerial information base.

In discussing the National Performance Review's successes and failures, Donald Kettl, nonresident senior fellow at the Brookings Institution and professor of public affairs and political science at the University of Wisconsin–Madison, observed: "They underscore an important point: that management reform is at least as much about politics and governance as it is about management."[2] Although the fierce play of politics helps make public-sector management fundamentally different from private-sector efforts, the basic rules of management hold equally for both if organizational goals are to be achieved.

Government Performance and Accountability

The domestic policy performance of the federal government ultimately comes down to how much its programs are improving the lives of citizens. That is, the bottom line is whether the federal effort helps its participants by producing positive outcomes or results (the two notions can be used interchangeably, but the latter reflects the newer usage). Unfortunately, the bottom line is both difficult to determine technically and subject to controversy over the appropriate measurement standard. As for the latter, former Harvard University president Derek Bok rejected both public opinion and programmatic outcomes.[3] He opted instead for a number of important societal goals, such as rising per capita income and an increasing percentage of the population owning homes, pointing out that public opinion may ignore reality and that the measurement of program performance results presents a number of well-known technical difficulties.

Bok's approach suffers from his choosing a technically sound measure because of its statistical strength, despite the fact that it is not an appropriate one for the task at hand. Although progress toward Bok's societal objectives are both indicators of national health and reflected in widely accepted statistical measures, the federal government's contribution may be negligible, as is the case with various economic measures. The key question concerning federal programmatic performance is not how well the nation is doing generally, but the extent to which specific government programs contribute to making their participants' lives better. The benefits could come from providing a valuable good or service, as would be the case when a government rent subsidy allows a large low-income family to move to a spacious house in a safer neighborhood or when a training program improves a person's capacity to earn a good income. The appropriate test of government performance should continue to measure how much a specific government program benefits its participants.

Technical and Political Problems

Determining the quality of the federal management effort and affixing accountability loom so large in the government performance equation because of several vexing problems generally absent in the private sector. The latter has objectives that generally can be well specified, with the needed assessment data emerging as a by-product of the accounting systems in use. Historically, market share and profits have these properties. However, the intense pressure in the stock market for higher and higher earnings per share during the 1990s produced "creative" accounting practices that overstated profits, with Enron being the most flagrant case.

The situation is far different in the public sector, where objectives, for political reasons, are often stated so broadly as to be amenable to several interpretations. Or conflicting objectives demanded by partisans may be "compromised" by putting them in different sections of a bill without any effort to reconcile the conflict. The accounting information generally developed does not allow the assessment of outcomes. For example, the records kept on a training project would not permit the determination of whether that project has raised a trainee's earnings capacity. To do so would require a soundly designed evaluation that would take into account the state of the economy by means of a control group of workers who did not receive the training and yet were comparable to the trainees for factors such as level of education and previous work history. Such a costly, time-consuming effort both demands a high level of competence and a kind of information that is much more difficult to build into the system than is the case with businesses. The discussion in this chapter is critical of the federal government's information development efforts, but it is important to keep in mind that the government's information problems far exceed those of the private sector because of technical and political demands in the public arena that are often in conflict.

Some elaboration is needed on the political difficulties. Federal managers of nationally funded but state or locally operated programs work with politically separate jurisdictions that have independent powers. States in particular have constitutionally based powers that may bring refusals to cooperate with federal managers, and such action can stand politically whatever the national legislation may specify. Also, public-sector managers must operate in an intense Washington political environment. They serve many masters in the executive and legislative branches who may make conflicting political demands on them or bar practices needed for sound management. Moreover, the fear of political criticism may make agency managers highly cautious or induce them not to develop information that can be used against them, even though it is needed both for sound management practices and for determining accountability.

At the heart of the accountability question is a lack of state-of-the-art data systems that would provide sound, timely, relevant information and analyses on the various activities of the federal government, particularly performance results. An international security case—the failure in the spring of 1998 of the Central Intelligence Agency (CIA) and its sister agencies, including the Defense Intelligence Agency, the National Security Agency, and National Reconnaissance Office, to detect India's nuclear testing—is an outstanding example of the basic weaknesses in the federal government's capacity to develop and use policy information. Particularly important is the fact that the failure occurred even though the available data were sound. Looking across the federal government, its information problems include too little investment both in computer capability and in staff competence to interpret data, as well as weak leadership in the White House and Congress in addressing the massive information deficit. The failure to detect India's nuclear testing underscores the three main culprits—overload, incompetence, and failed leadership—that make overcoming the information deficit so difficult.

Just a week before the Indian nuclear surprise, CIA director George J. Tenet's speech to his employees pinpointed the overload problem in arguing that the CIA intelligence analysts had been "overwhelmed" by information from historical, human, and technical sources, which he stated were ten times the volume of a decade ago.[4] The human factor loomed large in deriving a sound interpretation from the flood of relevant data. The competence level required is high because analysts face two tough jobs. One is to separate the good information from the dubious data, with the latter so often being far larger. It is a task demanding high skills. The second, even harder task may be to make sense out of the useful data. State-of-the-art equipment helps, but analytic competence is still indispensable.

The House Intelligence Committee pointed out in 1997 that the CIA and its sister intelligence organizations did not have "'the analytic depth, breath and expertise to monitor political, military and economic developments worldwide.'"[5] Gordon Oehler, who stepped down in 1997 as director of the CIA's Nonproliferation Center, claimed that intelligence analysts interpreting spy satellite photos were much less skilled than those serving at the end of the cold war.[6] One possible explanation for the declining competence is that the best analysts, who likely had more employment opportunities than their less able peers, found agency life after the cold war struggle less challenging and exciting, and so they moved on. The final element of the information deficit involved the lack of sustained political leadership. First, there was no continuing commitment by the president and Congress to provide the technical capacity and analytic competence needed to produce sound information and interpretation. Second, the polarized political leaders often refused to use sound numbers that did not fit their political beliefs or that could be politically embarrassing.

In an even higher visibility example, an agent of the Federal Bureau of Investigation (FBI) from Phoenix, Kenneth Williams, wrote a long memorandum on July 10, 2001, based on interviews with Arab students in American flight schools. He warned that followers of Osama bin Laden might be using training at these schools to stage attacks on the United States. Williams appropriately sent his memorandum to his superiors, but it never worked its way up the system so that no one at the top, including President George W. Bush, saw the document before September 11. Much later, when people found out about Williams's warning, the Democrats used the occasion to attack the president and the FBI for not making the document available sooner. Democratic senator Tom Daschle of South Dakota, the Senate majority leader, said: "'This isn't a question of why didn't the president act. This is a question of why didn't the agencies work? Why didn't the information get to the appropriate officials: the president, members of Congress?'"[7] The FBI had a well-deserved reputation for not sharing information, and presidents and attorneys general had never forced the issue. That would have meant taking on J. Edgar Hoover or his legacy. Now it is clear what harm bureaucratic pathology can do.

These two highly visible failures are only the tip of the iceberg of the federal government's information deficit. Unlike the CIA and FBI cases, the usual information systems problems are only garden-variety failures that come about because of obsolete equipment and too little useful data to make sense of them and are not likely to provoke extended media coverage unless scandal is suspected. For example, a 1998 U.S. General Accounting Office (GAO) report on the FDA pointed out: "The ineffectiveness [inefficiency] of FDA's approach is magnified by its inability to keep pace with rising levels of [food] imports. FDA's coverage of imported shipments has fallen from an estimated 8 percent in fiscal year 1992 to 1.7 percent in fiscal year 1997."[8] Although Americans eat much more imported food, with a 50 percent increase from 1990 to 1996 to $33 billion, efforts to hold down costs reduced inspections of such food by 80 percent. Running government on the cheap breeds institutional incompetence. This case shows that the government lacks the data it needs to protect consumers against harmful imported food and exemplifies the growing information deficit that threatens the health of U.S. citizens. Republican senator Susan Collins of Maine, who had requested the GAO report, maintained that declining FDA inspections were "'an invitation to trouble.'"[9] Senator Collins, in pointing out that the cutbacks in inspections were penny wise, pound foolish, offered a prescient warning a little more than three years before the September 11 terrorist attacks.

The Currency of Policymaking

Just as political information can be called the currency of citizenship, policy information might be christened "the currency of policymaking." Hard information should be central to crafting better policies and improving the management and operations of continuing policies—the bedrock for the critique of policies and programs by supporters and opponents. Policy analysts have long recognized that (1) all the needed numbers will seldom be available for deliberating on how well an ongoing policy is doing or how likely it is that a proposed policy will succeed, and (2) legitimate differences can arise in how competent analysts interpret information, even when they agree on its validity.

Although sound data alone seldom would or should carry the day, policy analysts believe that the development of hard numbers could drive out unsound information so policymakers would be able to start from an agreed-upon set of facts. With the erroneous information driven from discussion, the deliberations could be more realistic and push toward better policies. Such a hard-information–based setting might yield a virtuous circle where Democrats and Republicans would work together more productively. That environment can be critical in diminishing polarization. Getting to that point, however, requires traversing high technical and political barriers.

To start with, it will be both difficult and expensive to develop and integrate the needed sound information. Unfortunately, there is no wondrous technical fix. The spy satellite photos still needed competent analysts to shift the raw data and come up with hard information. Political difficulties loom larger yet. First, seldom is there much political mileage in making the case for sound numbers that require major outlays over time to pay for the needed computer capacity and/or analytic competence. The information deficit that threatens citizens' security and individual well-being will not go away without significant investment over time in equipment and people. The challenge is to muster the political courage to call for more hiring and for paying higher salaries to attract competent "number crunchers."

Second, the biggest political and bureaucratic barrier to the development of sound, relevant, timely policy information is that accountability is a double-edged sword. Program staff fear hard evidence of poor performance that reflects badly on the program itself and those responsible for it. For years, program people without solid outcome information have been masters at weaving a picture of success with anecdotes and the like, so they try to avoid the risk of a results-oriented evaluation that could show how poorly a program is working. Legislation will be enacted by Congress and signed by the president calling in clear terms for strong data systems to produce information that addresses performance results and the assignment of accountability. But once enacted, no one seems so sure that he or she actually wants to proceed down the long path to develop and use data that indicate whether or not a program is working and, if the program is failing, put in jeopardy those accountable for it. The reality is that evaluations seldom show striking program performance and are more likely to indicate limited progress at best. Programmatic results and the accompanying accountability are real threats to a program's funding and its managers' reputation, so it is small wonder that serious efforts to produce hard numbers are praised by presidents and political executives and enacted by Congress but are not effectively implemented.

Reagan's War on the Machinery of Government

This section treats the presidencies of Ronald Reagan and George H. W. Bush. The former launched an all-out attack on the federal government, and the latter did little to repair the damage. The consequences of President Reagan's war on the government are made most vivid by the U.S. Department of Housing and Urban Development (HUD) and S&L scandals. The former included top HUD officials and involved bribery to win the agency's low-income housing grants. Although the HUD case stood out both in how widespread the malfeasance was in the agency and how callous the crime was in taking scarce funds from the poor, the funds involved were small relative to the losses in the S&L case. The unbelievable chain of events in the S&L industry, which involved by far the worst federal government losses from a financial scandal in American history, mixed a lethal concoction of rigid ideology, nasty political action committee politics, business dishonesty and gross misjudgment, presidential and congressional pressure to block efforts by the permanent government to stem the losses, and undertrained, inexperienced examiners trying to cope with S&L examinations that were made more difficult to conduct because of deregulation and dishonesty.[10]

At the other end of the visibility scale is the Federal Managers' Financial Integrity Act of 1982 (generally referred to as FIA), which was couched in accounting language and aimed at internal financial controls and information systems. A GAO staff person told me that Congress views looking at internal financial controls much like "watching mud dry." The imagery is of faceless bureaucrats in green eye shades finding that a travel voucher claims $20.32 too much. Not so, however. The act aimed at upgrading federal agencies' internal control and accounting systems to produce timely, reliable information as a basis for enabling top managers to make better decisions, to safeguard the federal government's hundreds of billions of dollars of assets, and to stop waste, fraud, and abuse. The unsuccessful implementation of the 1982 act during the Reagan administration symbolizes the failure in that period to manage the federal government competently. Although FIA will be considered only briefly because of the more extended treatment of a similar, but more concerted effort in the Clinton administration, we will touch on how its failed implementation affected the S&L scandal.

As Reagan's successor, George H. W. Bush's main sin was not trying hard to restore the needed policy information capability. After the four years of the Bush presidency, GAO leveled some of its strongest criticism at the failure to develop basic financial and accounting data to support the management and operation of the legislatively mandated programs that the executive agencies are charged with administering: "Widespread financial management weaknesses are crippling the ability of our leaders to effectively run the federal government. . . . Not only does the government do an abysmal job of rudimentary bookkeeping, but it is also far from having the modern financial systems one would expect of a superpower."[11] Although President Bush made some limited efforts at improvement, his legacy, like Reagan's, left a government sadly lacking the information needed for reasoned domestic policy choices. Blame, however, went far beyond the two presidents to many of the other key actors in the American political system.

The Savings and Loan Scandal

Two legislative changes, one under Jimmy Carter and the other in the Reagan years, set the stage for a misguided deregulation effort marked by poor policies, inept management, and gigantic S&L industry losses. The Deregulatory and Monetary Control Act passed late in the Carter administration removed S&L interest rate restrictions and raised Federal Savings and Loan Insurance Corporation protection from $40,000 to $100,000 per depositor, thereby more than doubling the federal liability to individual depositors. Next came the Gain–Saint Germain Depository Institutions Act of 1982, which was pushed through Congress by Rhode Island congressman and House Banking Committee chair Fernand Saint Germain in cooperation with House majority leader Jim Wright of Texas. It permitted S&Ls to invest deposits much more broadly than in traditional housing loans—for example, to buy low-grade ("junk") bonds and to lend for speculative commercial real estate ventures—and lowered the already low 4 percent ratio of S&L net worth to deposits to 3 percent. Congress, Carter, and Reagan had set the stage for a government financial disaster of epic proportions.

In 1984, Federal Home Loan Bank Board (FHLBB) chair Edwin Gray begged President Reagan for 750 new S&L examiner slots. But adding examiners went against Reagan's deregulation principles. The president and Congress together thwarted the FHLBB efforts in 1984 to tighten up. James Miller, President Reagan's second director of the Office of Management and Budget, told Gray that "'this was a deregulated industry and that, therefore, you don't need any supervision anymore.'"[12] Economist Edward Kane, an expert on S&L financial structure, pointed out that "incredibly, examination and supervisory resources declined in 1983 and 1984, precisely when the economics of FSLIC's [Federal Savings and Loan Insurance Corporation] exposure to zombie [extremely high] risk taking was expanding and becoming harder to assess."[13] In 1982, the FHLBB conducted roughly 20 percent fewer field examinations of thrift institutions than it had in 1979. In the S&L case, the ideology of deregulation emerged in a particularly virulent form to produce both too few examiners and too little examination competence.

Culpability went to the top of the Reagan administration and Congress. Reporter James Ring Adams told of FHLBB chair Gray's travails, in which Congress, led by Wright, blocked him at every turn; but he then wrote that Gray "reserves his greatest vehemence, not for Jim Wright . . . or any Democrat in Congress, but for the second most powerful man in his own administration, White House Chief of Staff Donald Regan."[14] Congress joined President Reagan as coconspirators in creating a hollow, inept FHLBB, and it went further to block action when the understaffed, often inexperienced, underpaid thrift examiners tried to stop private-sector white-collar crime and gross mismanagement.

Looking back at the S&L scandal, it is impossible to determine how much of the losses came from criminal behavior; how much from gross mismanagement in the S&Ls and highly questionable behavior by the outside white-collar professionals, such as lawyers and accountants; and how much from reasonable management errors. As to the last, numerous financial institutions including commercial banks made what at the time seemed prudent loans on new commercial buildings only to see the loans become more and more questionable as others financed similar loans and the commercial real estate markets in city after city succumbed to overbuilding. Let us not think that criminal behavior or shady deals permeated the S&L industry. In a section of *The S&L Debacle* titled "Fraud and

Criminal Behavior," New York University professor Lawrence White, one of the three members of the Federal Home Loan Board in the period 1986–89, argued: "*The bulk of the insolvent thrifts' problems, however, did not stem from such fraudulent or criminal activities. These thrifts largely failed because of an amalgam of deliberately high-risk strategies, poor business judgments, foolish strategies, excessive optimism, and sloppy and careless underwriting, compounded by deteriorating real estate markets.*"[15]

In a 1993 study, CBO reported that various estimates of the S&L costs resulting from fraud ranged from 3 to 25 percent, and it argued that fraud alone probably caused only a few of the failures but had contributed to them and become a significant factor in the overall cost of cleaning up the industry.[16] The S&L case makes clear that neither market forces nor individuals in the private sector can be trusted to self-regulate so as to ensure honest behavior. In a number of the failed institutions, shady S&L operators had joined forces with outside appraisers and accountants, whose professional standards claim that they will be independent in their real estate assessments and audits and to the best of their ability will produce accurate information that can be relied on by government, business, and stockholders. Often only the thin ranks of government S&L regulators stood in the breach left by private enterprise, and they frequently were overwhelmed by the president's people and Congress.

Part of the S&L problem lay in the Reagan administration's misguided view of how to manage regulatory reform. The administration rightly believed federal regulation too rule bound. For the Reagan true believers, however, deregulation stood as a fundamental article of faith that translated into little or no regulation, combining a hands-off agency approach with "a slavish devotion to business interests."[17] The thinking created an ideal setting for deleterious behavior, with stupidity and stealing in the saddle. When regulatory redesign shifts toward the market to set standards, it requires a competent monitoring effort, sustained over time, to determine that the rules of the market are not subverted. Government regulators must search for a careful balance that benefits from the rigor of the market and yet protects the public against either imprudent or fraudulent acts by S&L officials and other participants such as appraisers and auditors. Moreover, the violations in a dynamic market setting will require a much higher level of substantive skills in determining, for example, when an S&L is insolvent or the market value of a piece of property that has passed through several bewildering transfers.

Only highly competent S&L regulators could have cut through complex efforts to hide questionable practices that well may have been adjudged as sound by outside private accountants. The central need is an adequate number of qualified specialists with the competence to engage in efficient government monitoring. Beyond this, there must not be violations of public trust. Malfeasance at the highest levels by the president's top staffers or Congress can thwart any monitoring system, no matter how competent the career civil servants. That is a hard political fact. Concomitantly, dishonesty can flourish with incompetent career staff persons, even if the president and Congress exert no pressure and speak out for exemplary behavior. That is a hard organizational fact.

The problem with the S&L scandal or the HUD scandal, as the term "scandal" itself implies, is that malfeasance dominates hollowness and incompetence. Could a sufficient cadre of competent federal supervisors and examiners with sound information systems have overcome the massive efforts of the White House, Congress, and the S&L industry to thwart them at every turn? I have the gravest doubts, for two reasons. First, the best policy information that can be attained in a reasonable time period at affordable costs with current techniques is likely to be inferior as measured by ideal standards. The more that relevant information is flawed or unattainable, the more likely that credible experts can offer reasonable conflicting opinions. Second, political forces generally can override information and analysis at the top of government, and the task is made easier by the technical limits of the currently available information tools and techniques.

At the same time, we should not underestimate the value of an orderly process of information development and monitoring by competent career staff. Kane wrote: "As the number and scope of problem [S&L] institutions grew, the size, training, and experience of the field examination force became progressively less adequate. This problem traces [in part to] . . . [the Office of Management and Budget's] unwillingness to pay high enough salaries or to establish a sufficiently attractive career ladder for examiners."[18] It is a long way from the lowly field examiners and information systems to Jim Wright and Donald Regan. Moreover, once the game becomes serious at this top level, the power of hard numbers pales, and political forces will bowl over mere information and analysis. But we can still speculate what would have happened if sound information, monitoring, and enforcement efforts had given loud warnings early so that corrections could have been made at lower levels of the federal decision-making process. The answer could well be tens of billions of federal dollars saved. In its analysis of the failed S&Ls in 1993, CBO argued, first, that closing S&Ls promptly when they became insolvent would have made "the collapse of the thrift industry . . . unquestionably apparent in 1982 rather than in the late 1980s" and, second, that the delays in closing insolvent S&Ls roughly doubled the ultimate cost.[19]

Culpability in the Reagan–Bush Years

Reaganism ranks first among the culprits responsible for the failed domestic policy leadership and management efforts during the dozen years between 1981 and 1993, but there are more to blame. The "Federal Managers" in the full title of the Financial Integrity Act did not apply to the faceless bureaucrats so often depicted in that period as underworked, overpaid obstructionists, but to the agency political executives—the president's appointees. As has been discussed, career civil servants had been pushed further and further down in the agency chain of command and likely were "out of the loop" when the big decisions were made by the cabinet secretaries and the other agency presidential appointees. The Reagan agency political executives often were ideologues with limited managerial competence, and they started off doubting the credibility of the career staff. They disdained staff advice, which offered more of a nonpartisan perspective, and failed to draw on their institutional memory.

Moreover, the political executives frequently attacked the career staff, as did President Reagan. Frank Carlucci, a successful public- and private-sector manager who served as Reagan's last secretary of defense, drew on his experience in that administration to observe: "'If I as a CEO [chief executive officer of a private firm] were to say that I had loafers, laggards and petty thieves working for me, one could hardly expect my people to perform. Nor would such talk inspire customer confidence; indeed they would wonder about us as a company and about me as a CEO.'"[20] Reagan and his minions, however, were intent on hamstringing the federal government to free the private sector from its dead hand.

President Reagan and his staff were in a crowd of culprits. The Democratic Congress passed FIA, but it went along with the administration's destructive management practices and, more often than not, aided and abetted them. One reason is that a popular president and his ideology of government as the principal problem fit so well with Americans' long-standing distrust of government. Risk-averse members of Congress sought safety by turning their backs on Reagan administration mismanagement and often by joining the attack on government. However, that institution's unwillingness to demand the execution of its own law to establish powerful large-scale control systems goes deeper. Members of Congress increasingly view service to individual constituents as a—perhaps *the*—primary means of getting reelected and tend to hammer the executive branch agencies on highly specific aspects of rules and regulations (e.g., limitations in Medicare coverage). The point is not that the agencies are usually right and the individuals seeking congressional help usually wrong but rather that such advocacy reinforces the growing tendency in Congress for members to overregulate and micromanage federal programs. Moreover, the typical member, as is discussed shortly, is likely to have limited concern for overall managerial problems, especially something as complicated and boring as large-scale financial and accounting systems.

During the S&L scandal, members of Congress did not want to take on the special-interest groups, which had helped fund their expensive congressional political campaigns, and they feared the local S&Ls and their supporters. In a detailed review of the scandal, *New York Times* reporter David Rosenbaum wrote: "As the crisis developed, Congress seemed to be in the pocket of the savings and loan industry, passing laws the lobbyists wanted, tying up bills they opposed, and hectoring regulators relentlessly to ease up."[21]

Rosenbaum went on to ask how the S&Ls gained so much political clout and answered that "money was only a small part of the close relationship." He quoted Democratic senator David H. Pryor of Arkansas, who was a member of the Ethics Committee: "'You've got to remember that each community has a savings and loan; some have two, some have four, and each of them have seven or eight board members. They own the Chevy agency and the shoe store. And when we saw these people we said, gosh, these are the people who are building the homes for people, these are the people who represent a dream that has worked in this country.'"[22]

It was a telling comment. For many years, the S&Ls had a well-earned reputation as hometown institutions conservatively financing individual housing. Although a number of S&Ls had been taken over by speculators in the "go-go" 1980s, the image and in many cases the reality of the S&Ls as good citizens of the community still held.

Another aspect of Congress seldom receives notice but is also of great importance: the members' own institutional incompetence arising from their lack of experience with and knowledge about large-scale public bureaucracies. We do not know whether Congress passed FIA to cover itself from attack or whether it sincerely wanted to significantly improve government management through more relevant, reliable, and timely information and to cut back on waste, fraud, and abuse. It is almost certainly the case, however, that many members of Congress had little idea of the organizational difficulties of making such improvements or of the huge outlays needed to upgrade agency staff competence and capacity, including the investment in state-of-the-art scientific equipment and computers. Members apparently have great difficulty in seeing how the often mundane programmatic numbers generated by efficient accounting systems build up to be the necessary base for their critical policy decisions. Add "honest" ignorance to the list of Congress's deleterious acts of omission and commission.

In assigning blame, two other culprits must not be overlooked. First is the press. Starting in 1990, no self-respecting newspaper was without its own in-depth S&L scandal coverage. The HUD scandal had received the same kind of treatment during much of 1989. But in the Reagan years, the press handled both scandals poorly. As Ellen Hume of Harvard University's Joan Shorenstein Center on the Press, Politics, and Public Policy wrote in 1990: "Every taxpayer deserves an answer to this question: Why did the well-educated and constitutionally protected press corps miss the savings and loan scandal, which is the most expensive public finance debacle in U.S. history?"[23]

Hume offered a host of reasons including (1) the scandal emerged as a "numbers," not a "people" story; (2) the story came in good part from outside the Capital Beltway, the segment of the Interstate Highway system that rings Washington, D.C.; and (3) the "villains" (her term) were a powerful political group with bipartisan support. Hume made another telling indictment against the press: "Journalists have gotten used to having their information pre-digested. . . . Serious investigative journalism has fallen on hard times." Competence and commitment were in short supply among a lazy press willing to be manipulated by White House news managers. Last but not least among the culprits, as the comic strip character Pogo once said, "is Us." As Adams said in closing his book on the S&L scandal: "Three years ago, we could blame the regulators for letting these debacles develop. Now we have to blame elected officials. The next time around, we can only blame ourselves."[24]

Federal information policy during this twelve-year period failed to provide the executive branch and Congress with the basic information and analysis needed to make reasoned policy decisions and to implement and manage them efficiently. In key decisions about programs and policies, federal decision makers relied on such weak information systems that much of the time, whether they understood it or not, they were flying blind. The formulation of policy from information that is faulty or unjustifiably missing (i.e., needed information that reasonably could have been attained) increases the likelihood of inept governance. Misguided and mismanaged information policy itself is a major aspect of the quiet crisis of hollow, incompetent government.

In the Reagan–Bush years, no Soviet mole from the old cold war period could have concocted a better strategy to produce such a serious, pervasive attack on the American system and yet elicit no public outcry. Though the public may be glued to the television news and weep over the plight of an endangered owl, it will hardly weep over endangered data. Good numbers are not an end in themselves; they are, however, one of the necessary ingredients for reasoned deliberation on critical decisions that affect the lives of the American people.

The Clinton Years

Unlike the years of Reagan's war on government and of Bush's indifference to the damage wrought by his predecessor, Clinton's presidency brought forth great concern in the administration and Congress about improving efficiency. First, the increasing distaste for the government in Washington intensified the efforts to devolve funds and responsibility to states and localities as a means of increasing domestic policy efficiency.

Second, Vice President Al Gore in September 1993 released his National Performance Review (NPR) aimed at reinventing government based on the four basic principles: Cut red tape, empower government employees to do the job right, put program participants first, and go back to basics. Third, the 1993 Government Performance and Results Act, which stressed the rigorous measurement of financial and program performance outcomes, aimed at changing how managers thought about federal programs and their accountability in them. The intent of this section is not to provide an extended critique of the three efforts but rather to consider a number of barriers that slowed each of them and are likely to block future attempts to develop and implement major institutional reforms in the federal government.

Devolution

The justification for devolving domestic policy responsibilities to subnational governments rests on two program-oriented propositions. First, state and local civil servants, by being more responsive than Washington bureaucrats to what citizens want, will provide better and less costly services. Second, subnational governments offer natural laboratories for new program ideas that can produce success models for other states and localities to adopt. After their 1994 congressional victory, the Gingrich Republicans sought a quantum jump in American federalism. This "Devolution Revolution" aimed at a dramatic shift of power over domestic policy to subnational governments through reductions both in federal grants-in-aid and in the level of the executive branch agencies' managerial responsibilities. The belief in the greater efficiency of governments closer to the people notwithstanding, however, the roadblocks to increased efficiency proved more daunting than expected.

First, the federal government itself did not surrender institutional power easily, whatever the rhetoric. Second, the states too kept to their old ways, as is illustrated by the experience of the states as laboratories: They generally have failed to undertake a rigorous effort to design, implement, and assess innovative programs. For instance, the 1988 Family Support Act empowered the Department of Health and Human Services to grant waivers on existing welfare regulations so that the states could experiment with major program changes and test these innovations in the field. *The Politics of Welfare Reform,* edited by Donald Norris and Lyke Thompson, provided in-depth studies of welfare waiver efforts in six states chosen because their governments were known for policy leadership.[25] In summarizing the results, the editors indicated that the six states in the main did little or no careful planning and implementation but instead undertook projects colored by ideology that focused only secondary attention on the needs of poor welfare recipients. University of Wisconsin–Madison public policy professor Michael Wiseman wrote in his review of *The Politics of Welfare Reform:* "The oft-cited notion that states are playing the role of 'laboratories'. . . in welfare reform receives little support. . . . The experiments are uncoordinated and ill-designed, no one seems to be keeping notes, and there is no peer and little federal pressure for serious and timely review of program contents or results."[26] The image of state and local folks laboring productively in bold natural experiments may be true; however, the proof of superiority requires hard data to show results and, when successful, to indicate what needs to be done to repeat the effort in other places.

Moreover, there is a more basic problem in that the real differences among the various levels of government are not necessarily that great. State and local civil servants also overemphasize rules and regulations; state government legislators are hardly immune from micromanaging programs or from making executive branch political appointees and civil servants pay for mistakes; and subnational government elected officials and their top political appointees may not want to transfer significant power by empowering government employees with greater managerial and operational freedom. The devolution of federal programs and managerial responsibilities did not repeal the iron laws of institutions that complicate implementation and management but simply transferred them to states and localities.

In his critique of devolution efforts, Kettl argued that there have been "widely heralded successes (cheaper, more effective, more responsive government)" but that the process undercut assigning accountability: "Especially compared with reforms in other nations, which sought to set sharp policy goals and then establish clear responsibility for results, the American reforms have blurred the process of setting and achieving goals . . . [and made] determining exactly who is responsible more difficult. *Management reform in the U.S. government has a unique style, very different from efforts elsewhere in the world.*"[27] Devolution is a double-edged sword. Shared governance has at times cut into local efficiency and effectiveness. Some localities, when not unduly constrained by a higher government (federal or state), have managed to overcome the usual political and administrative pitfalls and through good leadership and management build the strong institutional structures and processes needed for successful performance. There is a general consensus, even among those who still advocate a strong federal government, that local governments should have great flexibility in mounting federally funded programs but then be held accountable.

The other side of the coin is that states and localities may use federal funds and yet not carry out federal laws, divert the funds to uses not intended by these laws, or fail to develop the institutional competence needed for delivering the prescribed services efficiently. The shared governance issue has its political component, which goes back to the battles between the Federalists and Anti-Federalists concerning states' rights, and its institutional component whereby weak political leadership and managerial and staff incompetence at one or both government levels can undermine federally funded programs. If the focus is on the means for putting in place adequately funded, well-run programs that adhere to the spirit of the federal legislation establishing these grants-in-aid, devolution must confront both its political and institutional components.

Reinvention

By the time the Clinton administration came into office, a number of state and local governments and other nations were well into the heady process of reinvention. Washington was a laggard, and British prime minister Margaret Thatcher's New Steps Initiative, begun in 1988, provided a basic model for NPR. Next Steps had reorganized most British civil servants into executive agencies that were allowed much greater administrative flexibility to do their jobs than under the old civil service rules and charged the new units with reaching annual performance goals. NPR began as Next Steps was being acclaimed as a huge success that had transformed the hidebound British government and its stodgy civil servants into lean and mean executive agencies operating like businesses. However, Alasdair Roberts of Canada's Queen's University, in his late 1997 critique of "Performance-Based Organizations" (PBOs), which included both Next Steps and NPR, found that even the most modest claims about

Next Steps's success were either overstated or inaccurate, with the latter being in terms of the actual size of staff reductions.[28]

Roberts further argued that PBOs were unlikely to improve government performance greatly or to cut costs materially. As to Next Steps, he wrote: "One of the reasons for the modest impact of Next Steps may be the reluctance of many actors—including legislators, central management agencies, and parent departments—to permit radical deregulation of executive agencies. . . . The freedoms achieved may be useful, but they are not likely to produce widespread, dramatic changes in operating procedures."[29] He expressed even greater pessimism about NPR, in part because the British Parliament, which is far weaker than Congress, raises fewer high barriers to leap over than does the U.S. federal structure.

Two ideas were central to NPR: first, ending overregulation and micromanagement; and second, empowering government employees all the way down to where services are delivered. Both required Congress to back off from trying to manage agencies and to transfer to them considerable power to engage in more flexible actions. The agencies, in turn, had to shift power from higher to lower levels. As we will see shortly, Congress has great trouble following its own mandates. In NPR, the basic changes in how Congress should operate were not set out by that body itself but by the Clinton administration's initiative.

If this environment were not difficult enough in 1993 with a Democratic Congress, the 1994 election shifted congressional control to the Republicans. In light of these formidable institutional barriers, the limited changes Roberts found are hardly unexpected. Congressional overregulation and micromanagement continued while empowerment, which had been so central to the reinvention effort, did not pour down from Congress and the social agencies to the front-line workers who deliver services. Further, the administration itself may have severely undercut NPR in its haste to look good at the outset. Reagan's war on government did little to reduce the size of the federal career service, whereas Clinton made deep reductions in staff positions of more than 300,000 by 1998.

The essence of the Clinton administration's efforts at reinventing the federal government was doing better with less, but staff cutbacks can be costly. The S&L scandal is the showcase example of the danger of reducing monitoring staffs, but there are plenty of more recent ones. Take the Health Care Financing Administration, the nation's largest payer for home health care services, whose spending grew between 1988 and 1996 from $2.1 billion to $18 billion. A 1997 GAO report pointed out: "We found that the infrequency of the intermediaries' medical review of claims and limited physician involvement in overseeing home health care agencies' plans of care made it nearly impossible to determine whether the beneficiary receiving home health care services qualified for the benefit, needed the care being delivered, or even received the services being billed to Medicare."[30] Inadequate financial information and monitoring in a program such as Medicare can produce astronomical losses. By 1996, improper Medicare payments had risen to $23.2 billion, a staggering 14 percent of total outlays for that year.

In the face of these improper payments, the administration shifted resources to the problem of Medicare fraud, for example, going in five years from 12 assigned FBI agents to 400 by 1999. June Gibbs Brown, the inspector general of the Department of Health and Human Services, reported a 46 percent decline during 1997 and 1998 in improper Medicare payments, which reduced them to $12.6 billion—that is, only 7 percent of total program expenditures in 1998, as compared with 14 percent in 1996.[31] As this Medicare cost reduction of more than $10 billion for 1997 and 1998 indicates, the addition of a reasonable number of competent monitors (albeit in this case taken from somewhere else), whose salaries might have added up to tens of millions of dollars, can save the federal government billions of dollars. The experience with Medicare shows the payoff from an added monitoring effort. The return on competent monitoring is so high that one can only assume that the politicians, before the shocking level of improper Medicare payments in 1996, feared offending a group that through campaign donations and political threat had weight in the reelection equation. Concomitantly, the even greater fear of adverse public reaction to the Medicare loses in 1996 likely propelled action.

Reinventing government also ran afoul of the problem of the incompetence of executive agency political executives. Taegan Goddard and Christopher Riback attacked the administration's approach to reinvention by castigating the incompetence of "a government of novices, rookies to the sport," and they pointed out that government keeps getting reinvented again and again, observing pointedly: "What these new public officials really must reinvent is themselves."[32] Again, it is the "federal managers" coming up short as to knowledge and experience about implementing the NPR game plan. Yet, even if the incoming political executives were much more capable, the problem of turning over almost all of the management at the change of administrations would not go away. A new CEO, even if he or she wanted significant change, would likely start by removing only a handful of key managers. The business needs people with in-depth knowledge of the company in key managerial positions to maintain a degree of continuity. Institutions are made up of employees involved in organizational processes and relationships that have taken on importance, and these must be changed with due regard for the dangers of taking them apart too quickly. In the unique U.S. system of government, the political imperative of taking control has come to override the organizational imperative of continuity, as career civil servants have been pushed lower and lower down the chain of command and trusted less and less.

Kettl sets out this overall assessment of the reinvention of government effort that puts in perspective NPR's achievements and its failures:

> It saved a significant amount of money, brought substantive managerial reforms (especially in customer service and procurement processes), and promoted a performance-based discussion about the functions of government.... NPR demonstrated ... that the federal government is no longer organized for the job that law and the Constitution charged it to do. The federal government particularly had not built the capacity required to effectively manage a government increasingly operated through proxies.... The bottom line for democratic government is accountability—not profits or citizen satisfaction—and customer service does not provide a good proxy measure for accountability.[33]

NPR appeared to save money through staff reductions, which may have actually been costly if monitoring competence and capacity were reduced; rationalized procurement; and improved customer service, which is a means rather than an end. The last may have made program participants or clients more satisfied but not have improved their lot. NPR neither lessened materially the deep problems of shared governance nor increased accountability in the system. In the larger picture of U.S. federalism, NPR made a marginal contribution.

The Results Act

The Government Performance and Results Act (GPRA) of 1993 stands as Congress's most ambitious legislative attempt to base responsibility on the results programs produce. GAO, which serves the entire Congress, observed: "The Results Act seeks to improve the efficiency, effectiveness, and public accountability of federal agencies as well as to improve congressional decision-making. It aims to do so by promoting a focus on program results and providing the Congress with more objective information on the achievement of statutory objectives."[34] Under GPRA, all federal agencies were required to prepare long-term strategic plans indicating the general direction of their programs, determine their objectives and produce relevant performance measures, set out strategies for reaching the stated objectives, and report on their results in accomplishing their agency goals. Moreover, Congress recognized that earlier efforts to develop performance data had been unrealistic about how long it would take to change the institutional structure of the executive agencies and mandated that GPRA be implemented over seven years, beginning in 1994.

In this seven-year implementation phase, the Office of Management and Budget selected pilot tests to aid the agencies in gaining experience in using GPRA concepts and processes to develop their long-run strategies, with about seventy programs being designated as GPRA pilot projects. GAO's analysis of these projects and other GPRA efforts over the years has generated a number of studies for Congress and several of its committees that provide a fair assessment of the implementation effort. The main finding is that the agency information systems have not been improved nearly enough to yield the sound data needed to assess program results and affix accountability. In its February 1998 testimony before a House subcommittee, GAO described the lack of progress:

> The absence of both sound program performance and cost data and the capacity to use those data to improve performance is a critical challenge that the agencies must confront if they are to effectively implement the Results Act. . . . Most agencies still have a substantial amount of work to do before they are able to generate the reliable, useful, relevant, timely financial information that is urgently needed to make our government

fiscally responsible. The widespread lack of available program performance information is equally troubling.[35]

Neither Congress nor the executive branch agencies made the investment in people, equipment, and systems required to provide sufficient
technical and managerial capability to develop and use sound performance results in the policymaking process. In particular, the legislation mandated that Congress itself make major changes to benefit from the better
reporting of results by the agencies. Much like the case of the Financial
Integrity Act of a decade earlier, Congress passed a law that specified
major institutional changes in the federal government, including Congress itself, and GAO regularly delved into how the effort was being implemented, found grave deficiencies, and duly reported them to Congress.
Yet no amount of evidence propelled Congress into action to push the
agencies toward complying with the law. Such behavior could be interpreted as indicating that Congress either saw no value to performance information in supporting its own oversight and decision-making functions
or else feared that the results data would reflect badly on programs it favored. Whatever the reasons, Congress clearly did not see hard data and
rigorous analyses as a critical commodity worth concerted institutional
effort or political risk taking.

Nowhere does Congress seem more puzzling than in developing and
using data. Starting in the 1970s, it significantly upgraded the analytic capacity both of its standing committees and support agencies.[36] By the
1980s, it had the analytic capacity to challenge the president. CBO, a new
support agency started in 1974, gained the reputation for producing the
best budget numbers, much superior to those of the administration, and
supplied Congress with sound, nonpartisan information and analyses to
improve its decision-making process. With its widely accepted standing
as an analytic staff of exceptionally high competence and great internal
credibility with their peers, CBO symbolized the success of Congress's
remarkably rapid buildup of its staff capacity to develop and analyze the
policy information it needed to support its deliberations and choices.

But that is only half of the story. The dark side is Congress's use of
CBO's input in its decision-making process. An astute interviewee who
had served on policy analysis staffs in both the Executive Office of the

President and in Congress agreed with the positive judgment on CBO but asked: "'Why has the building of such formidable analytic capacity not been accompanied by better decisionmaking? . . . Do you really think those outcomes [Congress's budgetary choices] would have been worse in the absence of CBO? It is hard for me to believe so.'"[37] Are congressional efforts that on their face seek to strengthen the development of sound data and analyses in support of federal decision making "full of sound and fury, signifying nothing of substance?" Has Congress degenerated to the point that legislation's main function is to help members in their neverending quest for reelection? If so, this deeper reason for the failure of GPRA and FIA to materially improve the executive branch agencies' capacity to produce and employ sound decision-making data provides powerful evidence of political system deterioration and the lack of federal institutional commitment and competence to carry out the government's tasks as set out by law.

A Final Comment

No one understood the need for institutional competence better than Alexander Hamilton, who as secretary of the treasury dominated President George Washington's government. Hamilton wrote more than two centuries ago in *The Federalist* No. 70: "A feeble executive implies a feeble execution of the government. A feeble execution is but another phrase for a bad execution; and *a government ill executed, whatever it may be in theory, must be, in practice, a bad government.*"[38] In these seventeen italicized words, Hamilton captures the essence of governance. First, even if a concept of governance holds up to challenge in its theoretical stage, it must be well implemented and well managed to get off the ground. Second, such well-functioning government institutions come about because strong leaders and capable managers are able to build competent staffs and viable institutional structures and processes. The organizational genius of George Washington's administration built a sufficiently strong institutional framework underpinned by hard numbers to develop the national government monetary and budgetary systems that were needed to sustain the new American Republic. Hamilton's seventeen words are just as true today for governing the world's only superpower.

seven

The Media:
Linking Politicians and the People

Although the Constitution made eligible voters ultimately responsible for selecting able representatives and monitoring them over time, it did not address the logistics of good citizenry. That is, the electorate had no guidance on the operational question of obtaining the sound, relevant, timely political information needed for reasoned electoral choices. Today, that task is far harder than during the early years of the nation, when white males with property likely had personal knowledge of candidates' characters, and during much of the nineteenth century in the heyday of the political parties, when people were closely tied to party officials who provided information on why to vote the straight party line.[1] Pity the poor American voters of today who seek to find the political information and commentary that can help them pick wisely in national elections.

The key issue in this chapter is whether the media that are now the dominant source of political information and commentary can restore the institutional commitment and competence needed to provide a sound base for informed choice. This role is critical for the success of the American political system. Recall that Michael Delli Carpini and Scott Keeter were quoted above as observing that "political information is to democratic politics what money is to economics: it is the currency of citizenship."[2] Of late, the journalism effort has been plagued by the combination of high-speed technology, the misshapen politics of polarization, and the media's bottom-line mentality. First, vast quantities of information, often of questionable validity, spew forth in the postmodern world of extremely broad and rapid dissemination via electronic means. Second, polarized politics, which thrives on misinformation and slanted commentary, has converted political information and analysis into a primary weapon in the propaganda battles between Democrats and Republicans. Third, the media, like so many industries, became fixated on ever increasing profits during the long stock market boom. By the end of the 1990s, journalism's loss of institutional competence and credibility had become a central concern of responsible critics as the media challenged Congress for the title of the sickest of the major national political institutions.

Bill Kovach, then the curator of Harvard University's Nieman Foundation for Journalism, and Tom Rosenstiel, director of the Project for Excellence in Journalism, set out a devastating condemnation of the media: "In practice, the lowest standards tend to drive out the higher, creating a kind of Gresham's Law of Journalism."[3] There are now formidable barriers to a high level of professionalism, at which journalists concentrate on important political issues that affect people's lives, relentlessly check what they find for accuracy and fairness, and base their analysis on verified information. Kovach and Rosenstiel have also stressed the critical tie between professional journalists and their audience: "Whether serious journalism survives, first, is up to those who aspire to call themselves serious journalists. . . . In the end, [the change] depends more on citizens than journalists. If citizens value accuracy, balance, proportion, these qualities can succeed in the news."[4]

Journalists are not to be let off the hook. They need to recommit themselves to their profession's most basic responsibilities. If not, the plethora of biased political information and commentary can confuse people or convince them that unsound data are superior, especially if they fit their political predilections. The people, however, must see the value of such journalism. But that jumps ahead of the story. The immediate question is whether professional journalists can restore the credibility of the media by providing accurate information and well-reasoned analyses grounded in fact. Representative democracy cannot thrive on a debased currency of citizenship.

The Death of the Political Parties

The political parties dominated American politics in the nineteenth century with what have come to be seen as basic strengths as well as often criticized flaws. The parties during their years of political dominance found and vetted candidates, provided useful political information, encouraged citizen participation that was to reach its highest point in those years, and believed that successful policy performance offered the best means of winning elections. The once-castigated strong party system now is much praised. Writing in 1999, journalism professor Michael Schudson of the University of California at San Diego called parties in the 1800s "a fourth branch of government, responsible more than any other institution for the political education and mobilization of the voting population . . . and for the creation of a functioning leadership inside the . . . halls of Congress."[5] The same year, Columbia University's Michael Janeway observed favorably:

> They were parties in the business of legislating and governing first and foremost. They were partisan vehicles for shrill ideological name-calling—the modern model—a far distant second. And they involved average citizens who thought of themselves as "grass-roots" Democrats and Republicans, showed up at caucuses and campaign rallies, volunteered to assist their parties' candidates in election season, paid attention to their words and actions.[6]

The parties also were run by party bosses at all levels who chose candidates, even for president, in the legendary smoke-filled rooms; dished out public jobs mainly to reward loyalty, not merit; and gave lucrative contracts for buildings and roadways to those whose biggest credential too often was the generosity of their kickbacks. The politicians of that day did not search endlessly for large checks to fill their campaign coffers, but rather took cash under the table and put it in their pockets. The initiative process emerged near the end of the parties' great century because of rising concern that legislatures answered only to business interests. Because senators at the time were still being chosen by the state legislatures, business owned at least one house of Congress outright, or so it appeared to reformers with good reason. The process hardly fit textbook models of good governance, but despite the flaws, that era did tie voters to the politicians, encouraged citizen participation in a much more vigorous way than at the present, and stressed the business of governance.

The problems appalled the reformers in the parties' heyday. Yet, as is usually the case, the main difficulties were not in devising a better structural approach in theory but in probing for the threat of deleterious side effects and in figuring out how to implement the approach. As Schudson pointed out in *The Good Citizen*, the Mugwumps and later the Progressives sought a model of citizenship that centered on better-informed citizens using less-biased information and "helped transform voting from a social to a civic act . . . [that changed] the act of reading a newspaper and the process of political education."[7] The reformers wanted to provide voters with sound political information from sources independent of the political parties so that enlightened citizens could make a more reasoned judgment of their own interests and the public good.

Schudson quoted a striking 1914 statement by Yale University president Arthur T. Hadley (a political scientist) that highlights the institutional transformation problem: "'It is not by the personal influence which was characteristic of the old party system that nominations are now secured and the way made clear for the passage of laws. It is the influence of the printed page, which enables the man who controls it to determine thousands of votes for good or for evil.'"[8] The new model sought to shift institutional responsibility for developing and verifying the political information of the day away from the obviously partisan parties.

Yet the press, the only other institution with the capacity to take on the task, had earlier served the political parties and itself had won no accolades for Olympian nonpartisanship. Further, the political parties may have experienced a decline in power, but they and their candidates remained the major political actors still able to gain favorable treatment from the newspapers. The reformers had been transfixed by all the parties did wrong, not what they did right. This strong aversion to the party system seemed to blind the reformers to the institutional functions that needed to be replaced through a new or altered structural mechanism if there were to be a sufficient supply of sound political information offering timely, relevant political facts and hard interpretations grounded in such facts.

The reformers conceived of an energized citizenry ready to do the needed homework to sort out hard facts from party and press propaganda. Parties were no longer to be trusted to pick capable candidates, so the public had to have the necessary information to do the job and the skills and willingness to carry it out. The people needed to have greater civic virtue and more personal initiative if the parties were not to be trusted to choose representatives with the intelligence and wisdom to govern well. James MacGregor Burns has argued that "no polity on earth [has] put such civic demands on its citizens as [does] the American. . . . It is above all the decline of party in the United States that has made the citizen's task so overpowering."[9] Another key commentator, Austin Ranney, pointed out: "Since the early 1900s, the United States has been the only country in the world to choose most of its candidates by the direct primary system, in which anyone can enter the contest for a party's nomination and the selection is made, not, as in most other democracies, by small groups of party leaders, but by ordinary voters who have designated themselves as party members."[10]

In 1968, Hubert Humphrey, Lyndon Johnson's vice president, became the last presidential candidate to win no presidential caucuses or primaries and yet be his party's presidential standard-bearer. The Democratic presidential convention that year in Chicago, coming at the height of Vietnam antiwar fervor, still symbolizes the 1960s with its fierce clashes between police and demonstrators. After Humphrey lost to Richard Nixon, pressures in the Democratic Party led to taking the choice of presidential candidates away from party professionals. The changes were in place by 1972, and the United States started down a road traveled by no other country: Its political parties do not pick their presidential candidates.

Once the primary system became the means of choosing presidential candidates, the political party machinery lost relevance, except as a fundraising vehicle. The decline of parties meant that the U.S. political system no longer had a formal screening process for candidates by party members who knew the politicians' background, had seen them in action, and ostensibly had the kind of information needed to assess their capacity for presidential governance. The new breed of professional politicians choose themselves as candidates for all national offices. Further complicating presidential candidate choice, early caucuses and primaries, particularly those in Iowa and New Hampshire, could decide the ultimate presidential candidates prematurely by the votes of a few thousand persons with limited knowledge and certainly with criteria for choice that did not necessarily reflect a broad national consensus. After the institutional shift away from the party system as the vehicle for selecting candidates had been completed, the parties that had first been wounded by the reformers starting late in the nineteenth century now lay moribund without candidate selection responsibilities. They hung on and acquired a role in the money chase that came to dominate elections, but this new job was a pale reflection of their past glory.

To overvalue that party process would be a mistake, yet two terrible losses do stand out in retrospect. First, the parties in their prime did stress government performance as the chosen vehicle for winning elections. To be sure, the parties were simply following their own self-interest, but when that interest generally corresponded to the public's interest, that did not matter. Second, party members were partisan by definition, but they were not as cynical about politics as today's electorate. Now it needs noting that both of these losses may have come about even if the parties had remained important. Or the corruption the reformers attacked might have destroyed the parties from within. Finally, strong parties, whatever their earlier value as mediating institutions between politicians and the people, are not necessarily a feasible option for today. Their time may have passed as an institutional means for addressing today's political problems. What still makes the earlier experience so useful is that the losses described above remain important for thinking about the future.

The Rise and Fall of the Media

Today, the first question in considering the media is how to identify the beast. In *Warp Speed,* Kovach and Rosenstiel have sharply and succinctly spelled out journalism's myriad problems in trying to cope with "the newly diversified mass media" or "new Mixed Media Culture" in which the mainstream and tabloid press, entertainment, infotainment, television's political pundits and 24-hour news programs, and the Internet do not simply coexist but intermingle and merge.[11] The right imagery is from *Macbeth,* with the witches crying "Double, double toil and trouble; Fire burn and cauldron bubble" as they throw in various ingredients such as a frog's toe and a newt's eye.

The concoction tossed into the mixed-media culture pot is a laundry list that defies meaningful description; but trouble has at least doubled for the body politic as it boiled on. What emerged from this ungainly brew, however, can be conceived of in two distinct ways, both legitimate in the eyes of the beholder. The first is as a profit-maximizing industry no different in its economics than other businesses that must face the pressures for increased earnings growth. The second is as a special institution accorded First Amendment protection as the "fourth branch of government" so that it can freely carry out "the classic function of journalism to sort out a true and reliable account of the day's events" and to provide people the needed facts and analyses "so as to make sense of public problems."[12] The dilemma is that the two concepts, profit-making industry and hard news institution, are now far more at odds in their modus operandi than in the past.

Journalism and Corporate Profit Maximization

At an earlier time, such men as Joseph Pulitzer, E. W. Scripps, and William Randolph Hearst owned vast newspaper chains that combined a strong commitment to public service with a heavy dose of sex, crime, and yellow journalism to make profits. These men may have been ruthless in building their profitable empires, but they understood journalism's higher role. Pulitzer observed: "Our Republic and its press will rise or fall together. An able, disinterested public-spirited press, with trained intelligence to know the right and courage to do it, can preserve that public virtue without which popular government is a sham and a mockery."[13] In sharp contrast, the newspaper of today may be part of a chain that is part of a multimedia conglomerate that itself is only a division of a vast corporation. The corporation's commitment most likely will be to the bottom line, not to journalistic norms that may be little understood and of no great relevance to its top management.

Even without layers of owners, the clash between profits and norms will be intense because of the stress on marketing and cost-cutting in the news business. Take television. The emphasis is on programs involving commentary, punditry, opinion, and controversy. A favored format features several well-known political reporters and columnists all shouting invectives at each other, often without a hard fact in sight. Losing out have been programs grounded in the extensive use of reporters seeking and verifying information that cost far more to produce and likely attract a smaller audience. As Lawrence Grossman observed: "The commercial potential of major documentaries, serious discussions, public affairs forums, and analytical pieces about important issues is severely limited, especially if the issues involved are intensely controversial."[14]

From the business perspective, pleasing consumers and increasing profits is a "no-brainer," especially if the owners are not committed to providing hard political information or do not have ample resources to go against the trend. Bruce W. Sanford, a partner in the law firm of Baker &

Hostetler and a specialist in First Amendment law, wrote: "In earlier decades of the twentieth century, the missionary zeal of media leaders could not be mistaken. Nowadays, the public suspects that they are only driven by capitalist ardor. What else could account for the superficiality of the news?"[15] Neither Sanford nor I is trying to rewrite history and cast these often vindictive press barons of another era as selfless journalists, but they were not afraid to offend people in high places or take unpopular stands to fight for what they believed to be in the public interest.

The battle over journalistic integrity that has pitted the boardroom against the newsroom has not been much of a fight, for two reasons. First, with the stock of major media organizations now mainly publicly traded, the increasingly intense pressure for companies to meet or exceed quarterly earnings expectations has made the pursuit of costly journalistic norms more and more difficult. Second, the heavy guns—control over money and personnel—all belong to the owners. They have had the power to slash costs, cut staff, close foreign bureaus, stop covering the federal agencies, and reward managers for finding ways of making their product more salable by covering consumer interests. Janeway argued that with "the ascendancy of the corporate profit imperative in the news business . . . depth, breadth, and authority of coverage suffered."[16]

The primetime television news slots on the major channels have increasingly shifted away from hard political coverage; local television news is mainly crime, catastrophe, and entertainment; local newspapers have more and more consumer-oriented features offered in new special sections devoted on a periodic basis to such areas as automobiles and home computers and in beefed-up arts and entertainment sections. Notably absent has been the hard political news about major domestic and international events of consequence to national welfare and security.

Organizational competence has deteriorated. As Richard Morin, the director for polling of the *Washington Post,* pointed out in his column on a 1999 poll by the Pew Research Center for the People and the Press: "Four in 10 national journalists and more than half of all local reporters and editors agree that 'news reports are increasingly full of factual errors and sloppy reporting'—both double-digit increases from 1995."[17] The journalists in their poll reflected similar concerns to those of the public, but generally in lower percentages. For example, roughly half of reporters and media executives thought that news organizations often push controversy rather than follow it, whereas "'fully 72 percent of Americans say such reporting perpetuates scandal.'"[18] This increasing inaccuracy, poor reporting, and bad writing may be a major strategic error for the pursuit of long-run profitability.

Media organizations that lose credibility because of such practices could suffer costly consequences over time, facing declining revenues and profits as consumers turn away in disgust. Two factors reduce the likelihood of such change. First, as in other industries, the need for higher and higher earnings to bolster stock prices makes it difficult for most of the individual media organizations to move against the grain by undertaking expensive improvement efforts. Second, the public may praise sound reporting and in-depth coverage of important political news when queried in a survey and still opt for scandal, mayhem, catastrophe, and consumer-oriented features when they turn on the television or buy newspapers and magazines. For example, the *New York Times,* which ranks at the top among daily newspapers in its depth, breath, accuracy, and authority of coverage and is readily available throughout the nation, has not experienced large circulation increases as other sources have declined in thoroughness and accuracy. It seems fair to say that when media organizations are conceptualized as profit-maximizing businesses, they have responded appropriately to newly developing consumer tastes and to a stock market regimen marked by an intense focus on rapid short-run growth.

If the institution in the aggregate is assessed in terms of the second conceptualization as a fourth branch of government with the primary responsibility for providing the facts and hard analyses needed for good citizenship, it is now failing and moving further and further away from a passing grade. By the start of the twenty-first century, there was a litany of well-recognized weaknesses. First, journalistic competence deteriorated, with both the public and the professional journalists finding more factual errors, greater bias, and sloppier presentation. Second, the balance of coverage moved from a significant concern with serious news toward an obsessive seeking out of political scandal and a greater focus on mayhem, natural and human-made disasters, and entertaining human interest stories.

Third, the media, often not by design, fed and fostered the worst tendencies of the public (e.g., the distrust of politicians, the distaste for politics) and politicians (polarization, personal attack). Fourth, the media had thwarted serious political leadership and reasoned compromise by eliminating the private space where leaders might seek to induce change away from the glare of a critical press and by castigating realistic attempts at negotiating differences as unprincipled sellouts. That is, the media, both by intention and inadvertence, accentuated the negative and eliminated the positive. Fifth, serious journalistic efforts have been inhibited by the industry's profit imperative that drove media organizations both to press for speed in reporting without costly verification and for sensationalism and rumor mongering. Journalism, much like the comic Rodney Dangerfield, gets no respect and is also blocked at every turn from adhering to high standards.

Sixth, politicians, operating with growing sophistication in spinning the news to present themselves favorably, had come to view journalists as easy to manipulate and declining in importance to their reelection. Seventh, the public believed that the political information and commentary pouring forth from the many media sources were less and less credible and increasingly irrelevant to their lives. Sanford put the matter succinctly in observing that a "canyon of disbelief and distrust had developed between the public and the news media."[19] The rest of this section will discuss more fully the weaknesses of the institution and the barriers to correcting them, drawing at times on recent critiques of the media by practicing and academic journalists, many of the latter having been reporters, columnists, and editors. Their insights are often set out in ways worthy of being quoted extensively, as has been the case earlier in this section and will continue to be in what follows.

From the Word to the Image

For discussion purposes, it is useful to think of a long era when the word was king followed by a period when the television image dominated the media, if we keep in mind that the dichotomy abstracts from reality in three important ways. First, in between the two periods is a time of overlap without a clear date for the shift.

Second, television is not just an image but a composite of the image accompanied at times by words, music, and other sounds from, say, a lion roaring, a pistol firing, or a building collapsing. As Kathleen Hall Jamieson has argued: "The discussion of whether pictures dominate words or words pictures is confused by its assumption that one invariably dominates the other, that music plays no role in cueing recall, and that the impact of each remains the same with repeated exposure."[20] But image is the right metaphor.

Third, the electronic revolution that spawned television has now thrown the Internet into the equation as a further complication. Much of the interactive power of the Internet, such as e-mail, is word driven, and increasingly television programs use their Web sites to provide greater depth of treatment. Still, the word of hard print and the image on the television screen offer a handy means of comparing the time when the print journalism clearly ruled the media world and the era of television's dominance to see the immense repercussions from the transformation.

During the early postwar years, when the federal government seemed to work so smoothly, an elite press corps was intertwined with top Washington officials in a relationship where both respected and trusted each other and the former treated the latter with great deference. Janeway succinctly captured the scene: "In the media stone age, the great men of government and the great men of the Washington press corps did business about the great issues of the day in an atmosphere of great trust."[21]

Two aspects of this long-ago relationship stand out. First, the mutual trust paid off for the elite press by putting them close enough to the center of power to size up officials and to engage in policy discussions. As an implicit, if not explicit, quid pro quo, the press protected politicians from scandal, be it from excessive drinking or womanizing—with President John Kennedy still the best example of the latter. The young president's extramarital affairs reached epic proportions but went unreported, while the press joined in the myth of the loving husband and father at home by the fire in Camelot. Mutual respect provided the press with opportunities to take a hard look at the character and capability of the nation's leaders in a nonadversarial setting and facilitated a healthy self-restraint in probing political leaders' personal lives.

Second, much can be criticized about this earlier relationship—from old-boy elitism to the lack of transparency. The press was overly protective of politicians' reputations and too willing to trust them on substantive issues. Getting the balance right between journalists' skepticism of and deference toward political leaders and maintaining it in a dynamic institutional setting, however, is no small feat, as will be clear from additional discussion.

The press–politician relationship changed in the mid-1960s when rising turmoil at home and abroad shattered credibility. Vietnam and

Watergate showed media organizations—both reporters and owners—at their best, courageously seeking facts and standing up to the government in its attempts to suppress embarrassing information. In Vietnam, a number of reporters, including David Halberstam of the *New York Times,* covered the undeclared war in a hostile, dangerous setting and were able to find sufficient evidence to call into question the far too rosy picture being painted by Army and Department of Defense officials of U.S. and South Vietnamese success against the North Vietnamese. This extended effort by a handful of reporters, working on the ground in Vietnam to uncover information that belied the inflated claims and enraged the powers that be, still stands as an exemplary case of the fearless pursuit of the facts under adverse, at times life-threatening, conditions by journalists committed to the highest standards of the profession.

The owners became the heroes in the highly charged 1971 encounter over the Pentagon Papers, which contained embarrassing secret information about the still ongoing, increasingly controversial Vietnam war. Daniel Ellsberg, a former Defense Department and Rand Corporation analyst, protested the war by leaking a copy of the Pentagon Papers to the *New York Times* in June 1971, and the Nixon administration responded by obtaining a court injunction stopping publication. After the *Times* appealed, and during the time that the case worked its way to the Supreme Court, Ellsberg gave the *Washington Post* another copy of the Pentagon Papers.

The timing could not have been worse for the *Post* because its stock was scheduled to go public that week. Despite the dire warnings of her business managers and lawyers not to jeopardize the stock offering, *Post* owner-publisher Katherine Graham joined the *New York Times* in defying the Nixon administration by publishing the Pentagon Papers. It was a striking act of courage. Graham's defiance of the Nixon administration could have undone the stock offering. Even more threatening, her action exposed the Post Company to retaliation by that administration through a challenge before the Federal Communications Commission to its ownership of the Washington CBS affiliate WTOP-TV, which had become the company's "cash cow."[22] Graham's high journalistic standards, rather than a concern for corporate profits, dictated her judgment.

Watergate, if anything, made the press look even better, as Bob Woodward and Carl Bernstein of the *Washington Post* over an extended period relentlessly tracked down the Nixon scandal despite both the administration's effort to stop them and early ridicule as the *Post* pursued the scandal alone. Graham again put her newspaper at risk in supporting what appeared to be a Don Quixote–like attempt by two reporters who at the time had limited credentials. Watergate, in helping to bring down the Nixon presidency, was the high point of postwar investigative political reporting. Janeway pointed out that Watergate reflected "a dramatic, if transient, power shift from officialdom to the press. . . . Pen trumped sword— or so it appeared."[23] Yet the triumph contained the seeds of its own destruction as Watergate induced far too many reporters to seek their fame by chasing after corruption, cover-ups, and questionable personal behavior by public officials. Woodward and Bernstein had unintentionally created a Frankenstein's monster—or more accurately, a host of monsters stalking public officials, as if being elected to office rendered a politician's every act suspect and stripped him or her of any rights to privacy or civil treatment.

This golden period had other key elements that are no more. The notable achievements were led by elite press organizations, which set the professional norms for the media and had long traditions of being led by family owners and publishers who sought to maintain high standards at the expense of profit maximization. No longer do the *New York Times* and *Washington Post* or a somewhat larger elite group dominate the media. These two organizations, unlike so many others, have retained family leadership and sought to retain the professional norms, although their standards also have been compromised by lowest-common-denominator journalism. It may even be that family tradition and adherence to journalistic norms as basic values are not nearly as important as the discovery that solid, in-depth reporting of hard news is in demand in a subsector of the media market. These two newspapers and a small number of other media organizations, such as the *Wall Street Journal* and CNN, that feature hard news and accurate information do occupy an important niche in the media market. Sound data and hard analyses are not endangered species, but they are definitely not what sells best in the broad media market now dominated by television, titillating scandal, and entertainment. Writing in 1983, Austin Ranney argued:

> Television as the principal source of political reality for most Americans has altered the political game profoundly, perhaps more profoundly

than all the parties' rules changes and new state and federal laws put together. . . . Many observers, including myself, believe that the advent of television is the most important change since World War II in just about every aspect of American life, and certainly in the environment in which government functions.[24]

Moving from the word to the image had begun to transform electoral politics, but only with the election of Ronald Reagan did presidential success and high approval ratings come to depend so heavily on how the president came across to the public on primetime news. Had President Kennedy served two terms, the shift might well have occurred earlier. But President Reagan's personal comfort with and skill in being stage managed offered the ideal model for the first and the most successful television president thus far.

The Wondrous Reagan Image

In *The Primetime Presidency of Ronald Reagan,* Robert Denton claimed that the critical factor in maintaining presidential popularity was "controlling the videos in the evening news" so that television has become "the primary tool and background for governing the nation."[25] Television images—not just in the case of politicians but also in general—have come to dominate competing word-driven media in creating political perceptions. The images that emanate from national and local television news programs showing the destructiveness of wars and the horrors of crimes such as murders at schools now appear to be the main factors shaping how the public perceives political reality. These sights and sounds, if accompanied by comments, can enrich the public's political vision. The danger is the extent to which the entire package, whether by design or not, will misshape the underlying political reality, which in turn may misshape policymaking. For example, what politician would be so bold as to speak the truth by pointing out that few young people are shot while at school, that the number has fallen in recent years, and that increases in security outlays would be better spent elsewhere in protecting this age group?

Nowhere is this phenomenon better illustrated that by Reagan's uncanny capacity to lift appearance above reality, political spectacle above policy. Bruce Miroff captured an essential aspect of the Reagan presidency in calling it a "triumph of spectacle" and noted that "even the most egregious of these failures—public exposure of the disastrous covert policy of selling arms to Iran and diverting some of the profits from the sales to the Nicaraguan Contras—proved to be only a temporary blow to the political fortunes of the most spectacular president in decades."[26] Television, with its compelling presentation of the ever optimistic, always confident president, became the ideal vehicle for a politics of unreality that could draw Americans away from substantive political, social, and economic concerns.

The main casualty of the masterful manipulation of media was the reality of Reagan administration incompetence. In discussing the savings and loan and Iran-Contra scandals, Suzanne Garment, American Enterprise Institute scholar and former Washington columnist for the *Wall Street Journal,* has made clear that the often self-righteous media people were strikingly susceptible to the cover-ups:

> In each of these cases the great wrongs were those of politics and policy and should have produced a huge scandal by virtue of the incompetence involved. Instead, we seemed—and still seem—able to focus only on scandals of intention, moral failing, and criminal liability. In this sense, scandal hunting since Watergate has almost certainly made our government worse instead of better; in our pursuit of more virtuous politics and government we have fallen into a deep trap.[27]

That is, the issue became private virtue, as when the media focused on President Bill Clinton's sexual escapades, not public virtue, as when a president lies to mislead the electorate on his policy efforts.

President Reagan succeeded in substituting image-dominated propaganda for governance. The cardinal guideline for the Reagan handlers could have read: "It's managing the image, Stupid." And manage it they did. Never before had primetime television news been so adroitly manipulated. Yet success ultimately depended on Reagan's persona, which transformed the unbelievable into the believable. In his polemic *Culture of Complaint,* Robert Hughes made the strongest charge against Reagan and his television manipulation:

> The public face of politics, and especially of the Presidency, was radically overhauled to suit a public attention-span abbreviated by

TV. . . . In a sense, the President was TV—the world's most successful anchorman. Did he forget things? No matter: TV is there to help you forget. Did he lie? Oh well, never mind. . . . With somnambulistic efficiency, Reagan educated America down to his level. He left the country a little stupider in 1988 than it had been in 1980, and a lot more tolerant of lies, because his style of image-presentation cut the connective tissue of argument between ideas and hence fostered the defeat of thought itself.[28]

Writing in 1993, Hughes caught the most striking similarity between Presidents Clinton and George W. Bush: their use of distortion as a major weapon to protect their image and sell their policy proposals. And Reagan had paved the way.

Scandal and the Attack Culture

The media's role in misshaping American politics and undercutting the key institutions of the political system has been most visible in its fixation on political scandal. In the latest and most extreme version that emerged in the 1990s—the "attack culture"—journalists have had an important role in extended, all-out efforts to destroy politicians' careers, as exemplified by the cases of Clinton and Gingrich. Political scientist Larry Sabato titled his highly critical 1991 book *Feeding Frenzy;* in the same year, Garment called her harsh account of the media *Scandal.*[29] These and other authors have maintained that the media now practice "pack" or "junkyard" journalism, featuring a self-righteous search for flaws in less-the-perfect candidates, and "go after a wounded politician like sharks in a feeding frenzy."[30]

This brand of reporting evidences journalism's flight from policy governance to personal misbehavior and fuels the public's view of politics as a within-the-Beltway phenomenon not closely tied to the lives of ordinary citizens. Rosenstiel has made the key point that the media could no longer discriminate private from public, so journalists dug up almost any information and left the public to determine what was relevant, acting as if their product itself had no independent impact.[31] This jumbling together, which has eliminated a reasonable boundary between politicians' public and private lives, has led journalists to search for dirty linen rather than focus on political candidates' public experiences that would provide evidence for analyzing leadership capability.

The result of this excessive concern with personal character is that the public receives less and less sound, relevant information on two critical factors—public character and governance competence—needed by citizens to evaluate political candidates' potential for successful leadership. In the case of presidential candidates, journalists should inform voters about both the direction in which the candidates want to take the nation and the available sound evidence for considering whether they have demonstrated the leadership skills and commitment needed to accomplish their objectives.

The excessive pursuit of scandal reinforced the unwarranted claim that personal character is the critical element in future presidential performance. In a late 1999 column, Garry Wills argued that the notion of the president as moral role model stressed by writers like Gail Sheehy ("a self-styled character cop") and William Bennett ("the virtuecrat") continues to mislead voters about what it takes to be a strong leader: "The test of a leader is not temperament or virtue, but the ability to acquire followers. . . .Such leaders connect with others and influence them. What disqualifies a leader is the kind of flaw that would turn away followers. . . . [Forget] . . . theories on presidential character. Look at the real question: competence."[32] The media have much overplayed the importance of moral character. Moreover, the pressures to gain readership and not to be scooped on a breaking scandal can create a vicious circle in which rumor feeds rumor as the pack of reporters hounds a wounded politician at every turn.

In pursuing this attack culture, the media joined with the Washington political establishment in a corrosive relationship that weakened the connection of both institutions to the public. Kovach and Rosenstiel observed perceptively: "The attack culture could not exist without the press. The press, however, could not have engaged in it without the politicians. It has become their co-dependency, their self-destructive addiction."[33] The media's vicious investigations in the 1990s, however, garnered no praise, as had been the case with the earlier ones that exposed cover-ups in Vietnam and in the Nixon administration. In recent years, journalists have too frequently substituted unverified information and rumors for hard-nosed reporting or have become fixated on questions of personal character. Such efforts have damaged the credibility of both the attackers and their targets.

Politicians, as would be expected, have fought back by calling into question journalists' competence and motives. As to the former, evidence of sloppy journalism often was not hard to find, whereas motives were easily challenged because of the nastiness and relentlessness of the journalists' attacks. Or when being sharply criticized or in preemptory strikes to avert or blunt expected attacks, politicians employed "spin" to put themselves in a more favorable light, a practice taken to an incredibly high level by the Clinton administration. This joint destructiveness of the national political institutions unleashed by the attack culture during the last half of the 1990s distinguished that period from the last fifty years of the postwar era. The media suffered as much as any of the other main actors in the American political system from addictive involvement in joint destructiveness, as retaliatory efforts by those who were attacked by media organizations further reduced the media's already low institutional credibility.

Talk Shows as Total Political War

The longtime media correspondent of the *Washington Post* Howard Kurtz ended his book *Hot Air* with this observation: "America has become a talk show nation, a boob-tube civilization, a run-at-the-mouth culture in which anyone can say anything at any time as long as they pull some ratings."[34] There are still talk shows on which participants are not confrontational and seek to provide accurate information and reasonable analysis. The leader is the venerable *Washington Week in Review,* first seen on television in 1967. But it is not the model for many of the newer television shows that blend questionable information and analysis with a confrontational format.

The most striking feature of the confrontational television talk shows such as *The Capital Gang* and *The McLaughlin Group,* on which media pundits do battle, is that purposeful polarization is the driving force. Not only are the participants chosen well to the left or to the right of the political center, but they generally push their positions to the extreme without setting out reasonable reservations. Data are likely to be twisted to make points. Shouting and surliness are the tools of choice. The middle ground is to be avoided at all costs. Nor is any effort made to work toward a reasonable point of agreement. The battle is among heavyweights swinging for the knockout punch. This format is followed even though the pundits may be well-established journalists who would not think of such unprofessional behavior in crafting their written pieces. But they are not doing a column; they are engaged in staged entertainment.

Talk show participants may be highly professional in the same sense that the skilled fakery of professional wrestlers provides exciting entertainment that keeps audiences coming back for more. The best of the wrestlers-cum-actors seem to be so proficient that viewers believe the mayhem to be real—high praise indeed and likely of no harm, if some viewers know they are being entertained by skilled people who make the staged event look realistic and if others think it is a real battle. But when viewers believe that participants with their media credentials are playing it straight, the misapprehension is hardly benign. Polarized politics is given the media seal of approval by well-known and respected journalists. Distorted facts and slanted analyses are swallowed whole. Alternatively, many viewers are well aware that the no-holds-barred encounter of the pundits is really analogous to a wrestling match, hardly the image the profession wants to have. Ironically, the journalists may gain through wide exposure, leading to increased earnings and prestige through such opportunities as lucrative speaking engagements. It is a special form of hara-kiri in which the dagger miraculously passes through the journalist without a trace and strikes the institution.

Talk radio at its worst far exceeded television with, to quote the hard-line Republican Mary Matalin, "'the nutcakes like Gordon Liddy,'" who had served almost five years in prison as a Watergate conspirator and reveled in his killer image.[35] Far from the mainstream were a number of right-wing extremists much more off-the-wall than Liddy in their convoluted conspiracy theories, their obsession with one-world government that would destroy American freedom, and their denial of the Holocaust. Kurtz posed the question of whether talk radio had the responsibility to correct misinformation or give the people attacked on the programs an opportunity to respond and replied that, to his dismay, "many programs have settled on an anything-goes approach, leaving it to listeners to separate the rhetorical wheat from the chaff. The notion that obvious untruths or unproven gossip should not be disseminated over the airwaves is derided as an attempt at censorship. Talk radio, it seems, does not play by the everyday rules of journalism."[36]

This segment of the media industry is not alone in the lack of professional norms, but simply one of the worst offenders. The industry itself in the 1990s had become much more encompassing, and in this wide band were many who now could claim the title of journalist but did not operate under a code of conduct that stressed verified information, error correction, and fairness to those being criticized. Once the commitment to checking out the accuracy of information and grounding analysis in hard facts ceased to restrain media practitioners, it was a short, straight road to the scandal mongering and politics of distortion that came to dominate the inside-the-Beltway environment. *Washington Post* columnist Jim Hoagland captured the new mentality succinctly: "In Bill Clinton's Washington, truth is not always an important element."[37] Much too often, rules and standards ceased to apply in battles fought with distorted words and images.

In the Clinton years, politics became war by another means. The most damaging battles pitted politicians against each other or politicians against the media organizations and individual journalists, with all being fair during the eight years of war. The encounter in shifting from fisticuffs under Marquis of Queensberry rules to no-hold-barred alley fighting often benefited individual participants, but the institutions and the public were heavy losers. Although the historic role of the press to provide the sound information and critiques that the public needs to scrutinize and evaluate elected officials created tensions and an occasional casualty, the effort had been conducted within a well-established framework. The participants respected each other and interacted civilly, with the journalists expected to follow their norms of accuracy and fairness.

In the case of presidents, they and their staffs had long tried to present the leader in a favorable light and to downplay potentially damaging acts by the administration. White House journalists, in turn, sought both to expose inflated claims and to seek out what presidents would like to hide. The setting changed markedly for the White House press from that of insiders, who respected presidents and protected their image for a long period of time that ended with the Kennedy assassination, to that of outsiders ready to engage in sharp questioning and probing analyses. But even this new environment of more aggressive journalism turned out to be closer to the approach it replaced than to the uncivil, demeaning confrontational style the dominated the Clinton era.

The viscous new version of this interaction that began in the Reagan years and reached its full flowering during the Clinton administration differed from the past in several ways. First, the continuing hostile climate between the Washington media and politicians created a setting in which the two parties neither trusted nor respected each other and sought to score mortal wounds by any means at hand. Kurtz wrote of the journalists in the White House Briefing Room: "They were interested in conflict, in drama, in behind-the-scenes maneuvering, in pulling back the curtain and exposing the Oz-like manipulations of the Clinton crowd. It was their job to report what the president said, but increasingly they saw it as their mission to explain why he said it and what seedy political purpose he was trying to accomplish along the way."[38] Although not every Clinton move derived from a devious plot, as some journalists were prone to think, the president deserved the Machiavellian label as he and his aides undertook to protect his image without much concern for honesty or the rules of engagement.

Janeway, in a strikingly harsh observation, wrote of "the problematic environmental context in which a flawed and troubled journalistic culture was attempting to maintain a footing against an even more corrupted, even more manipulative, even more dead-end, even more cynical political profession."[39] Even discounting for Janeway's anger, it is true that neither of the institutions deserved much sympathy or respect as both of them heedlessly damaged the other's credibility while sullying their own reputation in the effort. That the two would continue this lose–lose game for so long is dramatic testimony to the extraordinary level of animosity shaping Washington politics in the 1990s.

Harsh Criticism from Within

The diverse media industry in the 1990s seemed hell-bent on destroying itself from within as the primary credible source of the political coverage needed for the exercise of civic virtue. Worse yet, the destructive behavior both damaged the credibility of the presidency and Congress and decreased their institutional capability by impeding strong leadership and sensible compromise. Grossman has pointed out that some segments of the public see any behind-the-scenes compromise as a sellout of a leader's principles and observed:

> This attitude is frequently reinforced by reporters, often so intent on appearing not to be "used" and on showing off their insiders' insight,

that the first thing they do is cast doubt on motivations and treat any compromise as a political retreat or defeat. One consequence, ironically, is that while television enhances both the visibility and the "bully pulpit" of the presidency by keeping the president on the screen front and center, it also makes it increasingly difficult for presidents to lead.[40]

The media's tendency to cast the reasonable outcome of bipartisan agreement as a sellout both undermines national leadership and feeds the public's cynicism that all compromises are crassly political.

Journalists, in prematurely attacking compromises, also violate one of their key professional norms by shirking their continuing responsibility to probe deeply into how and why the agreement came about so as to provide the public with a fact-based, thoughtful assessment. The press can help the nation's citizens make a sensible judgment and strengthen the political process by spelling out if a president is on firm ground in claiming that a final negotiated agreement shows his strong leadership in going beyond what could be reasonably expected in the face of fierce opposition, even though it does far less than he had called for in his campaign. If the press fails to do so, it can be criticized not only for poor service to the public but also for acting against its own long-run self-interest. As Kovach and Rosenstiel have cogently pointed out:

> In ways that most in journalism have yet to comes to grips with, the press today has a long-range economic stake in compromise and cooperation, a stake that the media's current investment in fragmentation and polarization undermines. . . . Perhaps the press's most fundamental purpose is to both educate the public about where the points of common ground are and to be a forum for that cooperation.[41]

It has been a formidable task as cooperation and compromise disappeared in the House after the Gingrich revolution and declined markedly in the Senate and the presidency. The national press, however, failed miserably during this period in executing this basic function and stands as culpable for pushing in the opposite direction in its emphasis on disputed terrain, not common ground. The media's destructive shortsightedness reinforced the growing political fragmentation and ensuing polarization that created often insurmountable barriers to reasoned bipartisan compromises.

James Fallows has succinctly set out journalism's two basic functions as being "the main tool we have for keeping the world's events in perspective ... [and] the main source of agreed-upon facts we can use in public decisions."[42] Above all, journalism can provide the nation's citizens with the verified information needed for considering public policymaking and put into broad perspective the political and socioeconomic dimensions relevant for making public choices. The mixed media culture failed miserably in meeting these goals. Profit-maximizing owners, scoop-driven editors, scandal-fixated reporters, and entertainment-oriented television journalists all were eager participants in the crime. The in-depth coverage during several months of the Lewinsky scandal provided a smoking gun with clear fingerprints in abundance.

As the highly respected journalist David Halberstam wrote in his preface to *Warp Speed,* in which Kovach and Rosenstiel condemned the media's treatment of that scandal:

> The past year [1998] has been, I think, the worst year for American journalism since I entered the profession forty-four years ago. ... What is disturbing about the bad odor of journalism today is that, I think, many of the critics are right, and the people who have been performing as journalists in the past year have in fact seriously trivialized the profession. ... Like many of my colleagues, I think that the proportion of the coverage given the story—compared to the news budget—is hopelessly out of synch, and that the standards for verifications, so critical to serious and fair reporting, have fallen dramatically.[43]

Although 1998—the most horrible year for journalism's reputation—stands as a distinct low point, it is not an aberration.

Summing Up

Halberstam's brief, highly critical observations set out in his preface for *Warp Speed* appear to encapsulate the consensus view at the end of the 1990s of how far journalists, editors, and owners had strayed from professional norms. The institution stands condemned, with the most eloquent and insightful criticism coming from those with long experience as journalists. The basic issue is how the industry can regain sufficient institutional competence to make it again credible, recognizing that Humpty-Dumpty simply may not be able to be put back together again in anything like its former configuration. The most daunting of tasks is to work out a means of changing the incredibly diverse creature now in place, which requires determining both a feasible institutional structure and a realistic implementation approach in the context of the current political environment. It is far beyond the scope of this book to try to spell out that structure and its implementation, but I agree with Halberstam that information verified by widely approved techniques is "critical to serious and fair reporting." The commitment to rigorous verification is a— perhaps *the*—defining mark of professional journalism.

If journalists and their organizations fail to fulfill their basic responsibility to inform the public on national policy issues, the institution either will remain on the intensive care list or escape it by abandoning its public functions and fully transforming itself into a twenty-four-hours-a-day, seven-days-a-week segment of the entertainment industry. Either status—a sick industry still seeking to inform the public on important public issues or a healthy one providing entertainment that attracts a large following—leaves unanswered the institutional question of how to provide U.S. citizens with the facts and the perspective needed for a reasonable consideration of public policy issues and an informed choice of their representatives.

Finally, it is useful to touch briefly on the media's relationships with the other institutions and key actors in Washington during the years of Reaganism. No one benefited more from the media than did Reagan. Television offered the ideal vehicle for selling the man and his political philosophy, making the media a significant contributor to the rise of Reaganism. But overall, the media may have done presidents and other politicians more harm than good through its unending search for scandal and the self-righteousness of journalists that damaged and often destroyed political careers.

The media also had a huge part in the explosive rise in campaign outlays as costly television commercials became the weapon of choice when politicians sought to reach large numbers of citizens. Corporate America gained great influence in Washington by bankrolling so much of these media costs for politicians. As for the federal agencies, the media's lack of interest in them left much of the public unaware of the agencies' mounting problems under Reaganism. The media's greatest disservice may have been its failure to inform the public as its low-level output increasingly became entertainment instead of news. In sum, the media were heavily engaged in an interactive process with other actors and attained a key place in the gang of culprits that did so much damage to representative democracy and the institutions meant to sustain it.

eight

The Will of the People

At its inception, the American Republic allowed only propertied white males to vote (about a fifth of the adult population); but in so doing, it became the first nation to grant ordinary citizens, as opposed to a privileged class of aristocrats, the power to choose those who make the laws governing their country. The new concept had at its core the revolutionary idea that sovereignty rested in the people, not in a particular government. As Gordon Wood has argued, the Federalists went beyond earlier theorists who had asserted that government power derived from the people: "Instead, they [the Federalists] were saying that sovereignty remained always with the people and that government was only a temporary and limited agency of the people—out to the various government officials, so to speak, on a short-term, always recallable loan."[1] Power to the people in this sense carried with it great responsibility for their recallable loan.

Representative Democracy in the Twentieth Century

Having looked earlier at the Madisonian model of representative democracy at its inception, it is useful to take a brief tour of twentieth-century thinking on representative democracy, beginning with progressivism and then jumping to the 1990s. The purpose is not to summarize current thought on representative democracy but rather to consider (1) the philosophy of the Progressive Party as the political party most committed to a strong version of representative democracy and (2) two well-stated modern notions of representative democracy that still incorporate the fundamental notions of the Founders as the basis for asking whether their conceptions remain realistic for the twenty-first century. The starting place for this discussion is the previously discussed key relationships between citizens and their members of Congress, one at the time the electorate votes and the other during the period when senators and representatives are in Washington.

The Progressive Era

The Progressive Party stressed that the electorate must engage in active citizenship, underscoring that the legitimacy of citizens' political power had to be earned through the hard work of acquiring political knowledge and employing it in deliberations to expand and refine that knowledge. If the needed effort was not forthcoming, citizens did not deserve political power. The Progressives were harder taskmasters than the Founders in demanding that popular sovereignty be earned, as Peter Levine has pointed out in his critique of the Progressive Party's 1924 nominee for president, Wisconsin senator Robert La Follette Sr., and such prominent supporters as Fiorello La Guardia, Lincoln Steffens, Louis Brandeis, Jane Adams, and John Dewey.

La Follette's statement at the 1910 Republican National Convention identified the core principle of his political philosophy: "Constitutions, statutes, and all the other complex details of government are but instruments to carry out the will of the people, and when they fail . . . they must be changed to . . . express *the well formulated judgement* and the will of the people. For over all and above all, and greater than all, and expressing the supreme sovereignty of all, are the people."[2] That statement mirrors Abraham Lincoln's "government of the people, by the people, for the people" set out in his Gettysburg Address. At the same time, La Follette had qualified his basic concept with a critical proviso captured in the italicized words of his quotation: The people's will took on legitimacy only if their deliberations had yielded a "well formulated judgement."

Like the Madisonian model, La Follette stressed the responsibilities of both the people and the elected officials in the extended political process underlying representative democracy. The electorate is obligated to interact so as to form reasoned opinions; members of Congress in turn are duty bound to use the people's "well formulated judgements." La Follette and his followers believed that the people's well-formulated judgments should guide policy deliberations by both Congress and the executive branch. At the same time, Levine, who argued that La Follette's ideas remain relevant for today, still warned: "It is a mistake to give people power without first asking them to deliberate, for only deliberation can tell us who should be empowered and how. Talk without power is empty; power without talk is blind."[3] The Progressive thinkers who supported La Follette in 1924 saw sound information as the crucial base needed to support the people's deliberations. Citizens had to have the political knowledge needed for developing the concrete dimensions of their popular will. Only informed deliberations could legitimize their power.

A Hard-Nosed Political Science View of Representative Democracy

Two teams of political scientists have provided rigorous current versions of representative democracy, with the knowledge–power relationship being important to each one. The first team, political scientists Michael Delli Carpini and Scott Keeter, have observed:

> [Our] book is an exploration of what Americans know—and don't know—about politics. Driving this exploration is a deceptively simple argument: that democracy functions best when its citizens are politically informed. Factual knowledge on such topics as the institutions and processes of government, current economic and social conditions, the major issues of the day, and the stands of political leaders on those issues assist citizens in discerning their individual and group interests, in connecting their interests to broader notions of the public good, and in effectively expressing these views through political participation. In addition, the more equitably information is distributed among citizens, the more likely it is that the actions of the government will reflect the public interest and, thus, that the public will be supportive of those actions. In short, a broadly and equitably informed citizenry helps assure a democracy that is both responsive and responsible.[4]

The authors' statement makes two main points. First, a high level of information is required to attain proficiency. Their listing of what needs to be known is both wide ranging in its call for information and challenging in the competence needed to interpret that information.

Second, a broad and equitable distribution of political knowledge among the citizenry is optimum for determining the public interest in America's representative democracy. Adequate knowledge for intelligent voting among a relatively small subset of the population and political ignorance in the main for ordinary citizens is elitist—even if it leads to wise choices. Moreover, in today's political environment, where the use of political misinformation has become the norm, the lack of political knowledge by most of the electorate can undermine responsive and responsible democracy. Delli Carpini and Keeter, like the Progressive Party, prove to be demanding taskmasters for the voting public.

In *Politicians Don't Pander,* the second team of political scientists, Lawrence Jacobs and Robert Shapiro, wrote: "The health of democracy rests, we argue, on responsible policymakers and an informed and knowledgeable citizenry that is engaged in rational and critical discussions about government."[5] These two authors expressed the concern that politicians have shifted away from centrist opinion, as indicated by the median citizen in the distribution of public opinion, and now look toward the views of highly active, ideological political party members who have more extreme, less changeable opinions than the centrists. Jacobs and Shapiro observed: "Without the immediate threat of elections, we expect politicians to perceive benefits in pursuing policy goals and discounting centrist opinion under conditions of rising political polarization, incumbency advantage, interest group proliferation, individualization of power within Congress, and intensified interbranch conflict."[6]

Such a statement apparently rests on the assumption that the average citizen has strong specific views about particular policy issues. The highly regarded veteran political pollster Daniel Yankelovich pointed out in his review of Jacobs and Shapiro's book that citizens generally do not formulate sharp views on policies on their own "without active leadership."[7] Except during elections, the critical period specifically excluded by Jacobs and Shapiro, the public's opinion is likely to be ill formed on most issues and amenable to change through the concerted efforts of political leaders.

Given that poll after poll has shown the public's lack of even rudimentary political information, Robert Shapiro and Benjamin Page, writing in 1992, provided a statistical explanation for how widespread citizen ignorance could turn into an informed judgment: "Collective public opinion (and, by extension, collective political participation) can be rational even if much of the individual opinion or behavior underlying it is not because the random views of uninformed citizens cancel each other out, leaving the true choices of more informed citizens to carry the day."[8] Collective rationality may emerge, but the result is hardly a tribute to broadly based democracy. After all, the uninformed voters avoid doing harm only because they cancel each other out. One cheer for democracy; three cheers for the law of large numbers. The statistical argument, moreover, had its Achilles' heel: *Large-scale voter ignorance means that concerted efforts to deceive the public can distort their opinion.* Page and Shapiro had raised a red flag about such political deception in their 1992 book, and Jacobs and Shapiro appeared even more troubled by it: "Manipulation and deception were routine in the 1990s.... Political success, politicians calculate, goes to the faction that most completely suffocates criticism and sets the terms of public debate."[9]

With the exception of George H. W. Bush's presidency, the last two decades of the twentieth century were marked by White House spin masters in the saddle. And the new millennium promised more of the same, as the Princeton University economist and *New York Times* columnist Paul Krugman asked rhetorically in discussing the selling of President George W. Bush's tax plan: "Has any previous administration been quite this shameless about misrepresenting the actual content of its own economic plan?"[10]

Bush's propaganda campaign for his 2001 tax proposal took presidential deceit to a level never before reached for economic policy. He went from city to city to sell his plan directly to ordinary citizens through a flagrant effort to mislead them about the key aspects of a major policy that was against their best interests, thereby grossly distorting the most important domestic policy legislation in at least two decades. Such concerted efforts at distortion mean that the statistical argument concerning the law of large numbers, whereby the random views of uninformed citizens cancel each other out, is unlikely to hold in the current era of incessant political propaganda. Generally speaking, when distorted political propaganda is widespread, the political ignorance of most of the public and the political knowledge of a well-informed minority of citizens will no longer sum up to collective wisdom.

A Little Political Knowledge Goes a Long Way

Whether the American electorate has sufficient knowledge to meet the requirements for good citizenship depends on the answers to two questions: How much sound political information, commentary, and deliberations do voters need to make informed choices in national elections and to reach reasoned opinions on the major policy issues facing the nation? How willing and able are citizens to cope with the plethora of data and commentary now so rapidly disseminated in national elections?

The English biologist and writer Thomas Henry Huxley observed in 1877: "If a little knowledge is dangerous, where is the man who has so much as to be out of danger?" Highly regarded specialists with impeccable credentials may reach highly questionable conclusions. Nobel laureates can look at the same set of data and arrive at opposite interpretations, in part because key information is unavailable. Yet Huxley notwithstanding, it does make sense to consider the other side of his question concerning the minimum level of knowledge needed for political literacy, recognizing that the level obviously varies with the question or issue at hand.

In pursuing this question, a distinction needs to be made between political information and political knowledge. The latter requires an understanding of the meaning and implications of political facts. Although political information and knowledge are not independent of each other, separating them conceptually is critical. I will argue that the capability component, as policies over time have grown increasingly complex and interrelated, frequently requires more concepts and tools than are likely to be in the kit of most citizens. Others maintain that Americans do know enough to meet their obligations of citizenship. None are as bullish as citizens themselves, as is shown by a typical response from a 1999 survey by the Center on Public Attitudes. In their answers, more than three-fourths of the survey sample thought that the public as a whole, rather than Democratic or Republican officials, was "'most likely to show the greatest wisdom on questions of what government should do.'"[11] Scholars of American politics also make the case, and this section considers two recent efforts.

In *The Good Citizen,* Michael Schudson seeks a sensible minimum effort that will allow citizens to cope with the mountains of sound and questionable political information and commentary pouring forth in the electronic revolution. He argues that "the obligation of citizens to know enough to participate intelligently in governmental affairs be understood as a monitorial obligation," and he thus elaborates on this concept:

> Monitorial citizens scan (rather than read) the informational environment . . . [engaging] in environmental surveillance more than informa-

> tion-gathering. . . . Print journalists regularly criticize broadcast media for being only a headline service, but a headline service is what, in the first instance, citizens require. ("The redcoats are coming!" said Paul Revere as he rode through every Middlesex village and farm, apparently not embarrassed by the brevity of his sound bite.)[12]

Schudson points out that the residents considered themselves British and would have been mystified if Revere had called out the version so many of us learned in school. The good (British) people of Middlesex surely knew what Revere's brief warning meant and what needed to be done to respond to it. Whether the same can be said for the readers of newspaper headlines or the slim coverage on the six o'clock television news is much less clear.

Schudson deems it sufficient for monitorial citizens to be defensive, which translates into leaving much to the specialists and delving in occasionally to check an issue, rather than being "full-time political back-packers."[13] Ordinary citizens cannot be expected to do all of the information gathering and analysis on their own and would be foolish not to utilize experts' political information and commentary. But being a good consumer is not easy. Picking the right experts demands the capacity to evaluate their output, and that task has never been more difficult than today, as experts spring forth everywhere ready to justify any argument. Schudson himself appears to go well beyond his minimum demands when he underscores the value for citizens in their political efforts in collective deliberation and in working together.[14]

But such endeavors are likely to bear fruit only when the participants have enough political information and knowledge for constructive discussion and action. The cry of a modern-day Paul Revere on the six o'clock news that "The Bush tax cut is coming!" hardly seems sufficient to alert people to the potential dangers to them and to the nation and indicate what they need to do. Schudson's monitorial obligation appears to much understate the political knowledge needed to meet the demands either of the political democracy he espouses or the specifications for representative democracy set out by the Progressives and the two teams of political scientists.

In *Everything You Think You Know about Politics . . . and Why You're Wrong,* Kathleen Hall Jamieson, dean of the Annenberg School for Communication at the University of Pennsylvania, claimed: "Although many studies have shown Americans' level of general political knowledge is low [she cited Delli Carpini and Keeter], our survey during the 1996 election indicates that by the end of a campaign, voters were able to accurately place the candidates on a wide variety of issue positions."[15] The survey showed that most people knew the major candidates for president and vice president and whether the incumbent Democratic president, former Republican senator Bob Dole, both, or neither supported such issues as expanding family leave, raising funding for job programs, making it more difficult for women to have an abortion, and a 15 percent across-the-board tax decrease.[16]

Jamieson also found that tax cuts and school vouchers confused voters: "In these two cases, the cognitive shortcuts on which voters would ordinarily rely were an unreliable guide. Republicans should be expected to cut taxes; [Bill] Clinton was promising this as well. Republicans are expected to support vouchers—but Clinton's support for 'choice' probably blurred the party distinction."[17]

These cognitive shortcuts in Jamieson's evaluation of the voters' political knowledge appeared to work only when the president or the former senator continued to follow the traditional party positions. Yet candidates increasingly position themselves close to each other and the political center to confuse voters. In the 1996 election, those surveyed often could not distinguish the extent to which the two tax cuts differed or how President Clinton's support for choice (charter schools) varied from Dole's voucher proposal. Despite such limitations, Jamieson claimed: "The bottom line in 1996, then, was that . . . voters learned a great deal about the central issues that mattered in their lives. . . . Indeed, one might even conclude in the tentative manner conventionalized in this cynical age that the evidence we have marshaled justifies optimism."[18]

Such optimism is unwarranted—unless the bar for good citizenship is set extremely low. Consider briefly the sample surveys employed over the years to assess the level of voters' political information. First, accurate scoring requires carefully worded questions that speak to the voters' stock of straightforward political facts, such as the names of the Republican and Democratic vice presidential candidates, not their capacity to analyze complex information. Second, surveys often indicate that what people thought they knew turned out to be wrong, such as believing that nonmilitary foreign aid is one of the biggest expenditures in the federal budget (it is less than 1 percent of the total budget). The argument can be made that it is simply not reasonable to expect the ordinary citizen to know the percentage of the federal budget that goes for such aid or that expenditures on Social Security, Medicare, defense, and interest on the national debt account for roughly 80 percent of the yearly budget. The nagging question remains as to how voters can determine whether a candidate's budget proposal, such as a major tax cut, makes sense for the future if they have no idea of what the current budget looks like.

The Primary Factors Leading to Political Ignorance

In this era of policy complexity and sophisticated political distortions, the American electorate lacks sufficient political information and analytic capacity to be responsible citizens, either as individuals or in the aggregate. This is not a claim that voters are fools but rather that they do not do the needed homework for what may be rational reasons from an individual perspective in the current political environment. Four main factors push citizens toward political ignorance. First, Americans labor 350 more hours a year than the average European and even spend more hours on the job than the workaholic Japanese.[19] Harried citizens may see the effort to acquire political knowledge as both detrimental to their careers and a relatively low claim on their tight time schedule.

The other three factors have already been introduced. Second, Americans often see themselves as more on top of the political facts and issues than they actually are. Third, the current policy complexity demands more knowledge than most citizens have. Fourth, Washington politicians are increasingly willing to employ sophisticated means to mislead the voters. For purposes of exposition, each factor will be considered separately, but the four likely are interrelated and often feed off each other. For example, the limited effort by citizens to acquire political knowledge encourages political propaganda, and the spreading of this false and misleading information and commentary adds to the difficulty of understanding complex issues.

A Matter of Time

Even though numerous American families in the 1990s earned significantly higher wages, they increased their work hours rather than opting for more leisure. One possible reason that this trade-off of work for leisure has not happened is that people seek status by spending their additional income on more costly goods and services: The Timex is replaced by the Rolex.

Dramatic changes in the job market also can help to explain the greater work effort. Individuals shift jobs frequently for faster advancement, whereas firms now quickly downsize their workforce in their increasingly intense search for higher earnings. President Clinton's first-term secretary of labor, Robert Reich, is among the growing number of analysts emphasizing the less secure job market of the globalized, information economy: "The faster the economy *changes* . . . the harder it is for people to be confident of *what any of us will earn* next year or even next month, what they will be doing, where they will be doing it. As a result, our lives are less predictable."[20] The greater job uncertainty can make the individual's effort at being a good citizen appear to be increasingly costly.

University of Michigan visiting professor Richard Craig found that even though only 7 percent of his extremely bright junior and senior students could name both Michigan senators, they were unconcerned. One student, somewhat offended at being quizzed on politics, asked: "When is any of this stuff going to matter in my career?"[21] These elite students wanted an education that would provide the kit of tools and techniques needed for well-paid, highly specialized jobs that put them on the fast track to economic success. They also felt that they lacked the time to focus on citizenship and were unclear as to why they should. The elite students were not simply selfish souls but perceived correctly that the job market demanded sophisticated skills and that these high-powered tools and techniques loom particularly large when graduates seek all-important initial fast-track positions. After graduating, the long hours of work needed for individual advancement could still keep them from exercising their political responsibilities. Craig asked: "But if our most promising young people have no appreciation for why democracy is worth preserving, how will they know it is threatened?"[22] The likely answer is that they will not know and will swell the ranks of the citizens who see the issue as unimportant to their lives or else assume that American democracy is able to flourish with only a minimum of political knowledge.

More Confidence than Knowledge

Voters typically exhibit great confidence in their knowledge in presidential elections. The Pew Research Center for the People and the Press's post-election poll conducted November 10–12, 2000, among 1,113 voters reported: "Fully 83% of voters say they learned enough . . . about the candidates and the issues to make an informed choice."[23] The reasons for confidence are not hard to find. First is the lavish praise of the people's wisdom. Most self-serving is that which politicians ladle out for the perceptiveness of the people as they race back to their states at frequent intervals to hear from their constituents. Even when students of American politics recognize the public's lack of knowledge, they still seem loath to strongly criticize this ignorance. To do so appears arrogant and elitist.

The tendency is to follow V. O. Key's maxim set out in *The Responsible Electorate* "that voters are no fools." But Key's study treated the years 1936–60, ending with Dwight Eisenhower's administration. Even then, Key immediately qualified his judgment by observing: "In the large the electorate behaves about as rationally and responsibly as we should expect, given the clarity of the alternatives presented to it and the character of the information available to it."[24]

Although the political environment in which the clarity of the alternatives and the character of the information play out today as compared with 1960 could hardly be more different, Key's "no fools" argument seems to have taken on a life of its own. Amid the praise, it is small wonder that the people believe in their own wisdom and the superiority of their choices to those of federal officials. Reinforcing their confidence is their fundamental faith in the superiority of the Democratic Ideal. If American democracy remains the light unto the world, citizens themselves must be doing their job. And who will say that it is not the emperor but the people who have no clothes on?

Policy Complexity and Propaganda

The increases in the complexity of policies and associated trade-offs and in the amount of misinformation are here considered together because the two are increasingly intertwined. Greater complexity opens the door wider for the undertaking of sophisticated misinformation efforts; the latter contribute to the barriers blocking the understanding of the implications of policies. Nowhere is the interaction between misinformation and complexity clearer than in President George W. Bush's proposal for an income tax cut, which he laid out in his February 27, 2001, nationally televised address to Congress.

The Bush plan is particularly revealing as to (1) the level of complexity in a policy issue that is vitally important to most citizens; (2) the increasing tendency to use misinformation in a heated, partisan controversy over a proposed policy; and (3) the interaction of propaganda and complexity that begets greater complexity. A vicious circle has emerged. The greater the underlying policy complexity, the greater the vulnerability of the public to misinformation; the greater the amount of misinformation, the greater the complexity. What stands out is how much sound political information and in-depth knowledge the president's tax-cut proposal demanded for citizens to assess its benefits and costs amid the plethora of misinformation and distorted commentary.

Caveat emptor has become the only sensible guide in today's highly partisan political environment, where extreme policy spin is the rule, not the exception. Being skeptical, however, only goes so far. In the case of the Bush tax-cut plan, the skeptic still needed enough political information and knowledge to sort out sound from questionable numbers and actual misinformation and to assess the quality of the proposal's claims.

A most disquieting development is that policy complexity has grown to the level at which just a little more citizen political information and knowledge will not do. The relevant policy issues, such as those raised by the Bush tax proposal, often demand a wide range of information and considerable capability to sort out fact from fiction. In the case of the Bush plan, the central issue concerned the fairness of the distribution of the tax cuts among the upper 10 percent of income earners, particularly the top 1 percent, and the rest of the American population. In assessing fairness, responsible citizens could have found useful such data as those showing (1) the burden of federal income taxes on different segments of the income distribution (e.g., for each quintile and for the top 1 percent) and the burden of all other federal taxes for these income categories; (2) the rates of income growth over time for families with different levels of income and education and/or skills and the associated changes in income shares; (3) changes in wealth over time for different income and wealth categories; and (4) international comparisons between the United States and its peers among the wealthy industrialized democracies as to poverty levels, the extent of income inequality, and the adequacy of the programs constituting the social safety net.

By the 1990s, efforts ranging from the outright doctoring of data to misleading statements about accurate information abounded. President Bush's February 27 speech to Congress made a number of technically true and/or seemingly reasonable claims, with the purpose of misleading people by covering over outcomes that could prove politically damaging. In one case, Bush asserted: "People with the smallest incomes will get the highest percentage reductions."[25] This technically correct statement concealed far more than it revealed. Despite the rhetoric about the great help afforded "people with the smallest incomes," the income tax cut provided limited relief or none at all for a large segment of the population.

Those at the top of the income distribution would be by far the biggest winners, whereas workers who paid a significant amount of Social Security taxes but no income tax received no reduction at all. The Center on Budget and Policy Priorities—a liberal policy research and analysis organization held in highest regard by other professional analysts for the accuracy of its data—indicated that the bottom 60 percent would receive just under 15 percent of the entire tax cut, less than one-half as much as the top 1 percent.[26] Deception with data had become a major presidential weapon that only knowledge could defend against. The uncomfortable truth is that such major economic policies as the Bush tax plan likely will set the political information and knowledge bar well above the level most citizens would be willing and able to leap over.

The democratic dilemma may be that economic literacy has become a necessary tool of responsible citizenship. The situation is analogous to that in other countries where the English language is no longer simply viewed as a desirable language for their citizens to have but is seen an indispensable ingredient for success in business and research. The English language has become a tool of the trade as the Internet and globalization have become the order of the day in an international marketplace dominated by the United States. If American representative democracy demands of its citizens both a goodly amount of specific information on policies and enough economic competence to determine such policies' implications, most citizens would fail the test and are likely to do so in the foreseeable future.

Power, Knowledge, and Representative Democracy

The extent of the people's influence on Washington politicians has stirred much controversy. On one side are those who claim that politicians slavishly watch opinion polls and simply have their policy stances reflect what the people say they want. Others maintain that politicians push their own left- or right-of-center policy proposals; but as the veteran pollster Daniel Yankelovich has pointed out: "Today's politicians use polls and focus groups to blindside voters—to find words and phrases to mislead and manipulate them in order to free themselves to pursue agendas that the majority of centrist voters reject, or would reject it they were clearer about what the politicians were actually up to."[27] In the game of polarized politics, elected officials need to pay attention to what the public appears to want; but they may be able to pursue a more extreme position with a relatively uninformed electorate by using various ploys to cover up how much it deviates from the political center. However, the main threat to representative democracy has not been citizens' lack of political power per se.

The energy and environmental areas in the first six months of George W. Bush's administration provide a pristine example of the power of the public's opinion. President Bush and Vice President Richard Cheney, both former oilmen, actively pushed for more intensive exploration for oil and gas in the United States by opening up areas to drilling in national parks and elsewhere that had previously been protected. The administration also took a hard line on environmental issues, including undoing some of President Clinton's efforts at greater protection that came near the end of his administration.

Major Republican contributors and their lobbyists could not have been more pleased. Then the people intruded on the desire of President Bush and his big contributors for a drilling-dominated set of policies. On June 21, 2001, the *New York Times* published the results of a national poll carried out with CBS News showing that the president's job approval rating had fallen by 7 points to 53 percent since March; 57 percent said "yes" to protecting the environment, even if it meant paying more for electricity and gasoline, as opposed to 36 percent answering "no"; and only 21 percent responded "yes" when asked whether a production increase in oil, coal, and natural gas should be a priority over conservation, as compared with 68 percent opting for conservation.[28]

The same paper reported the next day that the House had voted 247–164 for a postponement of six months for new leasing agreements for drilling offshore in the Gulf of Mexico "with 70 Republicans ignoring appeals from the White House and their own leadership" and that the Environmental Protection Agency was issuing rules to restrict old coal-fired power plants because they are the worst culprits contributing to the haze in many national parks and wilderness areas.[29] President Bush's falling approval rating and the unpopularity of his environmental and energy policies certainly did frighten a number of Republican House members enough to defy the president and their leaders. The poll also pushed the White House into setting out rules that were almost the same as those proposed by President Clinton, even though the administration with much fanfare had stamped out several other of Clinton's proenvironmental rules at the outset of the new administration.

The people's will thus had prevailed, even though the outcome disappointed some of the Republicans' biggest contributors, who had lobbied hard for the changes they wanted. Here is a striking example of the power of public opinion in eliciting rapid political responsiveness; but it represents the extreme case of straightforward information that is easy to interpret as to its meaning and importance. The task of convincing the public that the disturbingly visible haze did not greatly constrict views at Acadia National Park in Maine and the Great Smoky Mountains National Park in Tennessee, where the blight was the worst among the national parks, had indeed been a formidable one.

In contrast, most major domestic policy problems do not offer the smoking gun that the haze of atmospheric pollution provided but instead only such factors as mind-boggling data or complex economic relationships that facilitate the use of sophisticated propaganda tools to confuse information-deficient centrists. Elected politicians, government agencies, and special interests also conceal some useful information from the public. Still, they cannot control nearly enough needed political information to keep citizens in the dark. Insufficient citizen demand, not limited supply, is the central problem.

This need for enough political information and knowledge to understand the main policy problems facing the nation holds even when politicians want to do their duty as representatives of the people. Yankelovich went to the heart of the problem in his review of the Jacobs and Shapiro book *Politicians Don't Pander:*

> Even assuming that politicians have strong incentives to respond to the preferences of centrist voters, how are they to know what the preferences really are? Ironically, opinion polls, despite their proliferation, rarely reveal the public's real preferences on complex issues. Polls work best when people know what they want. But on most complex issues most of the time, people haven't worked through what they want, especially when painful tradeoffs are involved. . . . [The authors assume] that politicians have only two alternatives: to get the public to embrace their choices . . . or to pursue the public's choices. But in reality, without active leadership, the public does not ordinarily have clear-cut policy choices on its own.[30]

Three points stand out in Yankelovich's statement. First, opinion polls are unlikely to tell us what the public really thinks on complex policy issues. Second, part of the problem is that the people do not know what they want. Third, political leadership has the central role of helping the public reach clear choices.

Keeping questions simple on surveys of political opinion will increase the likelihood of respondents' understanding them, but this procedure can make the answers almost meaningless or actually misleading. Some respondents answering "yes" to the question "Do you favor President Bush's tax-cut plan" may have known the full details of the proposal and liked them all or believed that the desirable elements outweighed the undesirable ones. Others answering "yes" could have been mainly or totally unaware of the specific provisions of the Bush plan but generally favored tax cuts. The positive responses do not indicate how people felt about the various provisions in the plan (additional questions could address each of them but also would leave interpretation problems), whether respondents knew how much the proposal would cost and the implications of those costs, or if they were aware that the Bush tax cut greatly favored the extremely rich and did little or nothing for roughly half of the population.

Moreover, these simple questions seldom are cast in terms of trade-offs with a "yes" answer followed up by a statement that the tax cut could threaten the soundness of the Social Security system and an additional probe asking whether the person still favors the tax cut. On those occasions where such relevant information on potential trade-offs is provided, the decline in the percentage of "yes" responses can be striking. The political polls that have grown like weeds in a neglected garden frequently fail to capture the will of the people and may never do so because of technical, procedural, and cost problems.

If polling cannot miraculously detect the will of the people in part because they do not know what they want, political leadership offers another alternative. A transformational political leader could engage in a process of meaningful deliberations to seek a reasoned consensus among the people about the objectives to be sought and the policies to be used in trying to attain them, but the task is likely to be daunting. Telling the truth to the people generally demands setting out severe policy problems that can shatter conventional wisdom and self-serving myths and require sacrifices to attack the ills. All the momentum is in the opposite direction. Since the start of Ronald Reagan's administration, the propaganda presidency has come to the fore. In today's polarized political environment, the national institutions of government offer a platform that is too weak to hold up under the weight of politicians speaking the truth when their statements either threaten citizens' unrealistic but strongly held opinions or indicate that voters have been making choices that go against their own best interests—or in other ways show their political ignorance.

Presidents, Congress, and the media have performed miserably in helping citizens gain more hard facts and greater understanding of them. These institutions have employed misinformation and distorted arguments and told people what they wanted to hear even though it did not accord with reality. At the same time, the people's lack of political information—forget knowledge—is staggeringly low in contrast to their high levels of incorrect information and to their great confidence in having sufficient political knowledge to meet the obligations of citizenship. The political information deficit generates a vicious circle. The politicians who want to pursue their own agenda can get away with lying to citizens because of their lack of political information and knowledge. The lies, once believed, demand more lies to cover the truth. The growing web of misinformation and distortion requires more and more political understanding from the public if it is to cut through the propaganda to separate fact from fiction.

nine

The Costs of the Federal Government's Inefficiency

The terrorists' successful attacks on the World Trade Center's twin towers and the Pentagon suddenly and dramatically reshuffled the deck and dealt new cards to the key players in the American political system. People again looked to Washington to be the central actor. A policy window for meaningful institutional reform opened wide after the terrorist attacks and the Enron bankruptcy. Public opinion had shifted strikingly toward Washington as the means of providing homeland security and reining in unacceptable business practices.

At the same time, the badly damaged U.S. political system remained a critical barrier to restoring the institutional capacity of the federal government to meet the challenges of the early twenty-first century. More than twenty years of antigovernmentism had drastically cut into the competence and capacity to compromise of the federal institutions of domestic policy governance and the internal credibility within them. A snapshot taken just after the terrorist attacks and the Enron scandal would have revealed a fully opened window but with sadly deteriorated institutions of governance as the available vehicles for moving through it.

From Irrelevant to Indispensable

The level of fear aroused on September 11, 2001, when people suddenly saw themselves as vulnerable to terrorist attacks on Fortress America itself, drove the nation's citizens to a radical reassessment of their image of the federal government. After a day of exposure to the unforgettable television images of the destruction of the World Trade Center, the heretofore much derided federal agencies emerged as America's trusted protectors. The changed view, however, could not also transform the underlying reality of the inept federal agencies. Nor did the shift alter the

American people's lack of information and knowledge about the dollar costs of the needed improvements in the agencies and the tremendous amount of institutional change that would be required not just in the operating agencies but in Congress and the presidency.

Vulnerability: A Bureaucratic Horror Story

After September 11, Americans faced a markedly different world. They felt vulnerable within their borders to foreign enemies ready to kill themselves as they murdered ordinary citizens to strike at the hated United States. Not surprisingly, the greatest vulnerability lurked in the once "Friendly Skies." As fear of flying became a national mania, concern centered on security at the nation's airports. The people who did not cancel their flights were asked to come to airports at least two hours early to be put through beefed-up, intensified security procedures to protect against possible terrorists. It became a common experience to see large numbers of uniformed security personnel with weapons in hand or slung over their shoulders.

Nearly two months after the terrorist attacks, Subash Gurung walked easily through the security system at Chicago's O'Hare Airport with a carry-on bag containing a number of knives, a can of pepper spray, and a stun gun.[1] How this came to happen, not surprisingly, is a convoluted tale of a Washington bureaucracy—the Federal Aviation Administration (FAA)—and its tribulations over a number of years. Generally, the problem came from continuing garden-variety mismanagement that had no news value from the perspective of the media.

The FAA story in many respects mirrors the savings and loan saga, showing various problems that pop up in the federal agencies as profusely as skunk cabbage in a swamp. In the FAA case, the lethal mixture included (1) an agency with little political standing, incompetent personnel, and grossly inadequate funding; (2) firms with FAA contracts that engaged in unscrupulous and dishonest practices yet were not carefully monitored by the agency; and (3) top politicians running interference for powerful companies. Although we need not go through another extended example of the harmful interaction of politicians, business, and the federal agencies, it is worth treating the genesis of the FAA's security problems: low wages.

Using their great political strength built up through large campaign contributions, the airlines had been able to hold down the hourly rate for security workers. Potential passengers were happy to go along so as to keep down ticket prices, despite two deleterious repercussions. First, the people hired often had limited skills and/or interest, so turnover rates averaged 126 percent in 1998–99 at the nineteen largest airports and at one-fourth of them ranged from 200 to 416 percent.[2] Second, the pressures to fill these positions again and again, particularly as the labor market tightened in the mid-1990s, pushed companies competing for airport security contracts into a race to the bottom for employees.

Argenbright Holdings, the largest airport-security firm, paid its employees little more than minimum wages and provided no benefits. It also engaged in actions that brought "federal convictions on conspiracy to avoid performing background checks for employees in Philadelphia last year [2000] . . . and probation for the company in Pennsylvania and Illinois."[3] Despite the conviction and promises to start a program that would correct the earlier practices, Argenbright did not change. Attorney General John Ashcroft observed that "'Argenbright Holdings continues to violate laws that protect the safety of Americans who travel by commercial airlines,'" that screeners had been hired with criminal records, and that Argenbright had "'made false statements about its employees' backgrounds.'"[4]

In response to September 11, airport security was federalized; but that did not wipe away the issues of an adequate level of pay over time and of higher qualifications for security screeners. Billy H. Vincent, the director of FAA's civilian airport security in the 1980s, has made this key point:

> Argenbright was aggressive in getting its contracts, but they didn't do anything the others didn't do, either. These were terribly unattractive jobs, filled by people who were always looking for another job. To keep the jobs filled and meet the airlines' quota, they had to cheat, and I'm sure you could find exactly the same things at other airports, if you looked hard enough.[5]

Increased wages should attract more skilled security screeners over time, but a concerted effort likely will be needed to upgrade the education and/or skill qualifications so as to hire people who have the competence to cope with added responsibilities.

The newly created Transportation Security Agency, which has been charged by the Department of Transportation with that agency's mandate for aviation security, had indicated in a December 20, 2001, news release that "'screeners must be U.S. citizens, have a high school diploma and pass a standardized examination.'"[6] The agency quickly backed off, however, because the new rules would have eliminated thousands of screeners then on the job. Isaac Yeffet, once the security director for Israel's El Al Airlines, which is the most security conscious of the major carriers, observed: "'What we really need are people who understand how terrorists work, who can spot a false passport, who can ask the right questions of the right people. . . . Every screener is holding on his own shoulders a 747 full of passengers.'"[7] Few who fly would disagree with the list of skills that Yeffet set out, but such a high level of institutional and technical competence is not easily attained. Israel has stayed vigilant for years in its effort to deter hijackers and has maintained its high standards. The United States only had an open policy window and needed to act before it closed.

Vulnerability Writ Large

Although airports garnered the headlines about the lack of security after September 11, these facilities were veritable bastions of safety compared with the nation's 361 seaports. The Coast Guard inspects port facilities every two years; no more than 2 percent of the millions of shipping containers arriving at U.S. ports are inspected, whereas some ports in other countries inspect all cargo coming in; and a special presidential commission that studied 12 seaports around the country in 1999 found poorly trained security staff, inadequate clearance standards for those having access to sensitive areas, and cargo yards with no fences.[8]

New York Times writer Peter T. Kilborn ranked ports "among the greatest points of vulnerability," citing the poor security and the "tangled chain of authority" that complicated control. He noted that businesses and economic development agencies exerted great pressure on the ports to limit costly, time-consuming security measures so that cargo can move without interruption and maximize income for the shipping companies and the communities.[9] The limited federal monitoring effort meant that no one but the shippers would know what was in the containers. They could hold weapons for terrorists, including a nuclear device.

Also at risk from terrorists were the basics of life—food, air, and water. The secretary of health and human services, Tommy Thompson, informed

Congress that he had greater fear for the safety of the nation's food supply than anything else. And the food specialist Marian Burros, in commenting on Thompson's statement, pinpointed the inspection system as a primary reason for danger: "The system is so antiquated that it has been described as the regulatory equivalent of the Model T."[10]

One factor in this food inspection situation has been the uneven political clout that grossly misallocated inspection resources. The long-entrenched Department of Agriculture system employed 7,600 inspectors to monitor 6,500 meat and poultry plants. The Food and Drug Administration, with responsibility for 57,000 food-processing plants, could muster only 770 inspectors, of whom a mere 150 were assigned to the more than 3.5 million shipments of food that arrive in the United States each year from other countries. Without the aid of terrorists, food-borne illnesses have been responsible for an estimated 5,000 deaths and 76 million illnesses a year, and the misdirected, underfunded, mismanaged food inspection system had been one of the culprits. The food inspection system was consistent—continuing institutional incompetence provided unsatisfactory protection, both before the war on terrorism began and once it started.

Food is so basic to American life that the inadequacy of the efforts to ensure its safety seem puzzling until we look at the other side of the coin: The mammoth food industry possesses lots of political clout. Agribusiness and food processors contributed $13.9 million to both political parties in 2000.[11] When some members of Congress pushed for greater Food and Drug Administration food authority in bioterrorism legislation, eighteen trade groups in the food processing and marketing industry fought hard to stop or at least severely restrict the effort. Carol Tucker Foreman, an assistant secretary of agriculture in the Jimmy Carter administration and now with the Consumer Federation of America, observed: "'What this says is, Congress is willing to protect us but only to the extent that the new law doesn't offend the food industry, change existing federal bureaucracy, or cost much money.'" An alternative translation might be as follows: First, the reelection imperative drives the fear level in Congress higher and higher so that the overriding demand for any legislation is that it must be adroitly crafted to offend no group. Second, when trade-offs must be made among competing groups, big campaign contributors are at the front of the line whenever possible. Third, the public often loses out in the trade-offs because the other groups have greater intensity and far more political knowledge, so most of the public can be fooled or easily bought off with meaningless rhetoric.

The threat of bioterrorism has underlined the institutional weaknesses resulting from underinvestment in the nation's public health system. Tara O'Toole, director of the Center for Civilian Biodefense Studies at Johns Hopkins University, said: "'We have spent, in the last three years, one dollar per year per American on bioterrorism preparedness. We are basically getting what we paid for.'"[12] That is, the nation with by far the most costly health system in the world has allocated too few resources to cope with a major biological or chemical attack. More broadly, the nation badly underinvests in public health capability overall—a statement that applies to a number of other areas in which Americans are exposed to higher risks than they should be because of deficient public investment.

Plutocracy in America

Plutocracy is defined in *The New Oxford American Dictionary* as "government by the wealthy ... [by a] ruling class of people whose power derives from their wealth."[13] The British writer William Keegan has called the United States a "plutodemocracy," which he described as "a system under which the rich rule in the name of the people, but largely in their own interests."[14] Under Reaganism, the United States moved into early-stage plutocracy, as has been the case in earlier periods. Unlike the mature version, the nation does not have a small group of entrenched wealthy families supported by strong ties to a powerful military establishment. Nor is there a closely interlocked ruling aristocracy of wealthy families that has continued to hold their power over time, even though old money with staying power does exist.

The ruling class in America does have such longtime rich and powerful families as the Rockefellers; but the leadership comes primarily from the top executives of major corporations. Despite the fact that the composition changes as executives come and go, these individuals, in the name of their companies, do have great power. Their means of communication are varied, ranging from direct business relationships, such as those involving the major New York financial institutions, to membership in organizations that have lobbying as one of their main activities. At the top is the Business Roundtable, which, as John Judis has written, "[is] strictly limited to major corporations and their [chief executive officers]," includes numerous *Fortune* 200 companies, and has a membership that accounts for a significant portion of the nation's gross domestic product.[15] Early-stage plutocracy emerges when big business has strong influence over the national government's policies that have important implications for corporate practices and profits.

If we go back as far as the nineteenth century to start with the Gilded Age, the United States has passed through two periods in which corporate America dominated and two others when business's power was reined in by government. Plutocracy may have reached its high point in the Gilded Age, when big business—by "owning" the state legislatures that chose United States senators—also "owned" federal institutions.[16] The Progressive Era sought to curb the excesses of the Gilded Age. When its towering figure, Theodore Roosevelt, came to the presidency in 1901, this larger-than-life son of a blue-blooded New York family vehemently attacked the giant corporate trusts and sought to restore the needed balance of power between corporate America and the national government.

Plutocracy returned in the Roaring Twenties, as America again embraced unrestrained free-market capitalism. "The business of America is business," President Calvin Coolidge told the Society of Newspaper Editors in January 1925. In the 1920s, with rapid economic growth and corporate excesses, the stock market soared and business could do no wrong. After the Great Depression brought a sharp drop in the economy and massive unemployment, the balance of power shifted again when President Franklin Roosevelt, also a patrician son of wealth, turned on his class, attacking the "economic royalists" and "entrenched greed."

From Roosevelt's New Deal through Lyndon Johnson's Great Society and into the Richard Nixon and Carter administrations, the federal government maintained a reasonable power balance through a strong national government. Although any change could only go so far in the American version of capitalism, there was a marked shift toward the needs and concerns of ordinary citizens, and the period still stands as the high point of egalitarianism in the twentieth century.

The pendulum swung dramatically toward corporate America once Reaganism's antigovernmentism, with its basic tenets of deregulation and of tax cuts at the top, came to dominate American political thought. Enron, the huge Texas-based energy trading corporation, became the symbol of big-dollar politics. *New York Times* columnist Bob Herbert observed: "Enron is a case study in the dangers that will inevitably arise when unrestrained corporate greed is joined at the hip with the legalized bribery and influence peddling that passes for government these days."[17] Enron, which well may be the most spectacular case of deregulation gone wrong, shows starkly the dangers of plutocracy. Equally illuminating is how big business, driven by its fixation on increasing profits to fuel the surging stock market, used its political power during the final two decades of the twentieth century to force a sharp decline in the federal government's investment in the domestic policy arena, which had been of such great benefit to ordinary citizens.

The Failure of the Gatekeepers

Enron in many respects had been a 1990s rerun of the 1980s savings and loan scandal, with dishonest business executives, close corporate ties to the political system all the way up to the presidency, excessive deregulation, grossly inadequate monitoring by the federal government, and a failure of the private-sector gatekeepers responsible for protecting the public from unscrupulous corporate practices. One major difference is that Enron represented a particularly egregious example of the corporate practice of doctoring the numbers in response to the demands of the hyperactive stock market of the second half of the 1990s. Lanny Davis, special counsel to President Clinton from 1996 to 1998 and now a partner in the law firm of Patton Boggs, wrote of the Enron collapse: "The goal of 'meeting the numbers' projected by [stock market] analysts for each quarter has too often become the overriding goal—*to be achieved in the accounting department if it cannot be achieved in the marketplace.*"[18]

To escape detection, the internal fixing of the books demanded involvement by the various gatekeepers charged with ensuring accurate data, particularly Enron's outside auditor, Arthur Andersen. After the latter went along, Enron's manufactured profits in turn were used by Wall Street as the basis for unstinting praise and an unending string of strong buy recommendations. The results were astounding, as Enron's stock price rose to a level at which its capitalized value made the company the nation's seventh largest. Conflict of interest became rampant as supposedly unbiased investment house analysts touted Enron, in part so their firms would have a chance to qualify for the lucrative business of underwriting new Enron offerings.

After Enron started to fall apart, some of the big losers were ordinary stockholders, including the thousands of company employees whose 401(k) savings for retirement became nearly worthless. In contrast, top Enron executives, with their insider information, were able to sell their own shares early enough to make big gains. The belief that unfettered market capitalism would regulate itself so as to protect the public—one of Reaganism's fundamental verities—opened the nation to a level of individual and corporate greed reminiscent of the Gilded Age and the 1920s.

In playing the Washington game, Enron and its executives made campaign contributions to nearly half of the members of the House of Representatives and three-fourths of the Senate. Although Republicans had received 73 percent of Enron's campaign contributions, the firm spread its donations around. *Washington Post* reporter Dan Morgan quoted an unnamed former employee's comment about Enron's chairman, Kenneth Lay: "'Ken Lay would write letters and pick up the phone to call whoever was needed, and the party didn't matter that much."[19] Contributions to key Democrats and Republicans had become a necessary expenditure for corporations that wanted to play the Washington political game successfully and a way of life for members of Congress.

Businesses' campaign contributions that kept the Democrats competitive at election time demanded that their members of Congress go along with what *New York Times* columnist Bob Herbert labeled "the obsession with deregulation that has such a hold on the Republican Party and corporate America."[20] The Democrats could claim with justification that the system made them do it. The fact remains that their decision exemplifies the corruption of an institution in its purest form: The congressional Democrats supported deregulation without strong monitoring to gain sufficient campaign contributions so that they would stay competitive with a Republican Party that truly believed the regulatory prescriptions of Reaganism. When the Democrats over time have had to essentially adopt Republican positions to appease big business contributors, representative democracy has been struck a mortal blow. If the two major party candidates support the same probusiness position, citizens no longer are able to vote in a congressional election for a candidate who both opposes that stance and has a reasonable chance to win the seat. Money has squeezed out such a representative.

The lack of regulation and strong sanctions permeated the financial system. In particular, the private-sector gatekeepers—the first line of defense against unscrupulous financial practices by corporations—had expanded into new areas of business that created potential conflicts of interest. Traditionally, brokerage houses, which had primarily traded in already-issued financial securities, insulated their in-house security analysts from the firm's other activities to ensure their impartial assessment of individual securities for the firm's investors. But in the 1990s, after the underwriting of the securities of companies seeking new capital in the market became increasingly important to brokerage firms, the in-house analysts joined the cheerleaders by making strong buy recommendations for the securities being sold, even if they saw a company as a poor prospect. Jeff Madrick, editor of *Challenge Magazine,* observed: "Many businesses now aggressively 'spin' their information. Wall Street analysts, often the conduit of that information to the media, are increasingly accused of tailoring reports to please their investment banking clients."[21] Here is the kind of conflict of interest that converts the gatekeeper to culprit (the dishonest cop).

The ultimate private-sector gatekeepers are the "public accountants," a designation meant to indicate that the accounting firms and their professional staffs—even though paid by the audited company—are responsible for certifying the validity of the numbers for all who would use them. The public accountants' seal of approval is meant to specify that because an audited company had been subject to generally accepted accounting principles, its numbers are credible—hard currency to be trusted. When most of the accounting firm's income came from carrying out this public responsibility, the incentives worked in the right direction. The biggest asset was a sterling reputation for ensuring the accuracy and completeness of the financial information of the audited company.

After the major accounting firms became management consultants, often to the companies they audited, this long-standing incentive structure came crashing down. Samuel Hayes, a Harvard Business School professor, said: "'Auditing has become a stepchild, a commodity, to get your foot in the door.'"[22] In 2001, Enron paid Arthur Andersen $25 million for auditing and $27 million for its other services.[23] Not only did the incentives for rigorous audits by accounting firms decline, the inducements also increased not to challenge questionable accounting practices by companies being audited, lest this offend the clients paying large consulting fees. Given the stock market's fixation on fast-growing profits, ignoring the direction of the incentives put in jeopardy an accounting firm's earnings, the remuneration of its partners, the jobs of its employees, and possibly the survival of the company itself.

Starting in 1997, Enron overstated its profits by $586 million, using what Sherron S. Watkins, a company vice president, described as "an elaborate accounting hoax."[24] The behavior of Enron's auditor Arthur Andersen, one of the Big Five accounting firms dominating that industry, so severely tarnished its reputation that it had to declare bankruptcy. Enron's manipulation of its profits and Arthur Andersen's acquiescence appeared to be the tip of the iceberg. Numerous companies found it necessary to reduce past profits because of questionable financial practices that likely had received the needed certification by public auditors as complying with generally accepted accounting principles.

Adding to the problem, the Securities and Exchange Commission had allowed the accounting industry to regulate itself. The hands-off policy owed much to the fact that the commission, after being defanged under Reaganism, could not stand up to the accounting and securities industries, which had gained great political clout through major campaign contributors. When federal regulatory agencies are kept weak by the White House and Congress to satisfy politicians seeking campaign contributions, the setting becomes ripe for business practices that increase the maldistribution of income and wealth. This critical message from the Enron experience comes across clearly: A political environment in which the prevailing ideology holds federal regulation to be one of the deadly sins and in which corporate America dominates Washington politics has a high probability of producing toothless, incompetent government regulatory institutions that cannot control corporate malfeasance.

The Public Investment Deficit under Reaganism

During the first two decades of Reaganism, the United States underinvested in public goods aimed at improving the quality of life of all citizens. For example, the national parks have a staggering backlog of roughly $5 billion in maintenance and improvement projects; James Reynolds, the superintendent of Death Valley National Park in California, said: "Every park staff is struggling with operational issues—not having enough staff and funds to do what we know we need to to protect the parks and serve the users."[25] The failure to protect and preserve the national parks stands as a fitting metaphor for the public investment deficit that expanded rapidly as worship of unfettered capitalism grew among the disciples of Reaganism.

An adequate level of public investment is the mark of nations that seek to widen the social, economic, and political opportunities of all their inhabitants and provide them with protection against a variety of threats that individuals are unlikely to be able to cope with by themselves. Americans need infrastructure investments such as highways, streets, bridges, dams, and sewers; internal security investments to support the judiciary and policing functions; health and safety investments, such as hospitals, emergency response programs, and systems to ensure the quality of air, food and drugs, and water; and economic, social, and political opportunity investments, including education and training institutions, student financial support programs, and fair, technologically sound voting systems. Underinvestment in such public goods can limit the freedom of individual choice and make those goods that are available more dangerous (e.g., contaminated food), less enjoyable (dirty streets and parks), and more time consuming (inadequate public transportation and highways).

In the antigovernment climate of the 1980s and 1990s, businesses used their main political weapons of large campaign contributions and extensive lobbying to slow appreciably or stop federal agencies from making the investment needed to establish sufficient institutional competence in their inspection systems to enforce laws and regulations aimed at increasing the safety and security of the nation's people. The food supply offers a pristine case in point. Corporate America lobbied Congress and the executive branch to keep down the number of inspectors, to write loose regulations with numerous loopholes for avoiding compliance, and to impose only relatively small fines and no criminal sanctions for noncompliance. If all of these efforts failed, major corporate campaign contributors could still pressure the main recipients of these funds to step in and save the day. Hamstringing the federal effort meant that inspectors would lack the power to slow the production process or to stop companies from a number of practices that raised risks for the public but brought higher salaries and profits for the industry.

Public investment in the 1980s and 1990s had become a tarnished notion associated both with pork-barrel projects and an overly large federal government, despite the critical role it had played in the nation's success. *Washington Post* columnist E. J. Dionne pointed out that during the 1950s, President Dwight Eisenhower—a deeply conservative Republican in a complacent period—pushed through the Interstate Highway system and the federal student loan program "that paid off, as Vice President [Dick] Cheney might say, big time."[26] The huge infrastructure investment in the transportation system sought to increase business productivity and provide people with more job and travel opportunities. The large-scale human capital effort aimed at raising the levels of individual and business productivity and of economic opportunity for people with difficulties in financing the costs of higher education.

President Eisenhower's programs built on the 1944 GI Bill of Rights, which James Patterson, the Brown University historian, called "a remarkably broad piece of legislation, which not only offered veterans aid in purchasing housing, and loans to start businesses, but also provided monthly stipends for veterans who wanted help with educational costs."[27] The latter cost the then massive sum of $14.5 billion between 1944 and 1956 to provide benefits for more than 6 million veterans, of whom 2.2 million went to colleges and universities. This striking federal government investment increased the economic and social opportunities and political equality for millions of returning veterans. America's decision as World War II was ending to pass the GI Bill came to be seen as one of the nation's truly critical domestic policy decisions as the prudent long-term public investment become an important factor in greatly expanding the middle class and made the American Dream a realistic goal during the quarter-century of the strongest economy in the nation's history.

Democracy and Capitalism

Early during the 2000 campaign, presidential candidate Bill Bradley, the exceptionally thoughtful former democratic senator from New Jersey, spoke of:

a failure to understand that democracy and capitalism are separate parts of the American dream, and that keeping that dream alive depends on keeping one from corrupting the other. . . . There is still a very tangible relationship between the level of [economic] opportunity and security available to every American family and the extent to which we keep our democracy secure and separate from the force of money.[28]

In the world's most entrepreneurial nation, the continuing tension between democracy and capitalism means that the balancing act between the two must be well managed if representative democracy is to thrive. Without viable federal institutions of governance as a base for preserving democracy, the likely outcome is the capture of the political system by big-money interests, followed by a rapid increase in the maldistribution of income and wealth, the loss of political equality for ordinary Americans, and a decline in their economic security.

The Role of Elites

John Judis has argued that a factor contributing to business domination of the American political system in the last part of the twentieth century was the unwillingness of elites and elite organizations to seek to curb the excesses of corporate capitalism. He pointed out that earlier elite leaders—such as Theodore Roosevelt, Henry Cabot Lodge, Henry Stimson, Dean Acheson, and John McCloy—"placed public service above private gain and sought as public servants to represent the interests of the nation rather than those of a particular class, region, or industry. . . . In the past, elites and elite organizations had remained steadfast in their support for a politics that sought to reconcile democratic ideals of equality with the facts of corporate capitalism."[29] Such support is critically needed, lest the egalitarian ethos be crushed by the emergence of unfettered free-market capitalism.

Elites and elite organizations flourished during the Progressive Era, the New Deal, and the first two decades after World War II and, to a degree, offset the excesses of American capitalism. In these years, a form of representative democracy remained viable. National officials—far less dependent on large corporate campaign contributions—responded more to bipartisan leadership that sought to mitigate among various interests. Elites and elite organizations were able to strengthen pluralism and produce a more balanced perspective that was grounded in the national interest. The latter represented a variant of the Madisonian model, whereby these elites tried to make the needs of the people better understood in the political debate. The outcome may not have truly reflected "the will of the people," but in seeking to serve the national interest, these elites were guided more by the needs of ordinary citizens than the narrow concerns of business.

During recent decades, elite business leaders with a broad national perspective have all but disappeared, replaced by top corporate executives who only looked to the bottom line of the profit-and-loss statement and sought to weaken the power of the national government. The door had opened wide for Reaganism, as Judis observed:

> President Reagan fulfilled business's fondest wishes. . . . The new administration went after regulatory policies that dated from the Progressive Era. . . . [It] made a mockery of democratic pluralism by throwing its weight behind business and attempting to crush business's adversaries. Reagan would sometimes compare his administration with that of Eisenhower, but it did not show a trace of the "balanced" government that Eisenhower . . . had advocated. It was a throwback . . . to Coolidge and to the corrupt post–civil War administrations.[30]

To Ronald Reagan, as to Calvin Coolidge, the notion that democracy and capitalism could be in conflict would have been unthinkable.

The entrepreneurial spirit and the managerial skills of the nation's businesses have been the driving factor in making the United States the most productive nation in the world. However, a powerful force must be in place to counter business interests if U.S. political institutions are to strike a fair balance that can reconcile the movement toward greater economic, social, and political equality with the interests of corporate America.

The nation's unique brand of muscular capitalism has long posed the danger that the corporate sector will dominate and distort the political system. Three times—in the Gilded Age, the Roaring Twenties, and the Era of Reaganism—big business gained control of the national political process. In the first two eras, after corporate excesses tainted big business, the balance was restored by two strong leaders—one a Republican, the other a Democrat, both from the patrician Roosevelt family of New York. The excesses of corporate America in the 1980s and 1990s have again badly damaged its reputation and raise an intriguing question, whose consideration is postponed until the final chapter: Can the nation move back toward representative democracy, as it did after the excesses of the Gilded Age and the 1920s?

Is Representative Democracy Really Dead?

The argument that the Constitution's original concept of federal governance has died raises two issues that need to be addressed briefly. First, even if it is accepted that representative democracy has been pushed aside by Reaganism, the question remains as to whether the claim of its death is overly dramatic and misleading in that it has come back to life before. The second, larger issue concerns the extent to which the United States has actually been a representative democracy since its inception.

The starting point on the first question is to recognize that the demise of a political institution, concept, or practice does not necessarily have the same meaning as that of a human being. There can be finality as in the case of the Whigs as a major political party, even though some of its ideas continued in the same way that individuals' ideas live on. Conversely, representative democracy appears to have experienced a revival after the Gilded Age and again after the 1920s and a fall with the coming of Reaganism.

Such changes over time could be viewed as more of a cyclical phenomenon. I chose to use the term "death" because it is dangerous to assume that a self-correcting political process is operating to restore representative democracy, or, for that matter, to undo it. Capitalism and democracy may not return to a healthy balance without a catastrophic event like the Great Depression. Or, an adroitly managed plutocracy—George W. Bush's administration offers a good example—may become the accepted norm. The last point leads to the second question of the extent to which the United States has ever been a representative democracy.

Before addressing the issue directly, it needs noting both that business in America has generally been more powerful in the political arena than in other democracies, and that the highest form of representative democracy as conceived by Madison may have flourished only briefly or never actually occurred. The idealistic setting in which voters of virtue and intelligence select representatives of wisdom and virtue who strive as the people's agents to serve the best interests of their constituents would seem to demand more than fallible politicians and voters can deliver. More realistically, representative democracy has operated within a range with Madison's pure form at the generally unattainable upper point and a lower cutoff point below which representative democracy has ceased to work (exist). Both points, of course, are matters of judgment. The question is how often has the United States fallen beneath the lower boundary.

Going back to the Gilded Age, corporate America dominated Washington in part by owning the U.S. Senate, having purchased a number of senators in the state legislatures. Clearly, the nation had fallen well below the lower point of the range. The Progressive Era may have pushed the forces of business back sufficiently to reestablish representative democracy for a short period before the clear corporate domination of the 1920s, but it could be that the United States had not actually crossed the lower line into representative democracy before the Jazz Age began.

In the years since the start of the Gilded Age, representative democracy reached its highest point during the roughly fifty years from the presidency of Franklin Delano Roosevelt to that of Ronald Reagan. That period began during the worst economic years in American history and, before the economy had fully recovered, moved into a world war. After World War II, the United States emerged as an economic colossus and experienced nearly a quarter-century of exceptionally high levels of economic productivity and growth and of an underlying economic dynamics that greatly benefited low-skilled workers. During this time, the United States crossed the lower boundary point of representative democracy and stayed above it for roughly five decades.

The critical question now is whether this extended period of time had been driven by such extraordinary forces that it actually stands out as the liberal aberration on a long road away from representative governance. That is, the Age of Roosevelt, which is the nation's longest period of egalitarianism, and the burst of civil rights and social programs during the mid-1960s, which is the high point of American liberalism, may be the exception in U.S. history. Today, the norm increasingly looks to combine a rising maldistribution of income and wealth without much concern for the plight of poor people, plutocratic governance, and a tepid form of democracy dominated by consumer choice and the Democratic Ideal. Which one is the real America—an active federal government committed to increasing economic security and political equality or a plutocracy dominated by the wealthiest families and big business?

ten

American Democracy Today

To indicate where the nation is after a little more than two decades of Reaganism, in this chapter I focus on the movement of the United States from representative democracy to plutocracy and a much more watered-down version of democracy; on the reasons that this dramatic shift succeeded in the nation considered the exemplar of democratic principles; and on the difficulties in overcoming the massive barriers to institutional reform built by Reaganism and in returning to representative democracy. In looking to the future, the chapter reemphasizes the pivotal need to restore federal institutions of governance and stresses the dangers if plutocracy establishes deep roots in America.

Democracy in Decline

Because the nation earlier had been able to move back from plutocratic governance, the question arises as to the chances early in the twenty-first century for the restoration of Madisonian representative democracy and political equality supported by efficient federal government institutions. As we turn to this question, it is useful to have before us the primary external culprits in the assault on these institutions (there were also villains within) that began in the 1980s and gained renewed strength at the start of George W. Bush's presidency:

- *Reaganism,* with its antigovernmentism, its market fundamentalism, its belief that individual and family pure self-interest should guide behavior, and its embrace of national myths that together have made it the nation's dominant political philosophy and fostered a powerful ideology of the right;
- *big-money politics,* fueled by the growing maldistribution in income and wealth, which has filled the huge campaign war chests of reelection-fixated politicians in order to buy access and influence in Washington;

- *the information explosion,* which has yielded increased levels of information overload, incorrect or misleading information, and distorted commentary;
- *the media,* which have become profit driven and failed to provide enough sound political information and analysis to inform the American people about the major policy and political issues of the day; and
- *the American electorate,* which has failed to fulfill the obligations of citizenship because of its lack of sound political information and knowledge and its unwarranted confidence in its capacity to select good candidates and understand policy issues.

These five external culprits have interacted both among themselves and with other factors, including internal culprits, such as the reelection imperative, political propaganda, and party polarization. The combined force of the interacting factors appears to have driven the government's institutional competence, compromise capacity, and internal credibility to their lowest points in the postwar era.

It is my contention that nothing indicates the extent of the decline in the institutional efficiency of the federal government, the loss of full political citizenship, and the shift of House and Senate members away from their constituents toward corporate America as much as the death of Madisonian representative democracy. There is an alternative thesis: that Madisonian representative democracy simply died naturally after its relevance had ceased. However brilliant when first conceived, the venerable formulation for linking citizens and representatives became obsolete, despite its centrality at the start of the American Republic. The problem with the explanation of a benign death is that the public still holds strongly to the conviction that Washington officials should adhere to citizens' preferences on major policy issues, not those of others. Madisonian representative democracy may have died, but the public's desire for the representative as agent remains strong.

A Key Survey

A Kaiser–*Public Perspective* survey, based on a nationally representative random sample of 1,206 adults conducted through telephone interviews during the period January 3–March 26, 2001, ties together a number of the basic issues concerning the decline of democracy and is worth considering in some depth.[1] The survey employed two questions with slightly different wording to delve into the public's assessment of its own impact on Washington: "How much influence do you think the views of the majority of Americans *should* [or, in the second question, *actually*] have on the decisions of elected and government officials in Washington?"[2] These two questions and the two in the next paragraph offered four alternative responses, going from a great deal to none at all. Using only the first response shows the sharp differences between what people considered the appropriate behavior by members of Congress and what they believed the members in fact did. More than two-thirds (68 percent) of the public held that Washington officials should pay a great deal of attention to the views of the majority, but they thought that less than one in ten (9 percent) actually did.

Through two additional questions, the survey probed the sources of influence (paid attention to): "Generally speaking, when elected and government officials in Washington make decisions about important issues, how much attention do you feel they *should* [or *actually*] pay to . . . ?"[3] Nearly 60 percent of the public felt that citizens who contact officials merit a great deal of attention. In contrast, citizens put near the bottom on the normative question of influence both campaign contributors (18 percent) and lobbyists and special-interest groups (14 percent). When the question turned to the sources actually gaining the attention of Washington officials, the public placed campaign contributors in the lead at 59 percent and lobbyists and special-interest groups second at 45 percent. At the bottom in receiving a great deal of attention at only 14 percent were ordinary citizens who get in touch with Washington. The survey also asked: "Do you agree or disagree that the *main* reason elected officials consult polls is because they want to stay popular and get re-elected?"[4] While 58 percent of the respondents strongly agreed with the statement, only 5 percent expressed strong disagreement.

A key question concerned the public's capacity to make sound judgments: "For each of the following issues, please tell me if you think the public can make sound judgments about the details of laws and regulations debated in Congress."[5] Those surveyed show extreme overconfidence in assessing their ability to understand complex legislation: economic issues,

58 percent; health care issues, 70 percent; and education issues, 68 percent.[6] Making sound judgments on the specifics of densely worded, confusing legislation and putting what it means in the larger context of its impact is often a difficult tasks for policy experts. Be that as it may, the representative sample of American citizens perceived themselves as capable of understanding the intricacies of legislation on economic, health care, and education policies.

Ordinary citizens in effect were saying that despite their considerable knowledge, members of Congress either perceived them as uninformed or else paid attention mainly to moneyed interests. The Kaiser–*Public Perspective* survey results show how far away the public thinks it is from that still-desired bond between citizens and their elected representatives in Washington. How can the electorate hold that Washington officials listen mainly to those with money and special influence, even though citizens believe that they are well able to offer knowledgeable advice on major decisions, and still see American democracy as flourishing? The explanation likely stems from one of the nation's most cherished myths: that the United States unquestionably stands far above other nations as the world's foremost democracy. The myth's overriding of reality reveals much about both the rise of the Democratic Ideal and plutocratic governance and the increasing difficulty of returning to representative democracy.

Reaganism and the Freedom of Choice

The public's total conviction that the U.S. model of democratic governance is superior to the systems used in other nations and will continue to be successful over time is one of the two pillars upholding the Democratic Ideal. After this belief became unchallengeable, all else followed. It was easy for voters to conclude that they must be fulfilling the obligations of good citizenship. How else could American democracy stay so far ahead of the democratic systems elsewhere? Nor do true believers need additional evidence for verification once they have no doubts that their democratic system is and will continue to be far and away the best in the world. Contrary facts simply will not diminish this conviction in the eyes of the truly committed.

However flawed such reasoning may be, its power is not to be underestimated. Thus, in the discussion that follows, once individual voters took for granted that they were fulfilling their citizenship responsibilities, however little they actually did in that regard, they did not need to concern themselves with doing more to be good citizens and concentrated on their favorite activity of making consumer choices from the cornucopia of available goods and services.

Stanley Greenberg, the Democratic pollster, and his associates conducted 23 focus groups all across the United States after September 11, 2001, that asked the participants "what it means to be an American." He observed: "The great bulk of the responses raised the concept of 'freedom.' . . . People are defining freedom as the 'freedom to choose.' In America, we have 'options.' . . . Many people think that this freedom of choice is central to our way of life—and that it is now under attack."[7] Greenberg's examples indicate that freedom of choice revolves around highly specific decisions about getting on with one's life, such as whether to go to college, have children, or move to another area. At its center are a family's possessions, which define its socioeconomic status. Citizens' personal rights and freedom of choice appear to stand as the core concerns in the current version of democracy.

America has long had the widest array of consumer goods and services in the world. During the period of economic growth of the 1990s, the nation's freedom of choice soared far beyond that of any other country when viewed solely in terms of aggregate supply. An individual family's freedom of choice also depends on its "effective demand," a term used by economists to define a situation in which a potential buyer both wants an item *and* has the means of paying for it. Effective demand for an individual family varies with the level of its disposable income, wealth, and borrowing capacity. A broader definition of freedom of choice, which takes into account both supply availability and a family's effective demand, raises an important question: Will an individual family, when it suffers a fall in its available resources over time that materially restricts its effective demand, view its reduced ability to acquire goods and services as diminishing both its own freedom of choice and that of the nation?

Under some circumstances, it is reasonable for individual families to make a distinction so that their own choices are seen in terms of supply and demand, but the nation's freedom to choose is viewed as depending only on the aggregate supply of goods and services. If some families have their effective demand reduced by a job loss or an illness or injury, the country's freedom of choice is not affected. This interpretation appears to be reasonable when the declining circumstances of individual families arise primarily from the play of impersonal market forces, as in a recession, even though aggregate supply may decline temporarily. However, the interpretation does not hold up if the changes in economic circumstances have a powerful political (nonmarket) component, as has been the case under Reaganism.

Since 1981, explicit political choices at the national level, such as those that made deep cuts in top tax rates and decreased the relative investment in public goods and services, have strikingly increased the maldistribution of resources. So have decisions not to enact legislation that aids ordinary families when the needed policy choice might be costly to business. The lack of health insurance reform in 2002 by the Bush administration offers a telling example. In the face of rapidly rising health costs, businesses have been moving to reduce and/or eliminate insurance coverage. Drew Altman, head of the Kaiser Family Foundation, which sponsored a study with the Health Research and Education Trust, has said that workers will be paying higher premiums but receiving less coverage.[8] After pointing out that large firms are ceasing to offer health benefits to future retirees—this protection was available in 66 percent of large firms in 1988 but only 34 percent by 2002—Altman said: "If I were a baby boomer, I would be quite worried about that." The national government has done nothing to restrict firms from cutting out retiree coverage or to take up the slack through federal programs, steps that would infuriate corporate America.

Such systematic efforts over time likely reduce the probability that tens of millions of families will be able to obtain the goods and services needed to maintain their standard of living during their working years and/or in their retirement. Even in the booming 1990s, increases in workforce participation and hours worked still left numerous middle-class families struggling to maintain their standard of living. The main problem has not been the traditional one of sharp price increases during times of strong economic growth but rather the rising costs for middle-class families of upgrading their purchases to have the desired bundle of good and services demanded for their lifestyle.

Let us look more closely at how a middle-class family with a rising income could have ended up running harder and harder to stay in place. To start with, the distribution of the growing economic pie disproportionately favored the wealthy in part because that group had benefited so greatly from tax cuts in the highest tax brackets. This top income group in turn generally upgraded its purchases and thereby pushed up the cost of both its own living standard and that of those families below the wealthy on the income scale. In response, the middle-class family ratcheted up its outlays to buy the upgraded items and maintain its socioeconomic status. Americans emulated the proverbial grasshopper playing in the summer sun without concern for anything but the vast cornucopia of goods and services put before them. Higher income and increased consumption were in a dangerous race, with the latter winning. The family likely enjoyed its expanded freedom of choice and its upgraded bundle of goods and services. But to do so, like many middle-class families, it may have in effect entered into a kind of Faustian bargain, trading higher current consumption for its middle-class status at retirement.

Mishel, Bernstein, and Schmitt offered the critical insight that *"for most households, rising debt—not a rising stock market—is the real story of the 1990s."*[9] Economic security declined for many as the yearly savings rate fell toward zero and the increased use of credit cards and second mortgages on homes brought record personal debt. A high economic growth rate like that of 1995–2000 can still trap middle-class families in a catch-22 situation partly of their own making: Increase net savings sufficiently to sustain their standard of living at retirement, but cut deeply into the preretirement standard—or maintain the latter and suffer a significant fall in their living standard at retirement.

Reaganism's basic tenets have led to policies that threaten freedom of choice for ordinary citizens by impinging on their effective demand while disproportionately benefiting the wealthiest individuals and larger corporations. There are tremendous economic strains on large numbers of families striving to keep their middle-class status. The prevailing political philosophy in the United States today is the enemy of democracy—be it the version of the Founders or the newer concept of a Democratic Ideal.

Ignoring Future Economic and Political Dangers

During the 1990s, when federal institutions of governance were rapidly deteriorating, the United States—drawing on its great strength derived from its vast size and resources and its entrepreneurial capacity—

reemerged as the world's wealthiest and most productive country and its premier market for goods and services, without an economic challenger in sight. So the economic boom of 1995–2000 made clear that institutional inefficiency in the domestic policy arena (except macroeconomic policy) does not necessarily bring the nation to its knees in a state of economic chaos. Further, plutocracy likely stimulated economic growth with its probusiness decisions and its tax cuts, and the growing maldistribution of income and wealth did not dampen consumer buying. Family living standards often rose, even if family members had to put in more hours of work, increase their debt, and do little or nothing toward building an adequate retirement fund during the economic boom.

The good news had been that the economic sky did not fall quickly because of the deterioration of the institutions of governance and growing economic inequality. Yet it did not follow that all was well. In particular, the outlook over time for middle-class families being able to maintain their standard of living at retirement had become grim. Of the three components of retirement income, only Social Security worked moderately well, and it needed improving. The other two components—employer-funded pensions and personal savings—moved in the wrong direction, and pensions were likely to continue their downward spiral. There were also major problems in health coverage for the aged. Unless the federal government came to the aid of the grasshopper-like public or many more families acquired the savings habits of the ant, future retirees faced a rising threat to their middle-class living standard. But in an America that again dominated the world in geopolitical and economic terms, the public did not want to look beyond the present toward potential economic and political problems.

The Failed Opportunity

The open policy window after the al Qaeda attacks offered the nation its first real opportunity to end early-stage plutocracy since it had reemerged in the late twentieth century and taken hold in Washington. As the perceptive political and economic critic Kevin Phillips observed in the final paragraph of his 2002 book *Wealth and Democracy:* "The imbalance of wealth and democracy in the United States is unsustainable, at least by traditional yardsticks. Market theology and unelected leadership have been displacing politics and elections. Either democracy must be renewed, with politics brought back to life, or wealth is likely to cement a new and less democratic regime—plutocracy by some other name."[10]

Unlike final-stage plutocracy, in which the wealthy, often in conjunction with the military, would be in full control of the political system, the American version retained a strong element of democracy. Its early-stage plutocracy does not give moneyed interests enough political power to prevent the public from having a meaningful role in determining the winning candidate in the general election. Under dire circumstances, the reelection imperative can panic politicians and force them to confront the hard choice between the demands of the public and those of corporate America. In early-stage plutocracy, then, the wealthy dominate the political process but are not fully in control, so the nation can come back toward representative democracy.

The revelations that started in late 2001 about the extent of corruption in corporate America appeared to increase dramatically the chance for restoring the balance between capitalism and democracy. Yet the weakened national government did not undertake a concerted political effort to rescue the nation from plutocracy, as had happened after the business excesses of the Gilded Age and the 1920s. No political leader came forward to attack corporate America's hold on Washington, as had been the case with first Theodore and then Franklin Roosevelt in the Progressive Era and the New Deal. Representative democracy did not replace plutocracy. The policy window closed, with the only material effort at institutional strengthening coming in the area of homeland security. Why did the opportunity to restore the efficiency of the political institutions concerned with domestic policy fare so poorly?

Two Competing Forces and the Policy Window

During the first year of George W. Bush's presidency, two catastrophes each had a devastating impact on the nation. When terrorists attacked the World Trade Center and the Pentagon, these were the first major assaults by foreign forces within the nation's borders since the War of 1812. Nor had any foreign threat since Pearl Harbor raised such high levels of fear and anguish among Americans. In the other catastrophe, the financial scandals of Enron and a number of other major corporations, the level and scope of corporate malfeasance exceeded any similar corruption since the 1920s. The two events together seemed to demand immediate, dramatic action that potentially could sweep away barriers to institutional reform.

The murder of American citizens by terrorists shown live hour after hour on television made the events so vivid and frightening that the notion of personal danger became a compelling force over time. Both Republicans and Democrats committed immediately and fully to the institutional effort to track down possible terrorists in the United States and make airports more secure. Washington, however, only reluctantly took on the job of punishing corporate America. A weakened McCain-Feingold campaign reform bill passed after years of failure. Yet even if McCain-Feingold had been stronger, it would not have changed the underlying elective system. Some problems had reached a point at which piecemeal approaches would not bring much improvement and could do more harm than good. There is no better example than the current dysfunctional campaign-financing system, in which nothing will work as long as politicians must beg corporate America for the wherewithal to keep their seats in Congress.

When Enron could be assailed as a single rogue firm, business appeared to be escaping with only minor restrictions. Then more unscrupulous accounting practices came to light that revealed grossly misstated earnings by a number of corporations, including WorldCom, Global Crossing, Adelphia, Tyco, and Dynegy. WorldCom admitted it had improperly accounted for a staggering $3.85 billion in expenses in less than two years and became the largest bankruptcy in U.S. history at $102 billion, far surpassing Enron at $66 billion. Corporate America's callous disregard for the rules of the game infuriated the public and frightened Congress so badly in an election year that it enacted strong measures to curb these reprehensible corporate practices, including stiff jail sentences for executives.

A mid-July 2002 *New York Times* article summed up the situation: "The Senate bill passed tonight was a result of a frenzy of bill writing in which Republicans and Democrats seemed to compete to show who could be tougher on corporate malfeasance."[11] The enacted bill, known as the Sarbanes-Oxley Act, established a Public Company Accounting Board that no longer allowed the accounting industry to perform its own oversight. Auditors were restricted in the sale of consulting services to firms they audited, chief executive officers and chief financial officers of public corporations had to certify the accuracy of financial reports, securities fraud became a criminal offense, and the length of prison sentences for fraud was increased. The opportunity opened for the United States, despite its weakened institutions, to move through the policy window toward reining in corporate America.

Yet this chance slipped away, for three main reasons. First, the anger of the public and the politicians touched only the tip of the iceberg. The greatest concern centered on a relatively small number of top corporate officials, some of whom made hundreds of millions of dollars through nefarious practices, escaped jail, and kept their ill-gotten gains while shareholders, particularly ordinary company employees, suffered large losses. At the same time, putting some corporate executives in prison (no matter how satisfying to the public) would only treat the highly visible part of the iceberg. The far larger, more dangerous submerged portion—big business's iron grip on the federal government—still remained.

Second, the legislation's tough standards had little chance of being rigorously implemented and enforced because electoral politics and the mentality of Bush administration insiders raised major barriers. Earlier righteous indignation about corporate skullduggery in Congress—no matter how strongly felt at the time—ran a poor second for most legislators to their continuing insatiable demand for campaign funds. The Bush administration's moral concerns also had a short duration. In discussing the new Public Company Accounting Board created by the Sarbanes-Oxley Act, *New York Times* business page columnist Floyd Norris drew on the observations of Joel Seligman, dean of the law school at Washington University in St. Louis and an expert on the Securities and Exchange Commission, to write on December 27, 2002: "[Seligman] says no change in securities law ever had 'a slower or more inept' start. 'They don't have a full board, don't have a budget, don't have a staff, don't have an office, don't have a plan. It's as sad a beginning as one can imagine.'"[12] In its defusing of the Sarbanes–Oxley Act, the tremendous power of plutocratic governance is clear when in the hands of an administration that equaled those of the 1920s in its commitment to corporate America and exceeded them in its willingness to use whatever means needed to further the interests of the wealthy.

Third, the threat of terrorism at home and abroad remained the Bush administration's and the public's overriding concern and thereby continued to attract the media's attention, while business corruption faded from view as a newsworthy issue. Business had ample leeway to express strong opposition to restrictive measures and ultimately to thwart them. As Jonathan Weisman wrote: "The recently devastated retirement accounts of employees from Enron Corp. and WorldCom Inc. initially fueled a wave of indignation among lawmakers in Washington and solemn vows to protect their investments. But the anger that pushed tough new accounting standards past corporate opponents this summer has already faded, lawmakers and lobbyists say, allowing businesses to regain their strength on Capitol Hill."[13]

In sum, both the Bush administration and Congress, after passing powerful corrective legislation in the face of public indignation, watered down the Sarbanes-Oxley Act in the implementation process and in so doing protected plutocratic governance after the public had ceased to focus on the fate of the new accounting board. Congress and the president acted adroitly by first responding rapidly to mass public concern so as not to upset the people and then later, after calm had been restored, by responding to corporate America so as not to upset big campaign contributors. Political competence protected big-money interests and plutocracy at the expense of the nation.

Back to Square One

I cannot overemphasize the costs of the lost opportunity when the policy window opened by the terrorist attacks and the business scandals closed without significant improvements having been made in the overall federal institutional structure. Widespread financial corruption in business and government had opened a policy window that increased the potential for generating critical institutional reforms to restore the balance between capitalism and democracy. The opportunity had arrived for the United States to end its plutocratic form of government, resurrect representative democracy, and bring the institutions of federal governance back to a level of competence, credibility, and capacity to compromise sufficient to sustain representative government. But the chance passed. A closed policy window again blocked the institutional reform of the battered American political system. Did either the politicians or the people realize how much was at stake? I am almost certain that the public did not and fearful that the politicians did.

A look at what Americans thought and did just before the terrorist attacks and a year later yields further evidence of the return to square one in terms of broad institutional reform. Trust in the federal government, which had soared to 64 percent soon after the attacks, had returned to 40 percent.[14] Pollster Richard Morin wrote in September 2002: "Nearly nine in ten— 86 percent—said the United States will rank as the most democratic and free nation in history or 'right up there with the best of them.'"[15]

As usual, citizens' professed belief in the superiority of American democracy did not bestir them to vote. David Broder, disturbed that "70 or 80 percent or more of those eligible to vote" in the 2002 primary election did not choose to do so, admonished the public that he has often praised in the past: "The flight from politics, the mass refusal to participate in the most basic responsibility of a citizen of the republic, would be grounds for criticism at any time. It is particularly unworthy for citizens of a nation that claims before the world the right to judge the acceptability of leaders of other lands—a nation that promotes 'regime change' in Iraq and tells the Palestinians to replace Yasser Arafat."[16]

At the first anniversary of September 11, the American people still had great concern about terrorism and a heightened patriotism that made them at least as oblivious as before the terrorist attacks to what the federal government was doing in other areas. Only the institutional concerns about strengthening homeland security as broadly defined remained a critical national issue. Further, this effort, by draining away federal resources and political attention, made it easier for national elected officials, top political appointees, and the public to ignore or at least downplay any other institutional problems. As the public's disquiet dissipated in the other areas needing institutional reform, politicians and corporate America turned to their real concern in 2002: the battle for the control of Congress. This election showed that the fixation on campaign contributions from moneyed interests had grown even worse.

Generally, the amount raised in presidential election years is far more than in midterm elections, but not in 2002. The two political parties together ran roughly 20 percent ahead in the 2000 presidential election, whereas both parties raised more than 150 percent more unrestricted soft money than in 1998.[17] A "veritable feeding-frenzy" captured the scene as the parties encircled corporations and lobbying firms to pick out victims, surely well aware that the latter would seek recompense for their six-figure contributions when legislation affected their profits. Washington had returned to normal in the case of the reelection imperative. The very serious game of fund-raising had become even more serious. The nastier and nastier war between the parties made it increasingly difficult for the House of Representatives and the Senate to carry out their most straightforward duties. In a telling case, Congress had not even been able to pass one of the thirteen appropriation bills by September 30, 2002. The spirit of bipartisanship awakened after the terrorist attacks had vanished.

The Task at Hand

Well before the first anniversary of September 11, the policy window for strengthening the dysfunctional American political institutions had closed, plutocratic governance remained firmly entrenched, and the same barriers to structural change so apparent just before the terrorist attacks stood just as high. In the face of these blockages, I found it counterproductive to craft specific organizational approaches that might meet the test of logical consistency but not the one of political feasibility. A detailed spelling out of proposals, such as full federal funding of all national elections or a federal regulatory system with an adequate cadre of competent monitors, would focus on the pros and cons of the options, not the urgency of recognizing the overall danger facing the U.S. political system.

My basic argument is that tinkering at the margins, even if successfully undertaken, will do little or no good and that major proposals such as those mentioned in the previous paragraph have no chance at the present time to be passed in recognizable form and well implemented. Instead, the real need is to put forward a well-reasoned argument that (1) the American political system no longer works, (2) the continued poor functioning over time of government institutions blocks any efforts to perform federal responsibilities efficiently and effectively, (3) these defects already have severely impinged on political equality and threaten economic opportunity and security, (4) a concerted effort to improve the national institutions of governance should be the pivotal first step in addressing the nation's most critical domestic policy problems and in moving the United States from plutocratic governance toward representative democracy, and (5) the profound changes in the key national institutions of governance and in the dominant political philosophy in the years since 1981 now threaten the economic security of the broad middle class.

The Institutions: Still Battered, Still Pivotal

After the terrorist attacks, the anthrax scare, corporate corruption, a sluggish economy, and the first big stock market reversal that numerous younger investors had experienced, fearful Americans saw the federal government as their protector. Expectations much exceeded performance. The roughly fifteen-month period from the 2001 terrorist attacks to the beginning of 2003 supplied overwhelming evidence—about as close as one can come in the social sciences to being definitive—supporting the earlier findings on the dangers of inefficient federal governance. What distinguished the year after September 11 is that the evidence of institutional inefficiency came out of the shadows to become a prominent story on prime-time television and on the front pages of newspapers. The accounts of individuals making it through the airport security checks with various and sundry weapons and the difficulties both in protecting the population against anthrax poisoning and in tracking down the person(s) responsible for that crime became of great interest to the public. Government inefficiency no longer was humorous or irritating (as in the old case of a toilet seat costing a federal agency several hundred dollars) but potentially life threatening.

Although the national government sought significant institutional reform in the broad area of homeland security, structural weaknesses bedeviled efforts to increase security. Existing institutional problems proved to be daunting, despite the desire of politicians, the permanent government, and the public for the government to perform the needed tasks efficiently. The implications of the post–September 11 experience could hardly be clearer: The significant institutional damage inflicted on federal agencies in the past generally rules out quick fixes. Serious reform is likely to require difficult internal changes in organizational structure and processes and in bureaucratic norms. A federal agency that has been battered by members of Congress, its own political executives, and staff serving the presidency seldom can turn itself around quickly, despite strong political and public support. The evidence after September 11 on the performance failure of federal agencies underscores why time is of the essence in restoring their institutional efficiency, be it in the area of homeland security or domestic policy. A concerted institutional reform effort is pivotal.

Congress appears to be the most battered of federal government institutions, less and less capable of carrying out its most important institutional responsibilities. No loss is more clear or more critical than that of the reasoned deliberations needed for sensible compromise. This lack of meaningful debate became clear in the passage of the resolution that gave President Bush the broad power to "use the armed forces of the United States as he determines to be necessary and appropriate in order to defend the national security of the United States against the continuing threat posed by Iraq." In the October 9, 2002, *New York Times* reporter David Firestone described the purpose of the speeches before the final congressional vote on the resolution on Iraq: "Away from the microphones, members admitted that the three-day deliberation . . . was not a true test of ideas. . . . Though the buildup to Thursday's [October 10] vote is technically called a debate, members said it was more accurately a series of individual explanations from elected officials to their voters, justifying a difficult choice."[18] These were not the deliberations that James Madison and the Progressives had envisioned as integral to representative democracy.

Passion did not impel protagonists to try in the heat of battle to sway some of their peers in a last effort to win the vote. The Democratic senator from West Virginia, Robert C. Byrd, who at the time was well into his eighties and serving in his sixth decade in Congress, sharply protested against the lack of meaningful debate on the Iraq resolution:

> Titus Livius, one of the greatest of Roman historians, said all things will be clear and distinct to the man who does not hurry. Haste is blind and improvident. Blind and improvident. . . . For as sure as the sun rises in the east, this country is embarking on a course of action with regard to Iraq that in its haste is blind and improvident. We are rushing into war without fully discussing why, without thoroughly considering the consequences, or without making any attempt to explore what steps we might take to avert a conflict.[19]

Byrd's condemnation centered on deficient execution in the decision-making process—that is, on the means. Senators had shirked their fundamental institutional responsibility to deliberate and in so doing had failed their country. A resolution may still have passed after a real debate, but it would have emerged from the give-and-take that is central to a well-functioning Senate. To no avail, Senator Byrd had cried out that his colleagues had no clothes on. The Senate passed the resolution on October 11 with a vote of 77–23 after the House had voted 296–133 a day earlier in support of the president. In this momentous decision, serious debate aimed at clarifying issues, rather than scoring political points, had not served as either a base for constructive congressional compromises or a means of informing the public on the great issues of the day.

Senator Bryd's warning came before the vote in the Security Council of the United Nations that did restrain the United States from rushing into a war against Iraq when it mandated a serious UN inspection effort in that country. But the UN action hardly absolves Congress of its failure to undertake serious deliberations in search of a sensible compromise on United States policy on Iraq. That body lacked the capacity to compromise even when faced with the overriding policy decision about undertaking a preemptive strike against Iraq without a specific provocation. Congress as an institution had lost the competence, the capacity to compromise, and the internal credibility needed to be a functioning legislature.

A final note on what is required for institutional reform: Although a transformational leader such as either of the two Roosevelts is the most important requirement for restoring representative democracy, institutional reform is still pivotal. Even if an exogenous force such as a depression opens a policy window, a leader will be better off with strengthened institutions. An exceptional driver still needs a sound vehicle to perform well. There is a chicken-and-egg problem, however, in that institutional reform also demands leadership. At the same time, some important structural changes may be possible within the institutions before the transformational leader comes on the scene or an exogenous factor opens a policy window. But no one should doubt the difficulty.

Entrenched Plutocracy

During the time the policy window stood open, the nation made little or no progress toward restoring representative democracy and the federal institutions of governance needed to sustain it. No concerted effort was made to reduce the excessive power of moneyed interests sufficiently to restore the balance between capitalism and democracy. The United States missed out on the only real opportunity it has had, in the years since plutocracy returned, to break corporate America's grip on the federal government. Further, nothing appeared on the horizon that pointed to the coming of a similar opportunity. Nor did a new chance necessarily look so appealing, given that it might well come from a devastating occurrence such as an horrendous terrorist attack or a deep economic downturn with extended double-digit unemployment.

Had plutocratic governance become so entrenched that it was able to protect American business in the face of strong corrective legislation by thwarting its implementation as corporate insiders interacted with Washington insiders? This question is complicated by the fact that September 11 and the massive corporate financial corruption occurred in the same time period. The latter could conceivably have led to fundamental financial reform if Osama bin Laden had not come into the picture. That is, failing to enact stronger legislation could have been mainly a consequence of an exogenous catastrophe involving a horrendous attack and the fear of future assaults. Not surprisingly, the continuing deep concern kept the nation from giving full attention to the needed financial reforms. It is not warranted to infer, only on the basis of the lack of fundamental institutional change, that plutocratic government is now entrenched more deeply than in earlier periods of plutocracy. Nor is it possible to rule out the claim. What can be said is that plutocracy survived—be it because of fate (the juxtaposition of two unrelated events) or the excessive political power of moneyed interests—and in so doing became stronger.

President George W. Bush, with a handful of former chief executive officers (CEOs) among his top advisers, had the principal role in stabilizing plutocracy at the critical time when its hold on Washington was put in jeopardy by corporate corruption. But the Democrats' contribution must not be overlooked. Even before President Bush gained high political standing from his leadership after the terrorist attacks, the Democrats chose not to contest the most important tax legislation in at least two decades because they feared that their opposition might alienate voters who generally want tax reductions and bring down the wrath of their big campaign contributors. Together, the Republicans with their plutocracy-generating philosophy of governance and the election-fixated Democrats made an unlikely but ideal pair to quell the challenge to plutocratic governance in its hour of need.

After the Republican Party made striking gains in the November 2002 elections and regained control of Congress, the Bush administration moved quickly to seek benefits for the wealthy while mainly ignoring ordinary Americans. The White House's unrelenting commitment to Reaganism's tenet of repeated tax cuts at the top led it to support a reduction in dividend taxes that would mainly pass over roughly 90 percent of families and deliver by far the biggest bonanza to the top 1 percent.[20] To Bush, tax breaks for the rich became the preferred policy choice whatever the economic malady.

In the case of the environment, President Bush inflicted the lightest of punishments on owners of sport-utility vehicles—a 1.5-mile-per-gallon increase in gas efficiency by 2007. A *New York Times* editorial pointed out that the increase was "far less than what the National Academy of Sciences says is possible for all cars with existing off-the-shelf technology."[21] At the same time, the administration did not push for extra funds to the states, which were going through their worst financial crisis since the 1930s, so they could avoid cutting programs benefiting lower- and middle-income families. Under George W. Bush, plutocracy was on the march as the government engaged in class warfare for the benefit of the wealthy while spouting compassionate conservatism.

Unlike final-stage (pure) plutocracy, which allows tightly controlled elections but overtly holds down the people, America's unique brand of plutocracy is the bastard child of the pure version and the reelection imperative and gains strength from mimicking representative democracy. The current version can be employed to aggrandize American democracy as exceptional, while offering a lesser brand, and packaging it to appear as a form of representative democracy. What it takes to pull off the subterfuge are Washington's risk-averse politicians, who are adroit at misleading propaganda, along with a relatively uninformed, overconfident electorate, which worships but does not read its secular bible written in Philadelphia in 1787. The politicians praise the wisdom of the people and speak of the wonders of the world's greatest democracy, certainly not of the emergence of plutocracy or its dangers. They assiduously avoid any act that might overtly reduce the freedom of choice of consumers (it can be done so easily indirectly) and would be very reluctant to ask the American people to reduce engaging in some pleasurable activity, such as driving less, to reduce oil dependence. Plutocracy in its present guise carries an appealing patina of democracy without sacrifice that makes it quite palatable. It is also insidious. Plutocracy by stealth still favors the wealthy and holds back the institutional reform needed if the United States is to regain representative democracy as embodied in the Constitution.

In sum, Reaganism had been critical in the emergence of plutocratic governance by fostering a political environment conducive to the expansion of the imbalance between capitalism and democracy. The tenets of today's dominant political philosophy provided chapter and verse for regenerating plutocracy late in the twentieth century and continue to be the guide to its continuation. Moreover, plutocracy had been much strengthened in George W. Bush's administration and Congress protected it from the strong provisions of the Sarbanes-Oxley Act aimed at reducing corporate America's undue power in Washington. That new strength made clear the urgency of warning that plutocratic governance and a watered-down version of democracy now thrive and will continue to do so as long as Reaganism remains the nation's predominant political philosophy.

The Radically Changed Political Environment

If a modern-day Rip Van Winkle had fallen asleep before January 20, 1981, he would have been struck upon awakening by the changes brought by Reaganism. Numerous battles between the parties had left in ruins the national political institutions that had once been sufficiently sturdy to impose boundaries on naked politics and to foster a degree of bipartisanship. Institutional competence and internal credibility had long been hospitalized, whereas the capacity to compromise hardly breathed in the intensive care unit. Each election became a life-or-death struggle that justified the use of any weapons or the abandonment of principles that, if kept, might have political costs at the polls.

By the time President George W. Bush entered office in 2001, the political pollution level had soared to a far higher count than had existed at the start of the Reagan presidency. In discussing broad political developments, Robert Kuttner, coeditor of the progressive journal *The American Prospect,* wrote: "These trends, all of which debase politics, have been building for a long time; their full fruit is George W. Bush."[22] Labeling him as the "full fruit" of long-term institutional changes does not necessarily imply that President Bush has a more deeply flawed character than his predecessors. Federal Reserve chair Alan Greenspan, after calling the late 1990s a time of "infectious greed," made a similar point when he said to the Senate Banking Committee: "It is not that humans have become any more greedy than in generations past. It is the avenues to express greed that have grown so enormously."[23]

In more than two decades of Reaganism, not only had the tools of political lying grown sharper, the increasingly mean atmosphere had made current politicians more likely to use them. At the same time, political timidity also increased as the reelection imperative became a fixation for the individual candidate and the parties. Each election in the evenly split House and Senate involved the question of control. *Washington Post* columnist David Broder, who is the dean of today's political analysts and highly regarded for his balanced, judicious opinions, harshly criticized the Democratic Party's leaders in his late September 2002 op-ed piece for their failure to mount a stronger challenge to the resolution giving the president authority to wage war against Saddam Hussein and their earlier undue caution in the case of the 2001 tax cut:

> But there is something deeper—and less justifiable—at work. The Democratic leaders in Congress, in both the House and the Senate, largely have abandoned principle and long-term strategy for the short-term tactics they think will help them in this November's election—even on large and consequential matters. . . . The Democrats' refusal to face up to that fundamental issue [of the tax cut] leaves them without credibility for their entire critique of Bush's economic policy.[24]

The reelection imperative had reached its apex in so paralyzing the Democrats that they would not confront President Bush on the tax cut and Iraq—by far the biggest issues in his presidency until that time—lest they jeopardize winning the November election. Can there be better evidence that Congress has ceased to function?

When George W. Bush entered the presidential race, he also entered a terribly polluted political environment, where Marquis of Queensberry rules had ceased to be used. The path to the bottom had been well paved. This is not to say that the deeds of political leaders—such as President Bush's deception and the cowardice of the Democratic leadership—could be explained solely by the impact of outside forces. But it is equally untenable to think that the system-damaging behavior by both parties came about only because of the increasingly defective character of individual politicians. The better explanation is that politicians' personal flaws and the deterioration of the U.S. political system interacted to bring consistently unacceptable individual behavior that the weakened institutions of governance could not restrain. There were not just a few rotten apples in the barrel; the container itself had rotted.

George W. Bush is the full bitter fruit of Reaganism—the truest of true believers in its core principles. He restored that political doctrine at least to the level of its golden days in the reign of Ronald Reagan, after Presidents George H. W. Bush and Bill Clinton had failed to rigorously adhere to it. Like Reagan, President George W. Bush demonstrated his capacity to lead, in his case with his vigorous fight against terrorism. This ability, however, is necessary but not sufficient for bringing about the required institutional change. Without the needed policy objectives, strong leadership can be counterproductive. Hence, President Bush's ideological embrace of Reaganism produced the wrong leader when the wide-open policy window made it the right time to push hard for major structural repairs and for redirecting domestic policy toward greater economic security, individual freedom, and political equality.

Although the Bush administration may not have become more probusiness and less concerned with the plight of the low- and middle-income families than the Reagan administration, the structural changes after 1981 meant that President Bush could go well beyond Reagan, the godfather of Reaganism. A *New York Times* editorial succinctly captured the reality of Reaganism in the era of Bush's "compassionate conservatism": "The Bush budget is a road map toward a different kind of American society, in which the government no longer taxes the rich to aid the poor, and in fact does very little but protect the nation from foreign enemies."[25] Bush pushed the United States deeper into plutocracy as he carried the banner of Reaganism into its third decade.

Deus Ex Machina

Looking backward to see the many problems and forward to consider the likely barriers makes me feel much like the ancient Greek playwrights. They created a hopeless tangle by the start of the final act that defied the ability of mere mortals to save the day. But there are two big differences. First, the description of the lamentable political environment is about a real not a contrived situation crafted by a long-dead Greek playwright. Second, a solution lay at hand in that those who wrote plays could call forth the "god from the machinery"—deus ex machina—to save the day. Actors representing gods were physically suspended above the stage so they could intervene and miraculously sweep away all the thorny problems. 'Twas a wondrous device that never failed. With no equivalent of the ancient Greek gambit in today's tool box, a magical fix cannot provide a quick escape from the tangled political environment specified in detail in the previous chapters. The policy window for institutional reform is again tightly shut.

At basic issue is how to convince U.S. citizens that the nation itself needs fundamental change in moving back toward representative democracy and that they are a big part of the problem in blocking the needed institutional restoration. Americans laud the nation's brand of democracy at every turn. But such unqualified extolling of democracy papers over ordinary citizens' failure to participate in the political process. Not only do citizens vote less and less, much of the electorate apparently has little or no interest in acquiring political knowledge and instead sees it as taking away hours that could be used for work or leisure. When this limited interest is juxtaposed against the considerable time and energy entailed in sustaining representative democracy, the effort demanded looks to be more that the average voter is willing to bear.

Condemning the overburdened, manipulated American people for their adherence to Reaganism and their inadequate efforts in meeting the responsibilities of citizenship may seem unwarranted in light of all the other culprits. The electorate has been lied to and misled by politicians; deprived of political equality by corporate America using campaign contributions and an army of highly paid lobbyists to dominate the political process; and ill served by today's elites, who have sought to increase the imbalance between capitalism and democracy. The telling point, however, is that the Founders put the electorate on the spot by casting the people as the guardians of representative democracy, and that is where they remain more than 200 years later.

The beginning words of the Preamble to the Constitution are not "we the politicians," and certainly not "we the elites"—for the new nation rejected the rule of a monarch and a titled aristocracy—but "We the People." More than three decades after that document became the law of the land, James Madison, the man most responsible in 1787 for the original Constitution, still held fast in 1822 to the notion of the centrality of the citizenry in sustaining it: "The people who mean to be their own Governors, must arm themselves with the power knowledge gives."[26] Benjamin Franklin answered a question about the form of government decided upon in the Constitutional Convention by saying, "A Republic, if you can keep it." The people have not carried out their most basic responsibility of preserving the American Republic by acquiring the political knowledge needed to select national officeholders with the wisdom and integrity to serve them well. They have failed to "keep it."

Fixing blame, however, is far less important than the question of whether the maelstrom of the nasty politics of big money and the re-election imperative has raised insurmountable barriers to restoring representative democracy sustained by a firm foundation of sound federal governing institutions. At issue is whether citizens are willing and able to fulfill their historic role. They are suspect on both counts. Not only have citizens stayed away from the voting booth; they have clung to Reaganism with its certitude about the myths it upholds. After all, rejecting its tenets would force the people to call into question their own performance as citizens and their depth of commitment to democracy. That is, the refutation of Reaganism would deny that the public is meeting the responsibilities of good citizenship and that the American Republic is thriving.

Restoring representative democracy demands that the people be willing to accept a realism in which they cast aside their comforting beliefs that lack validity. No findings discussed above, however, indicate much of a chance that citizens will opt for reality. Even with much greater effort by the electorate, the issue of competence would remain. The American people are generally being inundated with too much political information and an abundance of tainted numbers and commentary and are left to sort out the good from the bad. Yet, working through complex policy issues, particularly those demanding numeracy and/or a degree of economic understanding, may be beyond what can be expected of the ordinary citizen.

Too many politicians, pundits, and professors either believe in the people's wisdom or at least join the crowd in praising it. But it ill serves the effort for major institutional reform to argue that citizens in some mysterious way can make wise choices on their own that will turn the system around. Neither the law of large numbers nor the god of the machine will bring a happy ending. The long-held notion of the people's miraculous wisdom "without the power that knowledge gives" is wrong. Madison was right in 1787 and in 1822 that the people could not be "their own Governors" without arming themselves with political knowledge. That proposition is even truer in the turbulent politics of today.

Besides greater effort on their own, citizens will need all the help they can get. The United States is going to throw off plutocracy only with wise leadership and well-functioning national political institutions in which there are serious debates and sensible compromises about policies that meet the nation's pressing needs. Honest deliberations and a high level of professional journalism must provide the electorate with sound data and commentary in a form it can use effectively. This discussion, although critical of the people's poor citizenship, is not meant to place all the blame for the current dysfunctional political system on the electorate. Restoring representative democracy will demand responsible efforts by the key actors in the system, and the barriers will still be high.

Plutocracy has become increasingly stable in the Bush administration, which protected it at its point of greatest crisis, when the people turned on corporate America. Paul Krugman has observed: "In retrospect, it's hard to see why anyone believed that our current leadership was serious about corporate reform. To an extent unprecedented in recent history, this is a government of, by, and for corporate insiders. I'm not just talking about influence, I'm talking about personal career experience."[27] Two of the most powerful players, Vice President Dick Cheney and Secretary of Defense Donald Rumsfeld, had long service in government before becoming CEOs. Interestingly, their careers followed almost the same lines, with both men having been President Gerald Ford's chief of staff, members of Congress, and defense secretaries in earlier administrations. And though the ex-CEO president, George W. Bush, had never been a Washington insider, he had gained considerable political experience through his father.

This government of insiders—who were experienced and knowledgeable about the two overlapping worlds of business and Washington and unalterably committed to business values and interests—provided strong support for continuing plutocratic governance. America's corporations had their own kind in control of the federal institutions of government.

Despite the country's history as the premier democratic nation, it is wrong to assume that plutocratic governance will fall of its own weight. First, American business has had far more influence on the U.S. federal government than the corporate sector has had in peer capitalist nations. Second, long-standing public distrust of the federal government and admiration of capitalist enterprise make it likely that citizens will tend to fear that Washington will hold back business more than they worry that corporate America will unduly influence the national government and diminish democracy. Once plutocratic governance has emerged in the United States, factors inherent in it will not necessarily bring that government down. That argument becomes far more compelling in the current political environment, in which Reaganism dominates political thinking and the Democratic Ideal holds sway. The two notions, both of which rest on a fundamental belief in the greatness of the nation and its form of government, reduce the likelihood that citizens will perceive that the United States has become a plutocracy.

Plutocratic governance in the United States does retain a degree of democracy. And a somewhat more benign plutocracy may satisfy most citizens as long as they can revel in the myth of America as the exemplar of democracy to the world and still obtain the bundle of possessions signifying middle-class status. To do so, however, substitutes a pale version of democracy for the Founders' towering concept of political equality built on the fundamental belief that the people should be their own masters.

Those who created the new nation accepted distinctions in income and wealth based on merit, but they also held that democracy was safest without significant inequality in resources among citizens. Tension between capitalism and democracy did at times widen the economic disparities among citizens too far, but political leaders came forth to restore the balance. In particular, the first quarter-century of the post–World War II era brought greater economic and political equality. Only in the last decades of the twentieth century did another dangerous imbalance arise between capitalism and democracy to threaten both the political equality of ordinary citizens and the economic security of the broad middle class.

Early in the twenty-first century, professing the greatness of American democracy has come to suffice for having the real thing. That is fine as long as citizens understand the full implications of choosing plutocratic governance and the Democratic Ideal. I write in the belief that first, they do not, and second, that they will want the real version back. If not, the need is for a fundamental rethinking of the American political system based on the rejected form of democracy established by the framers of the Constitution. But first things first. I have chosen to make the case for restoring representative democracy and the national institutions of government needed to sustain it and for rejecting the plutocratic governance and the tepid democracy that have emerged under Reaganism.

eleven

Epilogue

Since 1981, the nation has experienced a transformation in its political institutions and philosophy of governance unrivaled in the modern presidency, save for the New Deal era. The shift that had been striking in the first two decades of Reaganism gained speed under President George W. Bush. Twenty years of Reaganism afforded Bush the base for "out-Reaganing" Reagan in the rapidity of institutional change during his first three years.

President Bush's one–two punch—combining his huge tax cuts that disproportionately benefited the rich and his war on terrorism at home and abroad—materially strengthened plutocracy, further damaged the key institutions of governance, blocked new domestic policy spending, and put the economic security of the broad middle class in jeopardy. In assessing the damage wrought by Reaganism to the nation's political institutions and the American people, Ronald Reagan can be credited with doing greater harm overall because his political philosophy has dominated since 1981. In the first three years of his presidency, however, George W. Bush attacked the foundation of the institutions in the American political system more relentlessly and inflicted more damage than any of his predecessors during a comparable period of time.

I cannot overemphasize how profoundly the U.S. political institutions and the nation's view of their role have changed under Reaganism. It is not hyperbole to label the shift in less than a quarter-century as a *radical transformation*. Yet almost no one—neither the public nor the pundits nor the academic specialists—seemed to notice the speeding train pass by.

The Deceptive Propaganda Presidency

President Bush accepted completely the tenets of Reaganism, even apparently supporting the tax cuts for rich people and the interests of corporate America more than Reagan himself had. The critical difference between the two administrations emerged in Bush's mode of governance—in particular, the dramatic increase in the use of deception to sell proposed policies. President Reagan had ushered in the modern era of presidential propaganda as the first television president. His staff's masterly news management, however, usually sought the right television image on the evening news, such as President Reagan striding forth and waving to the crowd to show his vigorous leadership. Bill Clinton institutionalized spinning in the White House and excelled at it, but his staff mainly focused on polishing his tarnished image.

The extent to which deceptive propaganda had been employed in Bush's first three years to sell major policy proposals makes the Bush administration radically different from any earlier presidency. However, his deception as an offensive weapon only sold well with the home audience, as evidenced by Bush's success in convincing the U.S. public that a preemptive strike on Iraq had to be made and his failure to persuade people in other nations. *New York Times* columnist Nicholas Kristof pointed out that even in Britain—America's staunchest ally in the war—a poll found that "fewer than one person in seven trusted President Bush to tell the truth."[1]

Kristof offered this observation based on his discussion with a Chinese journalist covering the Iraqi war: "'This is propaganda,' he said brightly. 'I was born and grew up in a propaganda country, and so I know it well.' ... There's a Beijing-style rah-rah self-righteousness, too earnest by half, so the propaganda fizzles.'" People in other nations easily saw through the administration's distorted, moralistic assertions; Americans did not. Why U.S. citizens failed to question the claims can be explained in part by their intense patriotism. Equally or more telling was how fiercely they clung to the myth that their presidents would be moral and truthful in the Oval Office, having condemned President Clinton for failing to possess these attributes.

Bush's professed righteousness greatly appealed to the American public and underscored their continued belief in the institution of the presidency and the personal commitment to "faithfully execute the office of the President of the United States." After three years, even though distortion in pursuit of policy objectives has become second nature in the Bush administration, the president continued to be regarded by much of the citizenry as a moral leader willing to tell it like it is. This duality was striking in his 2003 tax reduction proposal, in which Bush went to extraordinary lengths to deceive the American people.

The Bush Tax Cuts

President Bush's 2003 tax relief proposal that over ten years would have cost $726 billion and eliminated taxes on most corporate dividends will receive extensive consideration. His initial proposal—not the later efforts to reduce its cost and shift to other means such as reducing the tax rate on capital gains—will be considered. The primary rationale for the extended discussion is that President Bush's gross distortions about a critical policy choice strikes at the very essence of constitutional democracy.

The president's concerted attempt to mislead the American people on his tax reduction proposal is cut from the same cloth as his successful effort to convince the public that Saddam Hussein had close ties to al Qaeda when he did not and that Iraqis were among the September 11 terrorists when none in fact were. *New York Times* columnist Paul Krugman's comments on Bush's misleading statements on Iraq also apply to his tax relief proposal: "A democracy's decisions, right or wrong, are supposed to take place with the informed consent of its citizens. That didn't happen this time. And we are a democracy—aren't we?"[2] If neither the president, Congress, nor the media tell the public the truth about major policy proposals, there can be no informed consent. Without it, democracy withers.

Tax Cuts and Economic Growth

Tax reductions for the wealthy started out as Bush's flagship policy, and after September 11, 2001, gaining tax cuts for the wealthy almost totally dominated his domestic agenda. The true believers on the Republican right could not have been more pleased. Strong antigovernmentism types hated the income tax above all taxes and held that it fell much too heavily on rich people. To make matters worse, the tax receipts were then used for programs that the Republican far right believed encouraged sloth, family breakup, and other behavior offensive to them. Staunch Reaganites also liked these tax cuts because the wealthy poured political contributions into Republican campaign coffers. Yet there was a problem. These reasons could bring the true believers to their feet in a speech, but they were unlikely to sell tax cuts for the rich to the general public.

An appealing proposition became the justification for disproportionate benefits going to the country's richest people: Tax cuts will provide strong incentives for the beneficiaries to engage in more work and investment, and all these efforts together will be a powerful stimulus for faster growth in the nation's gross domestic product. Further, the reduced federal tax receipts and the ensuing yearly budget deficits will block wasteful domestic policy overspending. Tax cuts, so the theory went, are the perfect fix for what ails a sluggish U.S. economy and an overweight federal budget.

Not surprisingly, advocates of Reaganism came to conceive of the positive relationship between tax cuts and national growth as a fundamental truth. Be that as it may, the actual experience over many years showed that tax cuts did not stimulate faster economic growth. As New York University economist William Easterly wrote in summing up what had actually happened: "'You can make a theoretical case that high taxes impede economic growth, but it is just not supported by the evidence in the U.S. or across countries.'"[3]

Researchers had found that workers did not reduce their hours of labor when taxes rose or increase them when tax rates dropped. Nor, as Jeff Madrick, the editor of *Challenge Magazine,* wrote did "high tax rates erode the entrepreneurial spirit."[4] The outstanding economic growth in the period 1995–2000 occurred even though the highest tax bracket had been increased from 31 to 39.6 percent in 1993. No serious research to date has suggested that the 1997 tax cut on capital gains induced the rapid economic growth of the late 1990s. The great cure-all of Reaganomics proved wanting when applied.

The hypothesis about the efficacy of tax cuts, however, was not just a theory, it was an unchallengeable proposition central to Reaganism. Empirical reality could not shake the true believers, including President Bush, from holding that tax cuts offered an all-purpose remedy. His 2003 stimulus package called for $726 billion in tax reductions over ten years, of which roughly $300 billion would go for the elimination of taxes on most corporate dividends. Joseph Stiglitz, a chair of the Council of Economic

Advisers in the Clinton administration, wrote: "It must have been hard for Bush to design a tax program that cost so much in revenue while at the same time doing so little to stimulate the economy."[5]

A well-designed tax stimulus to kick-start a sagging economy would immediately get money into the hands of those who would spend it quickly—for instance, unemployed persons or states and communities frantic for financial help to cover unmet needs. Such a stimulus, however, is anathema to the true believers in Reaganism because the tax cut would go mainly to lower- and middle-income people. Eliminating taxes on corporate dividends might lack the attributes of an effective stimulus, but it had the wondrous property of performing like a smart bomb with pinpoint accuracy in delivering the payload to the wealthiest taxpayers without the collateral damage of the funds falling on those having low incomes.

Policy versus Politics

Bush's proposal on taxable corporate dividends may have been egregious public policy, but it was crafty politics. In his January 22, 2003, speech in St. Louis, the president drew on the fact that stock ownership had risen during the 1990s to roughly 50 percent of the population to proclaim that "'92 million Americans will keep an average of $1,083 more of their money when this tax plan goes through.'"[6] Bush left unsaid that middle-income families mainly hold stocks in retirement accounts, such as 401(k)s that already have tax advantages and would not qualify for the proposed reduction in taxes. Estimates from the highly reliable Urban Institute–Brookings Institution Tax Policy Center showed that "80 percent of tax filers would receive less than the $1,023 'average' amount, while about half of the tax filers would receive $100 or less."

Bush's high "average" number that suggested tens of millions of tax filers would likely save a thousand dollars or more derived from combining (1) a relatively small group receiving large amounts of tax relief in the proposal, including those making over a million dollars a year who would average $90,000; and (2) a huge group including about half of all tax filers whose expected tax relief would be $100 or less. The Bush average— the arithmetic mean—had been calculated by dividing the full amount of the tax reductions for the ten-year period by the total number of tax filers. In statistical jargon, the extremely large incomes in the income distribution skewed (i.e., made higher) the average amount of tax relief in the president's proposal.

An example with five tax filers will help make clear the potential for distortion when there is a highly skewed arithmetic mean. Suppose a proposed tax plan, if enacted, would provide tax relief of $50 each to four tax filers, or $200 for all four, and $9,800 to the fifth for a total tax decrease of $10,000. The architect of this proposal—using the arithmetic mean and drawing on President Bush's St. Louis statement—could claim that each of the five tax filers will keep an average of $2,000 ($10,000 divided by 5) more of their money when this tax plan goes through.

This example of skewing, which shows 80 percent of the beneficiaries having their taxes reduced by only $50 after their visions of gaining $2,000 in tax relief, makes clear how a technically correct number can be used to deceive people that they will be big winners. President Bush liked this particular weapon of deception so much that he used it for other groups of tax filers—for example, telling his St. Louis audience that "'23 million small business owners will receive an average tax cut of $2,042 under this plan,'" when 79 percent would get a lower amount and over 50 percent would benefit by less than $500.[7]

Public-Sector and Private-Sector Deception

A private-sector example of several investment firms' deception offers another perspective on President Bush and tax relief. In late April 2003, Stephen Labaton of the *New York Times* reported a settlement by ten of the largest Wall Street investment firms: "The $1.4 billion settlement . . . resolved accusations that the firms lured millions of investors to buy billions of dollars worth of shares in companies they knew were troubled. . . . [The securities analysts] *wittingly duped* investors to curry favor with corporate clients."[8] The analysts' deception prevented their clients from making informed choices.

"Wittingly duped" also describes precisely what President Bush did to the American public in deceiving them about his tax proposal. Stiglitz wrote: "What is so impressive about the Bush tax proposals is the sheer brazenness with which they have been sold. Evidently thinking that the average American would not be able to understand statistics . . . and think that he will get the average benefit."[9] Both the security analysts and President Bush

engaged in purposeful deception to dupe their targets, but the latter's behavior is far more reprehensible. First, caveat emptor holds in the case of securities analysts; in contrast, citizens could be expected to be less suspicious of their president who had made so much of his good character compared with Clinton and had stood so tall after the terrorist attacks.

Second, Bush's deception was on a far greater scale than that of the investment firms. Joel Friedman and Robert Greenstein of the Center on Budget and Policy Priorities, drawing on the estimates from the Urban Institute–Brookings Institution Tax Policy Center, underscored how Bush's proposed tax elimination plan would actually work: "The group with incomes over $1 million—which consists of about 226,000 tax filers in 2003—would receive roughly as much in benefits as the 127 million tax filers with income below $140,000. Stated another way, the top 0.2 percent of tax filers would receive nearly as much from the tax cut as the bottom 95 percent of filers combined."[10] *Bush's use of grossly distorted propaganda in his attempt to provide roughly as much tax relief to less than a quarter-million tax filers with incomes of $1,000,000 or more as to the 127 million with incomes of $140,000 or less is both class warfare and unscrupulous presidential behavior at mind-boggling levels.*

Institutions under Siege

The British member of Parliament Julian Critchley in 1982 said of Prime Minister Margaret Thatcher (now Baroness Thatcher of Kesteven) that "'she cannot see an institution without hitting it with a handbag.'"[11] President Bush could bash institution for institution with the prime minister in her heyday. The new president immediately banged away with might and main at his own institution, inflicting major damage as he twisted the presidency out of shape. Using the White House as the base for deceptive propaganda on policy was but one aspect of his destructiveness from within.

The Bush administration has gone far beyond any earlier administration in controlling the presidency. First, George W. Bush and his inner circle excelled at keeping the administration on message and keeping Congress (except for their key allies) and the media in the dark about their machinations. Moreover, the administration sought to restrict access to information generally by such efforts as reclassifying documents as secret and limiting the Freedom of Information Act. At the very time when the need for transparency in government has been increasingly recognized by the world's democracies, the Bush administration mounted a successful effort to block access by the other political institutions to the information the public needed for informed consent.

Second, the administration was equally skilled in coercing individuals and institutions, with its greatest success coming from the intimidation of the congressional Democrats and the media. Punishment was swift and intended to do serious harm to those not supporting the administration's position. For example, the White House would coerce a Democrat in Congress who did not have a safe seat by threatening to find a strong challenger and pour out campaign money to support him or her in the next election. Bush did not invent intimidation, and there had been others who excelled like Lyndon Johnson, but the administration went much beyond those of the past with its single-minded efforts to punish harshly those who dared to defy it.

While President Bush was doing harm to Congress as an institution, that body continued to suffer from self-inflicted wounds. House Republican majority leader Tom DeLay, who as de facto leader of that institution became the most powerful person in Congress after his party recaptured the House in November 2002, exerted a level of control similar to that of President Bush. For example, Democratic representatives were kept from offering amendments on the floor. Mary Lynn Jones observed that this restriction has "made the House a one-horse show" and quoted Democratic representative Barney Frank of Massachusetts that the House "'is not in any way a deliberative body anymore.'"[12] The tight Republican control in the Oval Office and the House, combined with the further decline of the media, allowed a small number of Republicans committed to the tenets of Reaganism to dominate the agenda. This excessive control further degraded the institutional decision-making process that the Founders intended to be based on constructive deliberations and reasoned compromises within Congress and between that body and the president.

During his first three years, President Bush so intimidated the media that this institution failed to expose the administration's deception on the tax plan and Iraq, point up its mismanagement and its failure to provide reasonable levels of funding in the domestic policy arena, and to warn of the administration's fundamental threat to democracy. Moreover, the media's fawning over the president's morality and leadership after September 1, 2001, especially after the swift military victory in Iraq, was unseemly even in the era of bottom-line journalism. Intimidation by the administration joined with the profit motive and pushed the media to a distinctly lower level than in the Clinton years, when critics had lamented the precipitous institutional decline.

President Bush has figuratively swung the Thatcher handbag to strike a wide range of institutional structures and procedures. But let us consider only a single, particularly disturbing, case. A *New York Times* editorial observed: "[President Bush] has permitted his far-right base to take over vast swarms of domestic policy making. . . . The Department of Housing and Urban Development, for instance, recently announced plans to allow public funds to be used to help build churches, as long as part of the building is used to provide social services."[13]

Two centuries ago, Thomas Jefferson, who had the major role in writing the Declaration of Independence, and James Madison, the father of the Constitution, warned in no uncertain terms about the grave dangers of failing to build "a wall of separation between church and State," to quote Jefferson.[14] By attacking the wall of separation to please the Christian fundamentalists who had gained great influence in the Republican Party, President Bush has carried Reaganism in a new, system-threatening direction.

The Worst Income Tax Legislation in American History

The second shoe dropped just as this book went to press. With the tax cut and spending agreement finally worked out in late May 2003, George W. Bush had pushed through yet another massive tax cut in less than two and a half years. In 2001, with a huge projected budget surplus, the new president guided his first tax cut through Congress. As discussed, it was a disastrous piece of legislation that became a major factor in turning the projected yearly budget surpluses into deficits and in materially increasing the maldistribution of income. I consider the 2003 act, which adds to the projected deficits and further reduces distributional fairness, the worst piece of major income tax legislation in American history and the lowest point thus far in domestic policymaking under Reaganism.

Seen in broadest terms, the overall legislative package reduced taxes by $320 billion and made $20 billion available to the states over two years to cover Medicaid and other programs. It is important to note that the extensive use of sunset provisions, which offer popular new tax reductions for a limited number of years and then mandate that they expire abruptly, has a critical impact on the cost of the legislation (discussed below). As an example of this practice, the 2003 act reduces the tax rate on capital gains from 20 percent to 15 percent but then has that rate returning to 20 percent in 2009.

The total legislative package had a little something for almost everyone—couples facing the marriage penalty, families with children, and the states. But the big winners continue to be those at the top because of the reductions that lower the tax rates for corporate dividends, capital gains, and the highest tax brackets. The Urban Institute-Brookings Tax Policy Center has calculated that the 8.6 percent of taxpayers with incomes in excess of $100,000 will receive 58 percent of the benefits, whereas only 5 percent will go to those with incomes of $30,000 or less. The latter constitute over one-half of all taxpayers.

Deception has been a much-used weapon in selling both tax cuts. Paul Krugman wrote about the sunset provisions: "[The package] relies on exactly the same bait-and-switch tactics used to sell the 2001 tax cut. Since the scam involved in the 2001 tax cut remains one of the wonders of modern political economy, it is a measure of our leaders' contempt for the intelligence of the public—or maybe for the press—that they think they can use the same tricks a second time."[15] The extent to which Congress and the president employed unconscionable deception provides stark evidence of institutional bankruptcy and of the dominance of the politicians' concern for power over their concern for the health of the nation. The sunset provisions on tax reductions are as devious as any of Enron's lamentable practices. But in this case, the elected agents of the American people were cheating the American people and undermining the American Republic.

With a price tag of $350 billion, the legislation appears to cost less than one-half of the amount President Bush had initially proposed. But there is a catch in that the sunset provisions keep the estimated cost down. However, these sunset provisions will surely make almost no sense to most taxpayers who will be angered when their taxes are seemingly raised by fiat. The expected scenario is that the politicians will fear the wrath of the taxpayers and not let the tax increases actually come about. Hence, the more reasonable cost estimate of the 2003 legislation is *not* $350 billion that unrealistically includes the savings from cutting off the benefits under the sunset provisions, but $800 billion. The deficit barrier that blocks needed domestic programs is likely to go higher and higher.

President George W. Bush has "out-Reaganed" Reagan and become the biggest threat among the postwar presidents to the institutions of representative democracy and to the economic security and political freedom of the bulk of the nation's citizens. Warren Buffett, the chief executive officer of Berkshire Hathaway, Inc., and the second-richest person in the world, made this critical point: "Supporters of making dividends tax-free like to paint critics as promoters of class warfare. The fact is, however, that their proposal promotes class welfare. For my class."[16] Call it class welfare for the richest Americans, or class warfare against the middle class that over time threatens their economic status, or an abomination, it is a frighteningly dangerous domestic policy.

The nation's plutocratic government is being strengthened by true believers in Reaganism so as to enhance the welfare of the rich by engaging in class warfare against those of lesser means. In the process of aiding his class, President Bush is harming the institutions that support democracy and reasoned policymaking and reducing the likelihood that tens of millions of ordinary citizens will achieve political equality and middle-class status for their entire lives. There is no more clear evidence of Reaganism's destructiveness under George W. Bush than the 2003 tax cut.

Summing Up

The conclusions to be drawn from my arguments are straightfoward. Reaganism diminished the institutions of federal governance that were to support representative democracy and now stands as the major barrier to restoring those institutions. Reaganism's continuation almost certainly rules out strengthening them sufficiently to sustain representative democracy or any form of democracy materially stronger than the tepid version of today. Its continuation also makes the chances slim for appreciably greater political equality, economic opportunity, or economic security.

President George W. Bush—the truest disciple of Reaganism—started with the destruction wrought by that political philosophy during two decades and raised the barrier even higher for revivifying the institutions of democracy. He further entrenched plutocratic governance by increasing the role of big money and corporate America in the government's policymaking process. Through tax reductions that disproportionately benefit the nation's most affluent people, Bush's policies have moved the nation toward an ever increasing maldistribution of income and wealth and a further unraveling of the social safety net underpinning economic security, not only for poor people and those who are nearly poor but also for the broad middle class.

If the American political system is to recover, the nation must turn away from Reaganism and its current standard bearer. But that will come about only if ordinary Americans can understand the harm being done to them individually and to the United States in total. That will be difficult to do because the nation's citizens have been mesmerized both by President Bush's use of deceptive propaganda as a central element of leadership and by the mounting triumphalism of the terrorism war. In particular, the broad American middle class appears to be marching toward greater economic insecurity with limited comprehension that their journey owes much to the tenets of Reaganism and the harsh means used by President Bush to apply them early in the twenty-first century.

This indictment of Reaganism may strike readers as unduly harsh in the charges and in the call for a regime change in which the dominant political philosophy would be rejected. There is no question that my anger and frustration had risen as I saw the United States going in the wrong direction during the years of Reaganism. Then, President Bush returned to Reaganism's strongest version to attack the much weakened institutions twenty years after Reagan had come to the presidency. Equally disturbing was the lack of concern as the nation moved further and further away from the fundamental objectives of political equality and reasonable levels of economic opportunity and security and went from being the exemplar of democracy to an entrenched plutocracy as its political institutions crumbled.

After President Bush launched his 2001 tax plan, the appalling level of deception was followed by an equally appalling paucity of criticism from politicians and the press of what were brazen distortions that could not have been missed by goodly numbers of these generally well-educated professionals. As time passed, watching an oblivious middle class let its economic status be attacked by the Bush administration in aid of the wealthy underscored how much damage the American political system had already suffered and how much more could be dealt out by a popular president who could get away with unscrupulous deception. I came to doubt that there can be a turning back toward political equality and greater economic fairness without an economic calamity or some other catastrophe.

That I may have gone too far on occasion in making the case is the price paid for trying to push the charges to the limit to be heard in a political environment in which the politics of unreality reign supreme amid class warfare waged by the Bush administration against a docile middle class that cheers for its attackers. It does not vitiate the overwhelming evidence of both the great deterioration of the political institutions that must support a viable American democracy and the insurmountable barriers to restoring them as long as Reaganism is the dominant political philosophy.

The gravest threat to the American Republic is to ignore the radical and dangerous institutional transformation since 1981 and not to undertake the hard effort to restore the efficiency and effectiveness of the federal institutions of governance. Only then can there be a proper balance between capitalism and democracy that will end plutocratic governance and foster the fundamental objectives of political equality and economic opportunity for all citizens.

Notes

Chapter 1

1. John B. Judis, *The Paradox of American Democracy* (New York: Pantheon, 2000), 155.

2. Sean Wilentz, "A Scandal for Our Time," *The American Prospect*, February 25, 2002, 20.

3. Quoted in Peter Levine, *The New Progressive Era* (Lanham, Md.: Rowman & Littlefield, 2000), 236.

4. *Washington Post National Weekly Edition*, December 25, 2000–January 1, 2001.

5. Andrew Hacker, *Money* (New York: Scribner's, 1997), 41, 43.

6. The quotations in this and the next paragraph are all drawn from Cass R. Sunstein, "The Right-Wing Assault—What's At Stake, What's Already Happened and What Could Occur," *The American Prospect*, spring 2003, A2.

7. Sunstein, "Right-Wing Assault," A2.

8. The information in this paragraph is from Thomas E. Patterson, *The Vanishing Voter* (New York: Knopf, 2002), 3–4.

9. The quotation and data in this paragraph are found in Patterson, *Vanishing Voter*, 21.

10. Patterson, *Vanishing Voter*, 184.

Chapter 2

1. Elizabeth Drew, *The Corruption of American Politics* (Secaucus, N.J.: Birch Lane Press, 1999), 271.

2. Peter F. Drucker, "The Age of Social Transformation," *Atlantic Monthly*, December 1994, 57–58.

3. G. M. Trevelyan, *Lord Grey of the Reform Act* (London: Longmans, Green, 1920), 268, 272.

4. Trevelyan, *Lord Grey*, 272.

5. Bernard Asbell, *The Senate Nobody Knows* (Garden City, N.Y.: Doubleday, 1978), 452.

6. Walter Williams, *Washington, Westminster, and Whitehall* (New York: Cambridge University Press, 1988), 18, italics in the original.

7. Quoted in John M. Broder and David E. Sanger, "A New Economic Team: The Resignation," *New York Times*, May 13, 1999, A1.

8. This and the next paragraph draw on Walter Williams, *Honest Numbers and Democracy* (Washington, D.C.: Georgetown University Press, 1998).

9. Michael Schudson, *The Good Citizen* (New York: Free Press, 1998), 307.

10. Michael X. Delli Carpini and Scott Keeter, *What Americans Know about Politics and Why It Matters* (New Haven, Conn.: Yale University Press, 1996), 8.

11. Gaillard Hunt, ed., *The Writings of James Madison* (New York: G. P. Putnam's Sons, 1910), vol. 9, 103.

12. Delli Carpini and Keeter, *What Americans Know about Politics*, 10–11.

13. Lawrence K. Grossman, *The Electronic Republic* (New York: Viking, 1995), 182.

14. Grossman, *Electronic Republic*, 182.

15. Aaron Wildavsky, *Speaking Truth to Power* (Boston: Little, Brown, 1979).

16. Williams, *Honest Numbers and Democracy*, ix.

17. Kevin Phillips, *Wealth and Democracy* (New York: Broadway Books, 2002), 322.

18. Phillips, *Wealth and Democracy*, 69.

19. Quoted in Phillips, *Wealth and Democracy*, 419.

20. James T. Patterson, *Grand Expectations* (New York: Oxford University Press, 1996), vii–viii.

21. All of the income distribution data in this paragraph are from Frank Levy, *The New Dollars and Dreams* (New York: Russell Sage Foundation, 1998), 199 (table A.1).

22. Issac Shapiro, Robert Greenstein, and Wendell Primus, "Pathbreaking CBO Study Shows Dramatic Income Disparities in 1980s and 1990s: An Analysis of the CBO Data," Center on Budget and Policy Priorities, May 31, 2001; *Historical Effective Tax Rates, 1979–1997*, preliminary ed. (Washington, D.C.: Congressional Budget Office, 2001).

23. All data in this and the next paragraph are from Shapiro et al., "Pathbreaking CBO Study," 5 (table 3), 10 (appendix table 1).

24. Lawrence Mishel, Jared Bernstein, and John Schmitt, *The State of Working America 2000/2001* (Ithaca, N.Y.: Cornell University Press, 2001), 259 (table 4.1), 265 (table 4.5).

Chapter 3

1. Peggy Noonan, *What I Saw at the Revolution* (New York: Random House, 1990), 268.

2. Robert A. Nozick, *Anarchy, the State, and Utopia* (New York: Basic Books, 1974).

3. Quoted in E. J. Dionne Jr., *Why Americans Hate Politics* (New York: Simon & Schuster, 1991), 281.

4. Theodore H. White, *America in Search of Itself* (New York: Harper & Row, 1982), 161.

5. Noonan, *What I Saw*, 346.

6. Hedley Donovan, "The First Two Hundred Days: An Appraisal," *Fortune*, September 21, 1981, 65–66.

7. Murray Edelman, *Constructing the Political Spectacle* (Chicago: University of Chicago Press, 1988), 113.

8. Garry Wills, *Reagan's America* (Garden City, N.Y.: Doubleday, 1987), 94.

9. Paul D. Erickson, *Reagan Speaks* (New York: New York University Press, 1985), 123.

10. Lou Cannon, *President Reagan* (New York: Simon & Schuster, 1991), 364, 644.

11. Bob Schieffer and Gary Paul Gates, *The Acting President* (New York: Dutton, 1989), 89–90.

12. Schieffer and Gates, *Acting President*, 339–40.

13. Frances FitzGerald, "Memoirs of the Reagan Era," *New Yorker*, January 16, 1989, 92.

14. Paul K. Conkin, *The New Deal* (New York: Cromwell, 1967), 2, 18.

15. Herbert Stein, *Presidential Economics* (New York: Simon & Schuster, 1984), 63.

16. Cannon, *President Reagan*.

17. James MacGregor Burns, *Roosevelt* (New York: Harcourt, Brace, and World, 1956), 264, 314, 447.

18. Michael Kammen, *People of Paradox* (New York: Alfred A. Knopf, 1972), 291.

19. Ann Ruth Willner, *The Spellbinders* (New Haven, Conn.: Yale University Press, 1984), 142.

20. Burns, *Roosevelt*, 167.

21. Haynes Johnson has emphasized the air controllers' strike as critical to the Reagan image and provides a good account of it. See Haynes Johnson, *Sleepwalking through History* (New York: Norton, 1991), 163–67.

22. Cannon, *President Reagan*, 793–94.

23. Cannon, *President Reagan*, 341.

24. Linda L. M. Bennett and Stephen Earl Bennett, *Living with Leviathan* (Lawrence: University Press of Kansas, 1990), 135.

25. George P. Shultz, *Turmoil and Triumph* (New York: Scribners, 1993), 827.

26. John W. Sloan, *The Reagan Effect* (Lawrence: University Press of Kansas, 1999), 244.

27. Frederick R. Strobel and Wallace C. Peterson, *The Coming Class War and How to Avoid It* (Armonk, N.Y.: M. E. Sharpe, 1999), 26.

28. The comparative macroeconomic data in this and the next several paragraphs are in *Economic Report of the President* (Washington, D.C.: U.S. Government Printing Office, 2001), 277 (table B-2), 316 (table B-35), 367 (table B-78).

29. Sloan, *Reagan Effect*, 243–44.

30. *Washington Post National Weekly Edition*, June 14, 1999, 26.

31. Michael L. Detouzos, Richard K. Lester, and Robert M. Solow, *Made in America* (Cambridge, Mass.: MIT Press, 1989), 44–45.

32. Richard W. Stevenson, "Fed Chief Says New-Age Economy Can Have Old Problems," *New York Times*, June 15, 1999, C2.

33. The productivity growth rate data in this paragraph are from Sloan, *Reagan Effect*, 231; and *Economic Report of the President*, 27 (chart 1-3).

34. Frank Levy, *The New Dollars and Dreams* (New York: Russell Sage, 1998), 26.

35. Walter Williams, *Mismanaging America* (Lawrence: University Press of Kansas, 1990); for a more extended discussion of management and policy analysis in the Reagan administration, see pp. 64–104, and also see Walter Williams, *Honest Numbers and Democracy* (Washington, D.C.: Georgetown University Press, 1998), 156–63.

36. Paul Kennedy, *The Rise and Fall of the Great Power* (New York: Random House, 1987), 540.

Chapter 4

1. Robert A. Dahl, *How Democratic Is the American Constitution?* (New Haven, Conn.: Yale University Press, 2001), 121.

2. Gordon S. Wood, *The American Revolution* (New York: Modern Library, 2002), 166.

3. James McGregor Burns, *The Power to Lead* (New York: Simon & Schuster, 1984), 119.

4. Burns, *Power to Lead*, 102, 189.

5. Daniel Lazare, *The Frozen Republic* (New York: Harcourt Brace, 1996), 2–3.

6. Charles O. Jones, *The Presidency in a Separated System* (Washington, D.C.: Brookings Institution Press, 1994), 297.

7. Jones, *Presidency*, 295.

8. Jones, *Presidency*, 60–61.

9. Garry Wills, *A Necessary Evil* (New York: Simon & Schuster, 1999), 91–93.

10. Alexander Hamilton, James Madison, and John Jay, *The Federalist Papers* (New York: Mentor, 1961), 82.

11. Hamilton et al., *Federalist Papers*, 82–83.

12. Gordon S. Wood, *The Creation of the American Republic, 1776–1787* (New York: Norton, 1969), 472.

13. Quoted in Wood, *Creation of the American Republic*, 476.

14. Wood, *Creation of the American Republic*, 516.

15. Quoted in Wills, *Necessary Evil*, 100.

16. Wood, *Creation of the American Republic*, 510; italics added.

17. Dahl, *How Democratic*, 162.

18. Hamilton et al., *Federalist Papers*, 432; the capitalization is in the original.

19. Michael Schudson, *The Good Citizen* (New York: Free Press, 1998), 81.

20. Hamilton et al., *Federalist Papers*, 82.

21. Hamilton et al., *Federalist Papers*, 432.

22. Forrest McDonald, *Alexander Hamilton* (New York: Norton, 1979), 136.

23. Jack N. Rakove, *Original Meanings* (New York: Vintage Books, 1997), 79, 222, 239, 243.

24. Wood, *American Revolution*, xxiii.

25. Wood, *American Revolution*, 100.

26. Dahl, *How Democratic*, 135, 138–39; italics in the original.

27. Wood, *American Revolution*, 100.

28. Wills, *Necessary Evil*, 318.

29. Wood, *Creation of the American Republic*, 449.

30. Hamilton et al., *Federalist Papers*, 320.

31. Wood, *Creation of the American Republic*, 450–52.

32. Wills, *Necessary Evil*, 75; italics in the original.

33. Wood, *Creation of the American Republic*, 605; for Wood's more extended views, see the subsection "The Parceling of Power," 602–6.

34. Clinton Rossiter, "Introduction," in Hamilton et al., *Federalist Papers*, vii.

35. Herbert J. Storing, with Murray Dry, *What the Anti-Federalists Were For* (Chicago: University of Chicago Press, 1981), vii.

36. Wills, *Necessary Evil*, 82.

37. Hamilton et al., *Federalist Papers*, 287.

38. Wills, *Necessary Evil*, 75.

39. Paul P. Van Riper, "The American Administrative State: Wilson and the Founders," in *A Centennial History of the American Administrative State*, ed. Ralph C. Chandler (New York: Free Press, 1987), 12 and; Jerry L. McCaffery, "The Development of Public Budgeting in the United States," in *Centennial History*, 356.

40. John Patrick Diggins, *The Proud Decades* (New York: Norton, 1988), 136.

41. See Anthony James Joes, "Eisenhower Revisionism: The Tide Comes In," *Presidential Studies Quarterly*, summer 1985, 561–71, for a useful review of the revisionist literature. See Walter Williams, *Mismanaging America* (Lawrence: University Press of Kansas, 1990), 109–14, for a discussion of the strengths and limitations on Eisenhower's "organization man" presidency.

Chapter 5

1. Bill Kovach and Tom Rosenstiel, *Warp Speed* (New York: Century Foundation Press, 1999), 5; italics in the original.

2. Richard Reeves, *President Kennedy* (New York: Simon & Schuster, 1993), 19, 23.

3. Garry Wills, *The Kennedy Imprisonment* (Boston: Atlantic–Little, Brown, 1981), 167.

4. The Reagan–Bush managerial efforts are discussed in greater detail in Walter Williams, *Honest Numbers and Democracy* (Washington, D.C.: Georgetown University Press, 1998), 148–71.

5. Howard Kurtz, *Spin Cycle* (New York: Free Press, 1998). The quoted words were used on the dust jacket.

6. Paul Krugman, "Reckonings: The Hostage Economy," *New York Times*, March 28, 2001, A21.

7. *New York Times*, February 28, 2001, A14.

8. William Gale, Samara Porter, and Emily Tang, "The Bush Tax Cut: The Morning After," *Milken Institute Review*, third quarter 2001, 54.

9. Issac Shapiro, Robert Greenstein, and James Sly, "Under Conference Agreement, Dollar Gains for Top One Percent Essentially the Same under House and Bush Packages," Center on Budget and Policy Priorities, May 26, 2001, p. 2.

10. Paul Krugman, "The Bully's Pulpit," *New York Times*, September 6, 2002, A22.

11. Elizabeth Drew, *The Corruption of American Politics* (Secaucus, N.J.: Birch Lane Press, 1999), 20.

12. Paul J. Quirk, "Structure and Performance: An Evaluation," in *The Postreform Congress*, ed. Roger Davidson (New York: St. Martin's Press, 1992), 317–18.

13. Alan Ehrenhalt, *The United States of Ambition* (New York: Random House, 1991).

14. Drew, *Corruption of American Politics*, 19.

15. Quoted in Ehrenhalt, *United States of Ambition*, 242.

16. Quoted in Charles Lewis, *The Buying of Congress* (New York, Avon, 1998), 37.

17. Quoted in R. W. Apple Jr., "Odd Couple Cross Political Lines to Fight System," *New York Times*, October 6, 1997, A14.

18. Ehrenhalt, *United States of Ambition*, 235–36.

19. Drew, *Corruption of American Politics*, 265.

20. Ehrenhalt, *United States of Ambition*, 248.

21. Drew, *Corruption of American Politics*, 19.

22. Drew, *Corruption of American Politics*, 19–21.

23. Quoted in *Seattle Times*, November 8, 1998.

24. Thomas L. Friedman, "Foreign Affairs: Penny Pinchers," *New York Times,* October 20, 1999, A27.

25. Jim Hoagland, "America the Menacing," *Washington Post National Weekly Edition*, October 31, 1999, B7.

26. Thomas Mann, "Governance in America 2000: An Overview," *Brookings Review*, winter 2000 (vol. 18, no. 1), 4.

27. Anthony Lewis, "Abroad at Home: Hypocrites in Power," *New York Times*, November 9, 1999, A25.

28. Alan Ehrenhalt, "Demanding the Right Size Government," *New York Times*, October 4, 1999, A27.

29. Drew, *Corruption of American Politics*, 61.

30. Drew, *Corruption of American Politics*, 51; for a discussion of *Buckley v. Valeo*, see 44–58, and also see Jeffery H. Birnbaum, *The Money Men* (New York: Crown, 2000), 33–39.

31. Birnbaum, *Money Men*, 37.

32. *Seattle Times*, March 25, 2001.

33. *New York Times*.

34. Ellen S. Miller and Micah L. Sifry, "The Care and Feeding of Fat Cats," *The American Prospect*, August 28, 2000, 10.

35. *Washington Post National Weekly Edition*, March 12–18, 2001, 13.

36. Drew, *Corruption of American Politics*, 84–85.

37. Birnbaum, *Money Men*, 44, 171.

38. John B. Judis, *The Paradox of American Democracy* (New York: Pantheon, 2000), 132.

39. *New York Times*, March 21, 2002, A1. The main provisions of McCain-Feingold are summarized in this article.

40. Ellen S. Miller, "With Victories Like These . . . The Glaring Inadequacies of Shays-Meehan," *The American Prospect*, March 25, 2002, 14.

41. *New York Times*, March 20, 2002.

42. *New York Times*, March 20, 2002.

43. *Washington Post National Weekly Edition*, September 2–8, 2002, 12.

44. *Washington Post National Weekly Edition*, September 2–8, 2002, 12.

45. National Commission on the Public Service, *Leadership for America: Rebuilding the Civil Service* (Washington, D.C.: National Commission on the Public Service, 1989), 17.

46. *Washington Post National Weekly Edition*, May 28–June 3, 2001, 29.

47. *Political Appointees: Turnover Rates in Executive Schedule Positions Requiring Senate Confirmation*, Report GAO/GGD-94-115FS (Washington, D.C.: U.S. General Accounting Office, 1994), 2.

48. National Commission on the Public Service, *Leadership for America*, 7.

49. Paul Light, "When Worlds Collide," in *The In-and-Outers*, ed. G. Calvin Mackenzie (Baltimore: Johns Hopkins University Press, 1987), 163. The National Academy of Public Administration study on which Light's statement is based has been described as "the most comprehensive study of presidential appointees ever undertaken"; G. Calvin Mackenzie, "Introduction," in *In-and-Outers*, xiv; Mackenzie elaborates on the entire study at xiii–xix.

50. Charles H. Levine, "Human Resource Erosion and the Uncertain Future of the U.S. Civil Service: From Policy Gridlock to Structural Fragmentation," *Governance: An International Journal of Policy Administration*, April 1988, 118–19.

51. Walter Williams, *Mismanaging America* (Lawrence: University Press of Kansas, 1990), 84.

52. George P. Shultz, *Turmoil and Triumph* (New York: Scribner's, 1993), 33.

53. Shultz, *Turmoil and Triumph*, 917.

Chapter 6

1. The quotation is taken from *New York Times*, May 21, 2002.

2. Donald F. Kettl, *The Global Public Management Revolution* (Washington, D.C.: Brookings Institution Press, 2000), 29.

3. Derek Bok, "Measuring the Performance of Government," in *Why People Don't Trust Government*, ed. Joseph S. Nye, Jr., Philip D. Zelikow, and David C. King (Cambridge, Mass.: Harvard University Press, 1997), 55–75.

4. *Washington Post National Weekly Edition*, June 1, 1998.

5. Tim Weiner, "C.I.A. Study Details Failures: Scouring of System Is Urged," *New York Times*, June 3, 1998, A1.

6. *New York Times*, June 3, 1998.

7. Quoted in *New York Times*, May 22, 2002, A18.

8. *Food Safety*, GAO/RCED-98-103 (Washington, D.C.: U.S. General Accounting Office, 1998), 5.

9. Quoted in *New York Times*, May 11, 1998.

10. Congressional Budget Office, *Resolving the Thrift Crisis* (Washington, D.C.: Congressional Budget Office, 1993).

11. *Financial Management Issues*, Transition Series, GAO/OCG-93-4TR (Washington, D.C.: U.S. General Accounting Office, 1992), 4–5.

12. Don Van Natta Jr. and David Johnston, "Traces of Terror: The Intelligence Reports," *Washington Post National Weekly Edition*, May 14–20, 1990, A22.

13. Edward J. Kane, *The S&L Insurance Mess* (Washington, D.C.: Urban Institute Press, 1989), 100.

14. James Ring Adams, *The Big Fix* (New York: Wiley, 1990), 234.

15. Lawrence J. White, *The S&L Debacle* (New York: Oxford University Press, 1991), 117; italics in the original.

16. Congressional Budget Office, *Resolving the Thrift Crisis*, 17.

17. Sue Rose-Ackerman, "Deregulation and Reregulation: Rhetoric and Reality," *Journal of Law and Politics*, winter 1990, 300.

18. Kane, *S&L Insurance Mess*, 171.

19. Congressional Budget Office, *Resolving the Thrift Crisis*, 17.

20. Quoted in National Commission on the Public Service, *Leadership for America: Rebuilding the Civil Service* (Washington, D.C.: National Commission on the Public Service, 1989), 12.

21. David E. Rosenbaum, "The Savings Debacle: A Special Report," *New York Times*, June 6, 1990, A1.

22. Rosenbaum, "Savings Debacle."

23. This and the next quote are from *New York Times*, May 24, 1990.

24. Adams, *Big Fix*, 280.

25. Donald F. Norris and Lyke Thompson, eds., *The Politics of Welfare Reform* (Newbury Park, Calif.: Sage, 1995).

26. Michael Wiseman, review of the book *The Politics of Welfare Reform*, *Journal of Policy Analysis and Management*, vol. 15, no. 2 (1996): 286–87.

27. Kettl, *Global Public Management Revolution*, 28; italics added.

28. Alasdair Roberts, "Performance-Based Organizations: Assessing the Gore Plan," *Public Administration Review*, vol. 57, no. 6 (November/December 1997): 465–78.

29. Roberts, "Performance-Based Organizations," 474.

30. *Medicare*, GAO/HEHS-97-108 (Washington, D.C.: U.S. General Accounting Office, 1997), 6.

31. *New York Times*, February 10, 1999.

32. Taegan D. Goddard and Christopher Riback, *You Won—Now What?* (New York: Touchstone, 1999), 49, 221.

33. Kettl, *Global Public Management Revolution*, 29, 43.

34. *Managing for Results: Analytic Challenges in Managing Performance*, GAO/HEHS/GGD-97-138 (Washington, D.C.: U.S. General Accounting Office, 1997), 5.

35. *Managing for Results: Observations on Agencies' Strategic Plans*, GAO/T-GGD-98-66 (Washington, D.C.: U.S. General Accounting Office, 1998), 6.

36. Walter Williams, *Honest Numbers and Democracy* (Washington, D.C.: Georgetown University Press, 1998), 210–36.

37. Quoted in Williams, *Honest Numbers and Democracy*, 234–35.

38. James Madison, Alexander Hamilton, and John Jay, *The Federalist Papers* (New York: New American Library, 1961), 423; italics added.

Chapter 7

1. Michael Schudson, *The Good Citizen* (New York: Free Press, 1998), 81.

2. Michael X. Delli Carpini and Scott Keeter, *What Americans Know about Politics and Why It Matters* (New Haven, Conn.: Yale University Press, 1996), 8.

3. Bill Kovach and Tom Rosenstiel, *Warp Speed* (New York: Century Foundation, 1999), 7.

4. Kovach and Rosenstiel, *Warp Speed*, 98.

5. Schudson, *Good Citizen*, 132.

6. Michael Janeway, *The Republic of Denial* (New Haven, Conn.: Yale University Press, 1999), 59.

7. Schudson, *Good Citizen*, 147.

8. Quoted in Schudson, *Good Citizen*, 193.

9. James McGregor Burns, *The Power to Lead* (New York: Simon & Schuster, 1984), 160–61.

10. Austin Ranney, *Channels of Power: The Impact of Television on American Politics* (New York: Basic Books, 1983), 93.

11. Kovach and Rosenstiel, *Warp Speed*, 4.

12. Kovach and Rosenstiel, *Warp Speed*, 5; and James Fallows, *Breaking the News* (New York: Pantheon, 1996), 7.

13. Quoted in Bruce W. Sanford, *Don't Shoot the Messenger* (New York: Free Press, 1999), 47.

14. Lawrence Grossman, *The Electronic Revolution* (New York: Viking, 1995), 182–83.

15. Sanford, *Don't Shoot the Messenger*, 85.

16. Janeway, *Republic of Denial*, 169, 171.

17. Richard Morin, "Unconventional Wisdom: New Facts and Hot Stats from the Social Sciences," *Washington Post National Weekly Edition*, April 5, 1999.

18. Morin, "Unconventional Wisdom," *Washington Post National Weekly Edition*, April 5, 1999.

19. Sanford, *Don't Shoot the Messenger*, 11.

20. Kathleen Hall Jamieson, *Dirty Politics* (New York: Oxford University Press, 1992), 127.

21. Janeway, *Republic of Denial*, 76.

22. Janeway, *Republic of Denial*, 116–17.

23. Janeway, *Republic of Denial*, 77–78.

24. Ranney, *Channels of Power*, 89, 123.

25. Robert E. Denton Jr., *The Primetime Presidency of Ronald Reagan* (New York: Praeger, 1988), 71, 91.

26. Bruce Miroff, "The Presidency and the Public: Leadership as Spectacle," in *The Presidency and the Political System*, 3d edition, ed. Michael Nelson (Washington, D.C.: CQ Press, 1990), 301.

27. Suzanne Garment, *Scandal* (New York: Times Books, 1991), 289.

28. Robert Hughes, *Culture of Complaint* (New York: Oxford University Press, 1993), 40–41.

29. Larry J. Sabato, *Feeding Frenzy* (New York: Free Press, 1991); and Garment, *Scandal*.

30. Sabato, *Feeding Frenzy*, 1.

31. Tom Rosenstiel, *Strange Bedfellows, 1992* (New York: Hyperion, 1993), 57.

32. Garry Wills, "A Better Way to Test a Candidate's Mettle," *New York Times*, November 10, 1999, A23.

33. Kovach and Rosenstiel, *Warp Speed*, 83.

34. Howard Kurtz, *Hot Air* (New York: Time Books, 1996), 371.

35. Quoted in Kurtz, *Hot Air*, 249.

36. Kurtz, *Hot Air*, 258.

37. *Washington Post National Weekly Edition*, October 11, 1999.

38. Kurtz, *Spin Cycle*, xix.

39. Janeway, *Republic of Denial*, 161.

40. Grossman, *Electronic Republic*, 106–7.

41. Kovach and Rosenstiel, *Warp Speed*, 88.

42. Fallows, *Breaking the News*, 128.

43. Kovach and Rosenstiel, *Warp Speed*, ix.

Chapter 8

1. Gordon S. Wood, *The American Constitution* (New York: Modern Library, 2002), 161.

2. Quoted in Peter Levine, *The New Progressive Era* (Lanham, Md.: Rowman & Littlefield, 2000), xii; italics added.

3. Levine, *New Progressive Era*, 216–17.

4. Michael X. Delli Carpini and Scott Keeter, *What Americans Know about Politics and Why It Matters* (New Haven, Conn.: Yale University Press, 1996), 1.

5. Lawrence R. Jacobs and Robert Y. Shapiro, *Politicians Don't Pander* (Chicago: University of Chicago Press, 2000), 302.

6. Jacobs and Shapiro, *Politicians Don't Pander*, 296.

7. Daniel Yankelovich, "Guise and Pols," *The American Prospect*, September 25–October 9, 2000, 76.

8. The quote is from Delli Carpini and Keeter, *What Americans Know about Politics*, 44; also see pp. 41–49 for a good brief discussion of recent democratic theories, including that of Page and Shapiro.

9. Jacobs and Shapiro, *Politicians Don't Pander*, 309, 311.

10. Paul Krugman, "Reckonings: The Hostage Economy," *New York Times*, March 28, 2001, A21.

11. The quoted statement from the survey is from Jacobs and Shapiro, *Politicians Don't Pander*, 316.

12. Michael Schudson, *The Good Citizen* (New York: Free Press, 1998), 310–11.

13. Schudson, *Good Citizen*, 310–12; the quotation is found on p. 311.

14. Schudson, *Good Citizen*, 313.

15. Kathleen Hall Jamieson, *Everything You Think You Know about Politics . . . and Why You're Wrong* (New York: Basic Books, 2000), 8.

16. Jamieson's findings given in this sentence and the remainder of the paragraph, as well as her quoted arguments in the paragraph, are in Jamieson, *Everything You Think You Know about Politics*, 45–47.

17. Jamieson, *Everything You Think You Know about Politics*, 46.

18. Jamieson, *Everything You Think You Know about Politics*, 46, 221.

19. Robert B. Reich, *The Future of Success* (New York: Knopf, 2001), 6.

20. Reich, *Future of Success*, 7; italics in the original.

21. Walter Williams, "Rights Won't Be Guarded by Our Apolitical Students," *Seattle Times*, January 16, 1998.

22. Williams, "Rights Won't Be Guarded."

23. Pew Research Center for the People and the Press, "Post Election Poll," www.people-press.org/post00rpt.htm, 1–2.

24. V. O. Key Jr., *The Responsible Electorate* (Cambridge, Mass.: Harvard University Press, 1966), 7.

25. "Transcript of President Bush's Message to Congress on His Budget Proposal," *New York Times*, February 28, 2001, A12.

26. Issac Shapiro, Robert Greenstein, and James Sly, "Under Conference Agreement, Dollar Gains for Top One Percent Essentially the Same as under House and Bush Packages," Center on Budget and Policy Priorities, May 26, 2001, 2.

27. Yankelovich, "Guise and Pols," 75.

28. *New York Times*, June 21, 2001.

29. *New York Times*, June 21, 2001.

30. Yankelovich, "Guise and Pols," 76.

Chapter 9

1. *New York Times*, November 7, 2001.

2. *New York Times*, November 15, 2001, C2.

3. *New York Times*, November 9, 2001, A1.

4. Quoted in *New York Times*, November 9, 2001, A1.

5. Quoted in *New York Times*, November 9, 2001, A1.

6. Quoted in *Seattle Times*, December 30, 2001, A1.

7. Quoted in *Seattle Times*, December 30, 2001, A1.

8. *Seattle Times*, October 28, 2001, A1.

9. *New York Times*, November 7, 2001.

10. *New York Times*, October 31, 2001, E1. The data in the next paragraph were drawn from this article.

11. *Washington Post National Weekly Edition*, December 17–23, 2001, 29. The information and the quoted material in the rest of the paragraph were drawn from this article.

12. Quoted in *New York Times*, November 5, 2001, B1.

13. Elizabeth J. Jewell and Frank Abate, eds., *The New Oxford American Dictionary* (New York: Oxford University Press, 2001), 1314.

14. William Keegan, "Anyone Can Be President, If He's Rich," *Seattle Post-Intelligencer*, November 12, 2000, G1.

15. John B. Judis, *The Paradox of American Democracy* (New York: Pantheon, 2000), 120.

16. Kevin Phillips, *Wealth and Democracy* (New York: Broadway Books, 2002), 236–40.

17. Bob Herbert, "Joined at the Hip," *New York Times*, January 10, 2002, A27.

18. *Washington Post National Weekly Edition*, January 14–20, 2002, 23; italics added.

19. Dan Morgan, "Following the Money Trail: Enron Counted on Donations to Clear Regulatory Obstacles," *Seattle Times*, January 14, 2002.

20. *New York Times*, November 17, 2002.

21. *New York Times*, November 29, 2001, C2.

22. *New York Times*, November 29, 2001, C2.

23. *Seattle Times*, January 12, 2002, A3.

24. The text of the letter was quoted in the *New York Times*, January 16, 2002.

25. *Washington Post National Weekly Edition*, May 13–19, 2002, 29.

26. *Washington Post National Weekly Edition*, December 17–23, 2001, 26.

27. James T. Patterson, *Grand Expectations* (New York: Oxford University Press, 1996), 68; the data given in the paragraph are also found on that page.

28. Quoted in Phillips, *Wealth and Democracy*, xiv, 419.

29. Judis, *Paradox of American Democracy*, 16, 155.

30. Judis, *Paradox of American Democracy*, 150–52.

Chapter 10

1. Mollyann Brodie, Lisa Ferraro Parmelee, April Brackett, and Drew E. Altman, "Polling and Democracy: A Special Issue," *Public Perspective*, a Roper Center Review of Public Opinion and Polling, Special Issue, July–August 2001, 11–24. The survey also included policy leaders and journalists, but those results were not relevant to the discussion that follows.

2. Brodie et al., "Polling and Democracy," 17; italics in the original.

3. The quotation and all the data in the remainder of the paragraph are in Brodie et al., "Polling and Democracy," 20–21; italics in the original.

4. Brodie et al., "Polling and Democracy," 23; italics added.

5. Brodie et al., "Polling and Democracy," 20. A fourth area of foreign policy will be ignored (the ratings were somewhat lower).

6. Brodie et al., "Polling and Democracy."

7. Stanley B. Greenberg, "'We'—Not 'Me,'" *The American Prospect*, December 27, 2001, 26.

8. *Washington Post National Weekly Edition*, September 16–22, 2002, 21.

9. Lawrence Mishel, Jared Bernstein, and John Schmitt, *The State of Working America 2000/2001* (Ithaca, N.Y.: Cornell University Press, 2001), 283, italics added.

10. Kevin Phillips, *Wealth and Democracy* (New York: Broadway Books), 2002, 422.

11. *New York Times*, July 16, 2002, A1.

12. Floyd Norris, "Will Auditing Reform Die Before It Begins?" *New York Times*, December 27, 2002, C12.

13. *Washington Post National Weekly Edition*, September 16–22, 2002, 20.

14. *Washington Post National Weekly Edition*, September 16–22, 2002, 34.

15. *Washington Post National Weekly Edition*, September 23–29, 2002, 34.

16. *Washington Post National Weekly Edition*, September 23–29, 2002.

17. *Washington Post National Weekly Edition*, September 30–October 6, 2002, 11.

18. *New York Times*, October 9, 2002, A14.

19. "Threats and Responses: Excerpts of Speeches Made on Senate Floor Regarding Issue on Iraq," *New York Times*, October 4, 2002, A15.

20. *New York Times*, December 25, 2002.

21. *New York Times*, January 2, 2003, A28.

22. Robert Kuttner, "The Ideological Imposter: Run Left, Govern Right: The Fraudulence of the Bush Presidency," *The American Prospect*, June 3, 2002, 20.

23., Richard W. Stevenson and Richard A. Oppel Jr., "Corporate Conduct: The Overview," *New York Times*, July 17, 2002, A1.

24. *Seattle Times*, September 22, 2002, C2.

25. "The Axis-of-Inefficiency Budget" (editorial), *New York Times*, February 5, 2002, A24.

26. Gaillard Hunt, ed., *The Writings of James Madison*, vol. 9 (New York: G. P. Putnam's Sons, 1910), 103.

27. *New York Times*, October 22, 2002, A31.

Chapter 11

1. The quotations in this and the next paragraph are from the *New York Times*, April 8, 2003, A31.

2. Paul Krugman, "Empire of a Devil," *New York Times*, April 29, 2003, A31.

3. Jeff Madrick, "Economic Scene," *New York Times*, October 31, 2002, C2.

4. The material in this paragraph including the quotation are from Madrick, "Economic Scene," C2.

5. Joseph E. Stiglitz, "Bush's Tax Plan—The Dangers," *New York Review of Books*, March 13, 2003, 13.

6. This and the next quotation are from Andrew Lee, Robert Greenstein, and Issac Shapiro, "A 'Reality Check' on Recent Arguments in Favor of the Administration's New 'Economic Growth' Plan," Center on Budget and Policy Priorities, revised January 28, 2003, 1.

7. The quotation and the additional data in the paragraph are from Lee, Greenstein, and Shapiro, "'Reality Check,'" 3.

8. Stephen Labaton, "Wall Street Settlement: The Overview," *New York Times*, April 29, 2003, A1.

9. Stiglitz, "Bush's Tax Plan," 15.

10. Joel Friedman and Robert Greenstein, "Exempting Corporate Dividends from Individual Income Taxes," Center on Budget and Policy Priorities, revised January 17, 2003, 3.

11. Quoted in Walter Williams, *Washington, Westminster and Whitehall* (Cambridge: Cambridge University Press, 1988), 101–2.

12. Mary Lynn F. Jones, "The Republican Railroad: Squelching Democratic Voices on the Hill," *The American Prospect*, April 2003, 15.

13. "The War at Home" (editorial), *New York Times*, April 20, 2003, 8.

14. The Jefferson quotation is from Mary C. Segers and Ted G. Jelen, *Wall of Separation?* (Lanham, Md.: Rowman & Littlefield, 1998), 125.

15. *New York Times*, May 9, 2003, A9.

16. *Seattle Times*, May 22, 2003, B7.

Index

Index 289

See also